A Box Full of Tales

Easy Ways to Share Library Resources through Story Boxes

Kathy MacMillan

AMERICAN LIBRARY ASSOCIATION

Chicago   2008

While extensive effort has gone into ensuring the reliability of information appearing in this book, the publisher makes no warranty, express or implied, on the accuracy or reliability of the information, and does not assume and hereby disclaims any liability to any person for any loss or damage caused by errors or omissions in this publication.

The paper used in this publication meets the minimum requirements of American National Standard for Information Sciences—Permanence of Paper for Printed Library Materials, ANSI Z39.48-1992. ∞

Library of Congress Cataloging-in-Publication Data
MacMillan, Kathy, 1975–
   A box full of tales : easy ways to share library resources through story boxes / Kathy MacMillan.
      p. cm.
   Includes bibliographical references and index.
   ISBN 978-0-8389-0960-7 (alk. paper)
   1. Children's libraries—Activity programs. 2. Storytelling. 3. Library cooperation.
I. Title.
   Z718.3.M25 2008
   027.62'51—dc22   2007048794

ISBN-13: 978-0-8389-0960-7

Printed in the United States of America
12 11 10 09 08   5 4 3 2 1

Contents

Dedicated to the memory of Beth Dori and Claudine Hanner:
fine librarians, fine people, fine friends.

Preface

"Carroll County?" the big-city librarian said to me, nose wrinkling slightly. "Isn't that a little out-of-the-way, rural county? How many programs do you do there a week? Two or three?"

Imagine her surprise when I informed her that, at the time, we were offering three family programs, five infant programs, five toddler programs, three preschool programs, and two elementary programs a week—in addition to specials. And that was just at my branch.

"Oh," she countered. "Well, you must not have to work at the desk and do other jobs. Your job is just programming, right?"

No, I said—all the staff in my department did all the same jobs that other librarians do, in addition to programming.

She gaped at me. "How is that possible?"

"Story boxes," I replied.

I was lucky to start as a children's services supervisor at Carroll County Public Library (CCPL) at a time when sharing resources through story boxes was a long-established tradition. Like many of the staff members there, I took the amazing benefits of story boxes for granted—until I became involved in the Maryland Library Association and the American Library Association, and realized how few children's librarians have access to such a network of resources. Whenever I mentioned story boxes, I was peppered with questions from other librarians, all eager to offer more and better-quality programs with less time and effort.

This book is a guide to establishing a story box program in your library system, and it draws on the accumulated wisdom and knowledge of staff members at Carroll County Public Library, a system that has done story boxes—and done them well—for over twenty years. In the introduction, you'll find a comprehensive guide to setting up and maintaining a story box system, both for the individual programmer and for the system as a whole, as well as examples of programs developed by different programmers using the same box. Following the introduction, you'll find fifty ready-made boxes to get you started—all you have to do is gather the materials, make a few props, and you're on your way! Finally, you'll find a host of great resources for selecting materials for story boxes in the appendix.

Get ready for the best programming tool you'll ever meet: the story box.

ACKNOWLEDGMENTS

Thank you to the administration and staff of the Carroll County Public Library, without whom this book truly would not exist. I am forever grateful for the opportunity to work with such a creative and collaborative group of people. Special thanks to those who shared story box plans with me and whose ideas appear in this book: Christine Kirker, Amber Haslinger, Helen Sparks, John Clayton, Bettina Wesloh, Buff Kahn, Claudine Hanner, Dolores Schuyler, Debby Parker, Amy Schildwachter, Brenda Proper, Mark McKinney, Sharon Head, and Ginny Hurt.

Thank you to the kind folks at the Institute for Disabilities Research and Training, Inc., especially Corinne Vinopol and Jason Neubauer, for providing the graphics for this book.

Thank you to Brenda Conaway and Helen Sparks, who not only were willing to share their story box experiences for this book but also served as mentors for me when I arrived at CCPL.

Thank you to the circulation staff at CCPL, especially Pat Verdis and Mary Miller, who processed and somehow found space for hundreds of books on hold for me.

Thank you to Beverly Smoot for the best book-transporting suitcases ever!

Thank you to Laura Pelehach for guidance in the early stages of this project, and to Susan Geraghty and Carolyn Crabtree of ALA Editions for their eagle-eyed editing!

Thank you to the hundreds of librarians and storytellers who have influenced me with their creativity and planted the seeds for many of the ideas in this book.

Last but certainly not least, thank you to my wonderfully supportive husband, Jimmy, and to my son, J.X., who was the test audience for many of the ideas in this book.

Introduction

Storytime Outside the Box

How Story Boxes Were Born

When Brenda Conaway began working at Carroll County Public Library in the early 1980s, she was the only children's programmer for the entire library system. In the then rural Maryland county, this meant taking storytime programs sporadically to storefront locations around the county.

Big changes were in store; within six months of being hired, Brenda was joined by another full-time programmer, and by 1993, the county's library system grew to encompass five full-service branches.

The concept of sharing programming materials started early and stuck around. From the time a second person was hired, it was standard practice to share lists of materials used, and storing program materials in the central branch meant that all programmers had access to the same resources. Once the other branches gained full service, and a countywide delivery system was put in place, it seemed natural to take advantage of that system to share program materials. If one programmer can put together a great program on a theme, why not share it with other staff in other parts of the county? So the simple, elegant concept of story boxes was born.

What Is a Story Box?

Very simply, a story box is a thematic storytime resource box, designed for use by multiple programmers and for multiple age groups. The story boxes discussed in this book are designed for programming geared to toddlers, preschoolers, and families—the age levels that make up the bulk of most libraries' programs—but story boxes can be adapted for any level. Carroll County Public Library, in fact, now supplements its story box program with "Infant Boxes" designed for use in baby storytimes.

The key to effective sharing of programs using story boxes is a rotation and delivery system. By assigning themes to regular weekly storytimes in the library, every staff member presenting a program during that week is able to take advantage of the story box. Each season, children's staff members each make one to three story boxes, and then send them around on a scheduled rotation for others to use. A story box contains books, flannelboards, music, craft suggestions, puppets, fingerplays, and other props for use in programs. When presenting the program, staff members simply go through the box and choose their favorite items and those most appropriate for their audiences.

How to Do Twenty-five Storytimes a Week without Losing Your Mind; or, The Benefits of Using Story Boxes

Story Boxes Save You Time!

Saving time is the most obvious benefit of any resource-sharing project, and it's especially true of story boxes. Story box users don't have to gather books, wait for holds to be filled, or spend time making flannelboards and hunting down fingerplays—everything is already assembled! In addition, sharing craft samples at the beginning of the rotation period allows you to make better use of volunteers by having them prepare craft materials in advance. Using story boxes allows you to spend more time *presenting* programs, and less time *preparing* for them. Says Debby Parker, formerly of CCPL's Eldersburg branch, "Why reinvent the wheel on a weekly basis?" Indeed, at that very branch, the three full-time and two part-time children's librarians have been known to present twenty-five programs in one week, in addition to their other duties—a feat that would be impossible without story boxes.

Story Boxes Give You New Perspectives

Because story boxes are prepared by a variety of staff members, each one is unique. Two people preparing boxes on the same topic might approach it from completely different angles. Someone else might include a book or fingerplay that you never would have chosen. "I am exposed to more than just my old favorites," says Ginny Hurt, formerly of CCPL's Mount Airy branch. "Story boxes often contain materials I might not have access to or would never even think of using, and themes which might not particularly be of interest to me to create, but are to others and the kids love them," according to Claudine Hanner of the North Carroll branch.

Story Boxes Bridge the Gap between Staff Members

In an age when many public libraries are expanding rapidly, it's easy to lose track of staff members in other locations. In some cases, staff members who work at different branches may never meet! Story boxes encourage children's staff to share ideas and thoughts, drawing staff together even as they are physically separated. "I've sent e-mails to people I've never even met, just to tell them I really liked their boxes," says Brenda Conaway. She also points out that story boxes provide an opportunity to showcase the strengths of other staff members: "It helps to figure out whom to ask for help on specific topics or issues."

Story Boxes Provide Thematic Unity for Your Programs

Tying all programs in a given week to a specific theme makes publicity and displays easier. Many branches, for example, put up a display of theme-related materials at the entrance to the children's department each week, thereby promoting both programming and circulation. Claudine Hanner also points out that "children remember stories, songs, and fingerplays better if there is a united theme."

Story Boxes Set a Programming Standard for Your System

In many library systems, the programming levels and quality at branches vary greatly. By implementing an agreed-upon system like story boxes, you clarify expectations for your programs to staff, and everyone is on the same page.

Story Boxes Increase Your Program Quality

By reducing staff workload and providing standards, story boxes allow staff members to focus their energies in new ways. Rather than scrambling to procure materials for multiple programs, staff members can focus their efforts on creating more storytime materials and choosing the best items for their boxes. "When you can concentrate on one or two themes instead of fifty-two, you can do a better job and come up with a higher-quality product," says Helen Sparks of CCPL's Taneytown branch. Amber Haslinger of the Eldersburg branch agrees: "Programs done with story boxes are better because staff members are drawing from the same pool of material and can share what worked especially well during their storytimes with their coworkers."

Story Boxes Are Perfect for Training and Cross-Training

In systems where programs are regularly presented by staff members who have little or no background in programming, story boxes are the answer! By providing boxes of materials chosen by skilled programmers, novices to programming can get started with minimal training. Working from a story box is a perfect way to introduce new staff members and interns to storytime. In addition, training on putting together a story box gives new staff valuable information about how to select resources for programs.

Using story boxes can expand your pool of programmers as well—non-children's staff and volunteers can be trained to present programs easily and quickly with the resources provided. Kris Peters, an adult librarian at CCPL's North Carroll branch, says, "Without story boxes, I would be loath to present a storytime!" But with story boxes, customer service is improved: storytimes never have to be canceled just because a children's librarian is unavailable.

Story Boxes Change and Grow with Your Needs

The concept of sharing via story boxes is endlessly adaptable. Brenda Conaway points out that, in the beginning, boxes at CCPL were used only for preschool storytimes—the main staple of the library's programming twenty years ago. Today, CCPL focuses more heavily on programming for toddlers and families, so the contents of the story boxes have changed. Twenty years ago, before VCRs in the home were common, filmstrips were often included in story boxes. Today, the focus is more squarely on books and stories. Also, with a movement to drop-in instead of registered programs, the story box program at CCPL has expanded to provide each branch with a box every week of the year. "I think you can start where you are," Conaway says. "Story boxes can adapt to meet your library system's needs."

A Step-by-Step Guide to Developing a Great Story Box

Every great story box starts with a fun, kid-friendly theme. The theme can be as simple and standard as "Summer Fun," or creative and different like "Giant Vegetables." You might even want to develop a box around a prolific author's or illustrator's work. In every storytime rotation, it's best to have a cross-section of tried-and-true and original topics. Amy Schildwachter of CCPL's Taneytown branch advises, "Look for a topic that has a variety of materials for a variety of ages."

Brainstorm!

Begin by brainstorming everything that has to do with your topic. Look for unique angles that will entice kids. For example, if your topic is "Hands," you might list the many things we do with our hands, including arts and crafts, string games, fingerplays, and sign language. This list will give you a broader range of topics to search when you go looking for materials and will take you beyond the obvious resources.

Find the Best Books

Once you have your list of topics, search your library's catalog and start pulling materials. Check thematic storytime resources like *A to Zoo: Subject Access to Children's Picture Books* by Carolyn and John Lima (Westport, CT: Libraries Unlimited, 2001) as well, to make sure you've found items that might not be cataloged the way you expect. Use fellow staff members as a resource. Once you start making story boxes, you'll find yourself making mental notes about great books you want to use in the future—write those titles down, because you never know when one might inspire a unique story box!

Once you've found as much as you can on your topic, it's time to evaluate those books. Some will be too long, some will be inappropriate, and some might not fit your theme. Make sure that pictures are large enough to be seen by all in a group of about twenty-five children. If the pictures are too small for sharing but the story is terrific, consider making a flannel-board or stick puppet prop. Choose items by a variety of authors and illustrators, and make sure that the books themselves are in good physical condition. Don't include copies that are torn or scribbled on.

Winnow your selection down to no more than fifteen to twenty books. Remember to include a variety of materials for different age groups, and highlight materials appropriate for toddler storytimes.

Listen to the Music

A good storytime box should also include music. It's not always possible to find something related to your theme, but do your best. Music can be on CDs or cassettes included in the box itself, or simply be printed lyrics to well-known songs that you suggest using. Keep in mind that the best storytime music encourages activity—don't put in songs that require only standing and listening, because small children won't pay attention for very long! If you do want to include a song that doesn't have obvious actions, make sure to suggest actions to use with the song. *Children's Jukebox, Second Edition: The Select Subject Guide to Children's Musical Recordings* by Rob Reid (Chicago: American Library Association, 2007) is a great resource for finding music by subject. If you can't find songs that fit your theme, generic action songs are better than no music at all.

Find Fun Fingerplays

Fingerplays and action rhymes are an important part of storytime boxes and are great to intersperse between songs and stories. In the folder of materials accompanying your box, include printouts or copies of at least three fingerplays and action rhymes that follow your theme, with specific directions for performing them. A great way to encourage parental participation in toddler and family programs is to provide large printouts of the fingerplays and rhymes, suitable for posting in the storytime room.

Props! Props! Props!

One of the most fun aspects of story boxes is the opportunity to make props and see those made by other people. Look through the books you have chosen and see if any lend themselves to a flannelboard or stick puppet retelling—then get busy and make that prop! Look for puppets, stuffed animals, and other realia to enhance your theme, and note where they can be connected to stories and fingerplays in your box. Counting rhymes lend themselves especially well to flannelboard treatment. If you are hopeless at cutting felt, then make a magnetboard: by printing out and laminating large clip art items, then putting magnets on the back, you can create great-looking storytime materials in a short time. Make sure that you type up the text of the story or rhyme and include it with the prop, so that other programmers don't have to hunt down the original book in order to use the prop.

Prepackaged storytime materials are also available, if you have the budget for them. See the appendix for suggestions on where to purchase them.

Also, don't forget to take advantage of props other people have made. If your library has a storeroom of storytime materials, check it out before you make your own.

Get Creative!

You can include all kinds of activities in your story box: sign language (as this book's boxes include), suggestions for incorporating props or music into the books, simple games, ideas for making the stories more participative, or just about anything else that will enhance your theme. A perennial favorite is the "Pin the _____ on the _____" game, which can be used for everything from pinning the tail on a dog to pinning a vine on a giant pumpkin. Consult storytime resource books to find what others suggest about your topic, but don't let them limit you!

Remember Your Audience

When you're presenting a program, your audience is kids and parents; when you're putting together a story box, your audience is other library staff. Make your box as user-friendly as possible by including a folder listing all the materials in the box, fingerplays, music, and specific ideas for using the items. Don't make people guess why you included something! Also, remember to include a variety of materials—sometimes that means putting in books or fingerplays that you personally would never use.

Ask for Feedback

Include an evaluation form in your box to invite other staff members who use it to give you feedback on what they used. This will help you create even better boxes in the future. But remember that every storytime programmer is different—don't take it personally if someone hates the flannelboard you were so proud of!

Story Box Checklist

- 15–20 theme-related books
- Theme-related music
- 3 or more flannelboards, puppets, or other props
- A Materials Folder that includes
    a list of the books in the box, with items appropriate for toddlers starred or highlighted in some way
    3 or more fingerplays, with large printouts appropriate for hanging in the storytime room
    a list of music and props in the box, with specific suggestions on using them in programs
    other supplemental materials on the theme, including riddles, factual information, signs to share, game ideas, etc.
    an evaluation form or request for feedback

Smooth Story Box Sharing

Now that you have a great story box, how do you share it? The key is a great network. This network can be set up systemwide or as a consortium of a few branches that want to share resources.

Set Up a Delivery System

If you have a systemwide delivery program in place, sharing boxes may be no problem. However, buy-in from those who perform the deliveries and their supervisors is key. As soon as you consider implementing story boxes, invite those in charge of deliveries to assess how the program will impact their work and address any concerns they may have. Depending on how many branches you have, adding story boxes to regular circulation of materials can affect deliveries significantly. If necessary, you may want to have boxes delivered on certain days of the week when other delivery volume is lower.

Gather Supplies

Other than regular programming supplies, you will need a large supply of sturdy boxes in which to transport materials. Rubbermaid stackable totes are ideal for this. The fourteen-gallon size is sufficient for most story boxes, though larger props may require larger boxes, so you may want to purchase a few of the eighteen-gallon size as well. These boxes and similar products are available at such stores as Wal-Mart and Kmart, or can be purchased in bulk from office supply companies.

Another great time saver is to purchase a package of plastic sleeves from an office supply store and duct-tape one to the top of each box. Then staff members can easily slip a sheet showing the title and location/delivery dates for that box into the sleeve.

Centralize Programming Resources

Odds are, each of your branches already has a variety of programming resources and props that even its own staff may not know about. Make these resources available to all staff by either centralizing them in one place (unlikely to be practical space-wise, and certainly not a popular decision with staff members who have their favorite items at the branch) or creating a database for all staff to access. If you have a staff intranet, that's the ideal place to mount such a database. If not, something as simple as an Excel spreadsheet listing prop name, type, branch, and related themes is enough to get started. Find a volunteer to be in charge of this project, and make sure it is updated and distributed to programming staff at least twice a year.

Set Up a Schedule

A workable rotation schedule for your boxes is the key to effective resource sharing. This can be done in many ways, but the first step is to determine how many story box sessions you want to have during the year. Four (winter, spring, summer, fall) seems ideal and allows access to seasonal themes for all branches. Of course, you will want to coordinate story box rotation with your program publicity, so make sure your public relations department is involved.

Next, determine how many weeks each session will cover. Use this number to determine how many boxes you will need and how many boxes each staff member will be responsible for creating. (Make sure to include one or two extra boxes to allow for overlap.)

The next step is deciding how you want to set up your schedule. Helen Sparks remembers the early days at CCPL, when the entire children's staff would attend the meeting to set up the rotation of story boxes and essentially "bid" on which weeks they wanted which themes. That time-consuming system gave way to a more standard rotation, and now no meeting is even required to discuss it: one person is put in charge of setting the rotation. All staff members send their box topics to the scheduler by a specific date. The scheduler makes sure there is no duplication of topics, then plugs the box topics into a spreadsheet, allowing one week between each branch for delivery and staff preparation. After double-checking that none of the boxes overlap, the scheduler sends the spreadsheet to all the children's staff for use in publicity and program planning, and each staff member creates a rotation delivery sheet for his or her story box.

Getting Buy-In

Starting a new system like this has many advantages, but change, of course, always comes with concerns. How you present the concept of story boxes will determine how staff members accept it or not.

The major concern voiced by most children's librarians is that implementing a system like story boxes will limit their creativity and provide "canned" programs that they will be required to follow. In reality, nothing could be farther from the truth! By saving valuable staff time and providing a variety of resources, story boxes actually *encourage* staff creativity by allowing time to develop more and better materials and share the ideas of other programmers.

When introducing the idea of story boxes to staff, emphasize that the story box is designed to be a starting place. "This is just a beginning, a springboard from which to work," says Brenda Conaway. "Yes, your storytime must fit the topic, but it's possible to use nothing from the box." In addition, encourage staff members to add great materials to the box, or write notes about new materials on the evaluation forms. Encourage staff members to see the boxes as something to which everyone can contribute ideas, not as a predefined leech of creativity.

You might also run into concerns from circulation staff about keeping materials out of circulation for long periods. This concern is quite valid, especially for smaller systems that may not have the budget to purchase extra copies of books. If you think this will be an issue, invite your circulation supervisors into the discussion early and brainstorm ways to alleviate the problem. If necessary, consider placing limits on which books can be included in boxes—perhaps only titles of which the system owns at least two or three copies will be allowed. You might also consider applying for grants to purchase special copies of books for programming purposes. If keeping books out of circulation is still an issue, consider cutting down the length of your box rotations.

Training

Training staff to create and use story boxes is vital in making sure everyone is on the same page. Develop guidelines specific to your system's story boxes, and make sure everyone knows what the expectations are. Setting and maintaining a standard for program boxes is vital for creating a practical, user-friendly system. Utilize the resources in this book to show everyone what constitutes good storytime materials. Make sure new staff members are given these standards and training as well.

A Typical Season Timeline Using Story Boxes

Fall Session (September–November)
May 10: Story box topics due from all staff to scheduler.
May 15: Scheduler sends out box rotation schedule.
June 1: Publicity information due to Public Relations Department.
June–August: Staff members work on creating story boxes.
August 1: Each staff member sends copies of craft samples or coloring sheets to other branches.
Last week of August: Fall rotation begins.
First week of December: Boxes are returned to their creators, who dismantle them, return materials, and look at feedback.

One Box, Many Programs

Now that you've learned how to create a super story box, and you've got a great system in place for sharing story boxes, what do you do when those boxes start rolling in? The key to effectively using a story box made by another programmer is to use it as a springboard. With your particular storytime audience and your own style in mind, look through the materials and choose the books, songs, and fingerplays that appeal most to you. Feel free to add your own ideas and feedback to the box—and materials too, if they fit in the box and don't make it too heavy. A simple story box can become a creative connection for diverse staff in various locations, as everyone adds her or his own take on the theme. After all, many heads are always better than one!

In the following section, you will see examples of how programs designed from story boxes can be tailored to individual presenter styles and to audience needs for different age groups. These examples are outlines of programs presented by Carroll County Public Library staff members using the contents of the "Give Me a Hand" box found on page 79. Items in italics were added by the individual programmer.

Program Outline Samples

Outline 1: Toddler Program

Song: "If You're Happy and You Know It"
Book: *Here Are My Hands* by Bill Martin Jr. and John Archambault. New York: Henry Holt, 1985.
Song: "Put Your Finger On" from *Feel the Music* by Parachute Express. Walt Disney Records, 1991.
Book: *Hands Can* by Cheryl Willis Hudson. Cambridge, MA: Candlewick, 2003.
Stick Puppet Rhyme: "Hands Can"
Fingerplay: "Ten Little Fingers"
Flannelboard Rhyme: "Color Mittens"
Song: "Shake Your Sillies Out"

Outline 2: Toddler Program

Song: "The More We Get Together" (regular storytime opener)
Fingerplay: "Ten Little Fingers"
Discussion: What can we do with our hands?
Stick Puppet Rhyme: "Hands Can"
Book: *Hands Can* by Cheryl Willis Hudson. Cambridge, MA: Candlewick, 2003.
Song: "Put Your Hands Up in the Air" from *Learning Basic Skills through Music, Volume 1* by Hap Palmer. Educational Activities, 1969.
Flannelboard Rhyme: "Color Mittens"
Book: *Clap Your Hands* by Lorinda Bryan Cauley. New York: G. P. Putnam's Sons, 1992.
Craft: I LOVE YOU Sign Language Stick Puppets

Outline 3: Toddler Program

Opening: Introduce the letter H. "This is the sound you hear at the beginning of 'hands.'"
Song: "Hands Are for Clapping" from *Jim Gill Sings The Sneezing Song and Other Contagious Tunes* by Jim Gill. Jim Gill Music, 1993.
Book: *Clap Your Hands* by Lorinda Bryan Cauley. New York: G. P. Putnam's Sons, 1992.
Fingerplay: "Open, Shut Them"
Stick Puppet Rhyme: "Hands Can"

Book: *Ticklemonster and Me: A Play-Along Book* by Max Haynes. New York: Doubleday, 1999.

Fingerplay: "Ten Little Fingers"

Flannelboard Rhyme: "Color Mittens"

Book: *Busy Fingers* by C. W. Bowie. Watertown, MA: Charlesbridge, 2003.

Song: "Eensy Weensy Spider"

Book: *Hands Can* by Cheryl Willis Hudson. Cambridge, MA: Candlewick, 2003.

Song: "Rock and Roll Freeze Dance" from "So Big": Activity Songs for Little Ones by Hap Palmer. Hap-Pal Music, 1994. (with rhythm sticks)

Outline 4: Toddler Program

Song: "Welcome, Welcome Everyone" (regular storytime opener)

Discussion: Point out that we used our hands to clap in that song, then have the children guess the theme of storytime by showing book covers and large hand stick puppets.

Transition: "We used our hands to clap, now let's use them to point in the next story."

Book: Have You Seen My Cat? *by Eric Carle. New York: Simon and Schuster, 1996.*

Book: *Here Are My Hands* by Bill Martin Jr. and John Archambault. New York: Henry Holt, 1985.

Fingerplay: "Little Turtle"

Nursery Rhyme: "Hickory Dickory Dock"

Transition: "Some people speak with their hands."

Stick Puppet Rhyme: "Hands Can"

Activity: Learn signs for SUN, BLUE SKIES, MOTHER, ME.

Song: "May There Always Be Sunshine" from Nobody Else Like Me *by Cathy and Marcy. Rounder, 1998. (using signs above)*

Book: *Busy Fingers* by C. W. Bowie. Watertown, MA: Charlesbridge, 2003.

Song: "Eensy Weensy Spider"

Song: "Put Your Finger On" from *Feel the Music* by Parachute Express. Walt Disney Records, 1991.

Activity: Parachute play

Song: "Skinnamarink" from Six Little Ducks. *Kimbo Educational, 1997. (using sign for I LOVE YOU)*

Craft: Finger painting with vanilla pudding on watercolor paper

Outline 5: All Ages Family Program

Song: "If You're Happy and You Know It"

Book: *Hands* by Lois Ehlert. San Diego: Harcourt Brace, 1997.

Fingerplay: "Ten Little Fingers"

Book: *Busy Fingers* by C. W. Bowie. Watertown, MA: Charlesbridge, 2003.

Song: "Eensy Weensy Spider"

Book: *Hands Can* by Cheryl Willis Hudson. Cambridge, MA: Candlewick, 2003.

Stick Puppet Rhyme: "Hands Can"

Flannelboard Rhyme: "Color Mittens" (using signs for colors)

Song: "Shake Your Sillies Out"

Outline 6: Preschooler Program

Song: "If You're Happy and You Know It"
Book: *Bear Wants More* by Karma Wilson. New York: Simon and Schuster, 2003. (with sign for MORE)
Song: "Head, Shoulders, Knees, and Toes"
Fingerplay: "My Drum"
Fingerplay: "Ten Little Fingers"
Book: *My Two Hands, My Two Feet* by Rick Walton. New York: G. P. Putnam's Sons, 2000.
Fingerplay: "Open, Shut Them"
Flannelboard Rhyme: "Color Mittens"
Stick Puppet Rhyme: "Hands Can"
Book: *Hands Can* by Cheryl Willis Hudson. Cambridge, MA: Candlewick, 2003.
Song: "Shake Your Sillies Out"
Craft: I LOVE YOU Sign Language Stick Puppets

Outline 7: Preschooler Program

Opening: Introduce the letter H. "This is the sound you hear at the beginning of 'hands.'"
Book: *Bear Wants More* by Karma Wilson. New York: Simon and Schuster, 2003. (with sign for MORE)
Song: "Shakey Shakey" from Yummy Yummy *by The Wiggles. Koch Records, 2000. (with shaker eggs)*
Book: *Hand Games* by Mario Mariotti. Brooklyn, NY: Kane/Miller, 1992.
Stick Puppet Rhyme: "Hands Can"
Song: "Head, Shoulders, Knees, and Toes"
Pop-up Book: Take Me Out to the Ballgame *by John Stadler. New York: Simon and Schuster, 2005.*
Song: "The Wheels on the Bus"
Fingerplay: "Our Hands Say Thank You"

Fifty Ready-Made Story Box Plans

In the pages that follow, you will find fifty Story Box plans to get you started. Each topic includes fifteen to twenty recommended books as well as suggested recordings, fingerplays and songs, props, and crafts to go along with the theme. Items especially appropriate for toddlers are preceded by an asterisk. In addition, each topic features an illustration of an American Sign Language sign that relates to the theme and may be used during the songs, fingerplays, and stories. The sign language graphics in this book are from the CD-ROM *American Sign Language Clip and Create 4* (Institute for Disabilities Research and Training, 2003), and appear with the permission of the publisher. To find out more about the Institute for Disabilities Research and Training, see www.idrt.com.

Ah-choo!

Sign: **SICK**

BOOKS

Elmo Says Achoo! by Sarah Albee. New York: Random House, 2000.

Farm Flu by Teresa Bateman. Morton Grove, IL: Albert Whitman, 2001.

The Big Sneeze by Ruth Brown. New York: Lothrop, Lee, and Shepard, 1985.

Who's Sick Today? by Lynne Cherry. New York: Dutton, 1988.

Goldie Locks Has Chicken Pox by Erin Dealey. New York: Atheneum, 2002.

Dr. Duck by H. M. Ehrlich. New York: Orchard, 2000.

Barnyard Song by Rhonda Gowler Greene. New York: Atheneum, 1997.

Don't You Feel Well, Sam? by Amy Hest. Cambridge, MA: Candlewick, 2002.

Guess Who, Baby Duck! by Amy Hest. Cambridge, MA: Candlewick, 2004.

I Am Sick by Patricia Jensen. New York: Children's Press, 2005.

Buster Catches a Cold by Hisako Madokoro. Strongsville, OH: Gareth Stevens, 1991.

Bronto Eats Meat by Peter Maloney and Felicia Zekauskas. New York: Dial, 2003.

The Grandma Cure by Pamela Mayer. New York: Dutton, 2005.

The Big Little Sneeze by Katja Rader. New York: North-South, 2002.

Rooster Can't Cock-a-Doodle-Doo by Karen Rostoker-Gruber. New York: Dial, 2004.

Imogene's Antlers by David Small. New York: Crown, 1985.

Dear Daisy, Get Well Soon by Maggie Smith. New York: Crown, 2000.

Felix Feels Better by Rosemary Wells. Cambridge, MA: Candlewick, 2001.

How Do Dinosaurs Get Well Soon? by Jane Yolen. New York: Scholastic, 2003.

RECORDED MUSIC

"The Sneezing Song" from *Jim Gill Sings The Sneezing Song and Other Contagious Tunes* by Jim Gill. Jim Gill Music, 1993.

FINGERPLAYS/SONGS

"I Godda Code"

I godda code,
A code in my node.
Ah-choo! Ah-choo!
Have I got a code!

"When I Am Sick"

When I am sick, I stay in bed.
   (mime sleeping)
I fluff the pillow under my head.
   (fluff pillow)
I rest all day and drink some tea
   (mime drinking)
Until I feel all better, you see!
   (make "ta-da" gesture)

"When Do We Wash Our Hands?"

When we're done playing outside, do we
   wash our hands? YES!
When we've been petting the dog, do we
   wash our hands? YES!
When we've picked icky-sticky chewing
   gum off of our shoes, do we wash
   our hands? YES!
When we're done using the toilet, do we
   wash our hands? YES!

*Ask for other examples of times when we should
wash our hands.*

Wash your hands and keep them clean,
   and you'll keep away those germs so
   mean!

"Tissue, Please"

If you feel you need to sneeze,
Cover your nose with a tissue, please.

*Pass out tissues to each child and repeat this
rhyme, practicing covering noses. Then have
each child take a turn sneezing, and have
everyone else say "Bless you, _____!" or
"Gesundheit, _____!"*

"Old MacDonald Had a Cold"
(to the tune of "Old MacDonald")

Old MacDonald had a cold, EIEIO.
And with this cold he had the sniffles,
   EIEIO.
With a sniff sniff here and a sniff sniff
   there,
Here a sniff, there a sniff, everywhere a
   sniff sniff.
Old MacDonald had a cold, EIEIO.
. . . and with this cold he had a sneeze
. . . and with this cold he had a cough

"If You're Sick and You Know It"
(to the tune of "If You're Happy
and You Know It")

If you're sick and you know it, rub your
   tummy.
If you're sick and you know it, rub your
   tummy.
If you're sick and you know it, then your
   face will really show it.
If you're sick and you know it, rub your
   tummy.
. . . blow your nose
. . . cover your sneeze
. . . take your medicine
If you're better and you know it, shout
   hooray! . . .

PROPS

*Flannelboard Song

"Balloons"
(to the tune of "The Twelve
Days of Christmas")

PIECES NEEDED: *5 balloons in blue, purple,
yellow, red, and green*

The first day I was sick, my mommy gave
    to me
One blue balloon, you see.
The second day I was sick, my mommy
    gave to me
One purple balloon and
One blue balloon, you see.
The third day I was sick, my mommy
    gave to me
One yellow balloon and
One purple balloon and
One blue balloon, you see.
The fourth day I was sick, my mommy
    gave to me
One red balloon and
One yellow balloon and
One purple balloon and
One blue balloon, you see.
The fifth day I was sick, my mommy gave
    to me
One green balloon and
One red balloon and
One yellow balloon and
One purple balloon and
One blue balloon, you see.
The sixth day I felt all better!

*Flannelboard or Prop Song

"Old MacDonald's Farm Gets Sick"
(to the tune of "Old MacDonald")

PIECES NEEDED: *cow, chicken, sheep, cat, pig*

Old MacDonald had a cow, EIEIO.
And this cow, it had a sneeze, EIEIO.
With an AH-MOOOO here
And an AH-MOOOO there,
Here an AH-MOOOO, there an AH-
    MOOOO
Everywhere an AH-MOOOO.
Old MacDonald had a cow, EIEIO.
Chicken had a cough . . . cough, cough
Sheep had a tummyache . . . MAMA!
Cat had a headache . . . me-OWWW!
Pig had the sniffles . . . sniff, sniff.

Prop Rhyme

"My Medicine"

PIECES NEEDED: *bottle, spoon or medicine cup*

My mom says I have to take my
    medicine, but I don't wanna!
It's going to taste yucky, I just know it's
    gonna!
She says it will make me feel better, but I
    don't care!
I won't take that medicine anytime,
    anywhere!
Now she says I have to do it, she says
    there's nothing to it.
I open up (*make hesitant, disgusted face*)
And in goes the medicine . . .
HEY! It tastes like grapes! Yum!

*Prop Story   *Soup* by Cathy Goldberg Fishman. New York: Children's Press, 2002.
PIECES NEEDED: *pot, spoons, napkin, bowls, cheese, crackers, rice, and ice*

*Flannelboard Story   *Ah-choo* by Christine Taylor-Butler. New York: Children's Press, 2005.
PIECES NEEDED: *1 bowl of soup, 2 teacups, 3 board games, 4 puzzles, 5 books, 6 teddy bears, 7 sheets, 8 pillows, mom, dad*

Prop Story *I'm Not Feeling Well Today* by Shirley Neitzel. New York: Greenwillow, 2001.

PIECES NEEDED: *a bathrobe for storyteller to wear, box of tissues, blanket, pillow, stuffed cat, finger puppets, puzzles on a tray, remote control, toast and teacup, bear, book*

*Flannelboard or Prop Story *Monkey Soup* by Louis Sachar. New York: Knopf, 1992.

PIECES NEEDED: *basket, Band-Aids, balloons, crayons, tissues, blanket, buttons, bubbles, bar of soap, toothbrush, napkin, monkey, stick horse*

CRAFTS

Cover Your Sneeze Paper Plate Craft

MATERIALS: one paper plate for each child, crayons, paper fastener for each child, construction paper, yarn, gluesticks, tissue for each child, hole punch

DIRECTIONS:
1. Draw a face on the middle of the paper plate.
2. Cut an arm out of construction paper.
3. Use the hole punch to punch a hole in the side edge of the paper plate (at about the 7 o'clock position.)
4. Punch a hole in the bottom of the construction paper arm.
5. Put the arm over the paper plate and use a paper fastener to attach it to the plate.
6. Glue the tissue to the hand of the arm.
7. Glue yarn onto the plate for hair and decorate as desired.
8. Move the arm up and down to cover the nose with the tissue.

Get Well Cards

MATERIALS: one piece of construction paper for each child, crayons or markers, preprinted get well messages, gluesticks, stickers or other decorating materials

DIRECTIONS:
1. Fold the construction paper in half to make a card.
2. Select a get well message and glue it onto the inside or the front of the card.
3. Decorate your card.

All about Red

Sign: **RED**

 BOOKS

Red Fox Dances by Alan Baron. Cambridge, MA: Candlewick, 1996.

The Little Red Hen by Byron Barton. New York: HarperCollins, 1993.

Clifford the Big Red Dog by Norman Bridwell. New York: Scholastic, 1963.

The Grouchy Ladybug by Eric Carle. New York: HarperCollins, 1977.

The Little Red Hen by Barry Downard. New York: Simon and Schuster, 2004.

Little Red Caboose by Steve Metger. New York: Scholastic, 1998.

Ten Red Apples by Virginia Miller. Cambridge, MA: Candlewick, 2002.

Flashing Fire Engines by Tony Mitton. New York: Kingfisher, 1998.

*Fire Engines by Anne Rockwell. New York: Puffin, 1986.

*New Shoes, Red Shoes by Susan Rollings. New York: Orchard, 2000.

*Who Said Red? by Mary Serfozo. New York: Simon and Schuster, 1988.

Fire Truck by Peter Sís. New York: Greenwillow, 1998.

Pete's a Pizza by William Steig. New York: HarperCollins, 1998.

*Red Light, Green Light by Anastasia Suen. Orlando, FL: Harcourt, 2005.

Shy Guy by Gilles Tibo. New York: North-South, 2002.

Apples, Apples, Apples by Nancy Elizabeth Wallace. Delray Beach, FL: Winslow Press, 2000.

"Hi Pizza Man!" by Virginia Walter. New York: Orchard, 1995.

*Apple Farmer Annie by Monica Wellington. New York: Dutton, 2001.

Firefighter Frank by Monica Wellington. New York: Dutton, 2002.

*The Little Mouse, the Red Ripe Strawberry, and the Big Hungry Bear by Don and Audrey Wood. London: Child's Play, 1984.

RECORDED MUSIC

*"Hurry, Hurry Drive the Fire Truck" from *Barney's Favorites*. Barney Music, 1993.

"Mary Wore Her Red Dress" from *Everything Grows* by Raffi. Rounder/UMGD, 1996.

*"Big Red Car" from *Here Comes the Big Red Car* by The Wiggles. Koch Records, 2006.

*"Little Red Caboose" from *Travelin' Magic* by Joanie Bartels. BMG Music, 2003.

"Are You Ready for Red?" from *Songs about Colors and Shapes*. Kimbo Educational, 2003.

*"The Strawberry Shake" from *Strawberry Shortcake: Strawberry Jams*. Koch Records, 2004.

"Little Red Wagon" from *Wiggles, Jiggles, and Giggles* by Stephen Fite. Melody House, 2000.
   (Follow directions in the liner notes—have children crawl on all fours, each time a wheel goes flat, they have to stop using one arm or leg. By the end of the song they will be lying flat on the floor unable to move.)

FINGERPLAYS/SONGS

"The Big Red Firetruck"

The big red firetruck races down the
   street
Full of ladders and hoses, isn't that neat!
Hear the siren blare: NEE NAW, NEE
   NAW
See the water blast: WHOOOSH
The ladder goes up. *(stand on tiptoes)*
The ladder goes down. *(hunch low)*
I'm so glad the firetruck is in my town!

"Way Up High in the Apple Tree"
(traditional)

Way up high in the apple tree
3 little apples smiled at me.
I shook that tree as hard as I could.
Down fell the apples, and
Mmmmm, they were good!

"Ladybug, Ladybug"

Ladybug, ladybug, turn around.
Ladybug, ladybug, touch the ground.
Ladybug, ladybug, swing and sway.
Ladybug, ladybug, fly away!

"P-I-Z-Z-A"
(to the tune of "BINGO")

There was a kid who loved to eat
And pizza was his favorite.
P-I-Z-Z-A, P-I-Z-Z-A, P-I-Z-Z-A,
And pizza was his favorite.

Repeat, gradually replacing each letter with a clap.

"A Perfect Pizza": An Acting-It-Out Story

To make a perfect pizza, you start with the crust. Can you pretend to push out the dough? Now let's roll it flat. Now we throw it up in the air. Uh-oh! Mine stuck to the ceiling! Now we pinch up the edges. Mmmm, looking good! Let's put on some tasty red tomato sauce! Now comes the cheese! What else do you want on your pizza?

Solicit suggestions from the audience, and intersperse your own silly suggestions, such as ice cream, worms, and dirty socks.

Now it's time to bake the pizza . . . and it's ready. Take a bite, but be careful not to burn your mouth!

PROPS

*Prop Rhyme

"Red Means Stop"

PIECES NEEDED: *double-sided Stop/Go sign*

Red means stop and green means go.
This is something you should know.
When you see green, just go ahead.
But be sure to stop when you see red!
Go ahead and DANCE!

Play the freeze game. Children can do the activity when the green Go sign is facing them, but when you turn it to Stop, they must freeze. Repeat with jumping, turning, clapping, and waving arms.

Puppet Story   "The Wolf and Granny's Lost Glasses" from *One-Person Puppetry Streamlined and Simplified* by Yvonne Awar Frey. Chicago: American Library Association, 2005.

PIECES NEEDED: *wolf puppet, granny puppet, red cloak, basket*

***Flannelboard Story**   *Ten Red Apples* by Pat Hutchins. New York: Greenwillow, 2000.

PIECES NEEDED: *farmer and wife, tree, 10 apples, horse, cow, donkey, goat, pig, sheep, goose, duck, hen*

Flannelboard Story   *Farmer Dale's Red Pickup Truck* by Lisa Wheeler. New York: Harcourt, 2004.

PIECES NEEDED: *red pickup truck, farmer, cow, sheep, pig, goat, rooster*

***Prop Story**   *Hobbledy-Clop* by Pat Brisson. Honesdale, PA: Boyds Mills Press, 2003.

PIECES NEEDED: *red wagon, snake, horse, cat, dog, tea set, tablecloth*

***Prop or Flannelboard Story**   *Ten Rosy Roses* by Eve Merriam. New York: HarperCollins, 1999.

PIECES NEEDED: *10 flannelboard or artificial roses*

***Prop Song**   "Big Red Car" from *Here Comes the Big Red Car* by The Wiggles. Koch Records, 2006.

PIECES NEEDED: *red Frisbees or cardboard circles to use as steering wheels. Act out buckling up and driving around the room.*

***Prop Song**   "Little Red Caboose" from *Travelin' Magic* by Joanie Bartels. BMG Music, 2003.

Have children line up in a train and take turns being the caboose. For extra fun, have a red shirt or hat for the "caboose" to wear.

ADDITIONAL SUGGESTIONS

Poetry

"A Pizza the Size of the Sun" from *A Pizza the Size of the Sun* by Jack Prelutsky. New York: Greenwillow, 1994.

CRAFTS

CD Pizzas

MATERIALS: 1 CD for each child; a circle of red construction paper for each child, cut to the same size as the CD; pizza "toppings" cut from library processing stickers or construction paper (red circles for pepperoni, yellow strips for cheese, etc.); glue; crayons or markers

DIRECTIONS:
1. Glue the red circle onto the CD to represent the sauce.
2. Decorate your pizza with "toppings" as desired.

Ladybug Stick Puppet

MATERIALS: Ladybug body shape cut from black construction paper for each child, 2 wings cut from red construction paper for each child, paper fasteners, craft sticks, black dot stickers, glue, crayons

DIRECTIONS:
1. Place the wings on the ladybug's body and push a paper fastener through all three layers.
2. Decorate the ladybug with black dots and crayons.
3. Glue the ladybug to the craft stick and move the wings to make her "fly."

Animals at Night

Sign: **NIGHT**

 **BOOKS**

"I'm Not Cute!" by Jonathan Allen. New York: Hyperion, 2005.

Raccoons and Ripe Corn by Jim Arnosky. New York: Lothrop, Lee, and Shepard, 1987.

Night Cat by Margaret Beames. New York: Orchard, 2000.

Hoot and Holler by Alan Brown. New York: Knopf, 2001.

While You Were Sleeping by John Butler. Atlanta, GA: Peachtree, 1996.

Stellaluna by Janell Cannon. San Diego: Harcourt, 1993.

Where Are the Night Animals? by Mary Ann Fraser. New York: HarperCollins, 1999.

Oliver's Wood by Sue Hendra. Cambridge, MA: Candlewick, 1996.

Desert Song by Tony Johnston. San Francisco: Sierra Club Books for Children, 2000.

Sweet Dreams: How Animals Sleep by Kimiko Kajikawa. New York: Henry Holt, 1999.

Up All Night Counting: A Pop-Up Book by Robin Koontz. New York: Simon and Schuster, 2006.

Ahwooooooooo! by Yannick Murphy. New York: Clarion, 2006.

Animal Lullabies by Lila Prap. New York: North-South, 2006.

Night in the Country by Cynthia Rylant. New York: Bradbury, 1986.

North County Night by Daniel San Souci. New York: Bantam Doubleday Dell, 1990.

The Owl Who Was Afraid of the Dark by Jill Tomlinson. Cambridge, MA: Candlewick, 2000.

Owl Babies by Martin Waddell. Cambridge, MA: Candlewick, 1992.

Where Does the Brown Bear Go? by Nicki Weiss. New York: Greenwillow, 1989.

Bear's New Friend by Karma Wilson. New York: Simon and Schuster, 2006.

Owl Moon by Jane Yolen. New York: Philomel, 1987.

RECORDED MUSIC

"Raccoon Rock" from *Animal Walks* by Georgiana Stewart. Kimbo Educational, 1987.

"Do the Owl" from *Wiggly Safari* by The Wiggles. HIT Entertainment, 2002.

FINGERPLAYS/SONGS

"The Raccoon"

Let me tell you about the raccoon.
He stays up all night by the light of the
    moon. *(hold hands up to make moon)*
He searches and searches for something
    good to eat, *(put hand to forehead and
    look around)*
Then scurries away on silent feet.
    (run in place)

"Night Noises"

What noises do we hear at night?
Owls say whooo . . .
Crickets say chirp . . .
Wolves say a-rooooo . . .
What other noises do we hear at night?

"If I Were a Bat"

If I were a bat I would fly all night.
    (flap arms)
I'd have great hearing, *(point to ears)*
but not good sight. *(point to eyes)*
I would wake up when the sun went
    down, *(jump up as if waking up)*
And I would sleep all day hanging
    upside-down! *(hook 2 fingers from one
    hand onto index finger of other hand to
    represent bat hanging)*

PROPS

*Flannelboard Rhyme

"Five Little Owls"

PIECES NEEDED: *5 owls*

5 little owls sitting in a tree.
The first one said, "You can't catch me!"
The second one said, "Let's fly through
    the air!"
The third one said, "Sure, I don't care!"
The fourth one said, "Please, after you!"
But all the fifth one said was,
    "Whooooo."
Then whoosh went the wind and out
    went the light
And 5 little owls flew out of sight.

*Flannelboard Rhyme

"Where Are the Night Animals?"

PIECES NEEDED: *enough bats, owls, cats,
wolves, and other nocturnal animals for each
child to hold a flannelboard piece*

We can find the night animals, if we look
    carefully.
Use your eyes, use your eyes, use your
    eyes and see.
If you have a/an _____, bring it here to
    me!

*Flannelboard Story

"Going on a Wolf Hunt"

PIECES NEEDED: *house, grass, river, trees, mountain, wolf puppet*

Refrain: We're going on a wolf hunt!
We're going to catch a big one.
Here we go! We're not afraid.

Uh-oh! Here's some tall grass.
Can't go over it, can't go under it.
We'll have to go through!
Swishy-swishy, swishy-swishy.

Repeat refrain.

Uh-oh! It's a river.
Can't go over it, can't go under it.
We'll have to go through!
Swimmy-swimmy, swimmy-swimmy.

Repeat refrain.

Uh-oh! It's a forest, a dark scary forest.
Can't go over it, can't go under it.
We'll have to go through!
Shiver-step, shiver-step.

Repeat refrain.

Oh look! It's the mountain!
Can't go over it, can't go under it.
We'll have to go . . . up!
Climby-climb, climby-climb . . .
A-roooooo!
What's that? It's a wolf!
A big scary wolf!
Hurry down the mountain (stumble-trip, stumble-trip).
Hurry through the forest (shiver-step, shiver-step).
Hurry through the river (swimmy-swimmy, swimmy-swimmy).
Hurry through the tall grass (swishy-swishy, swishy-swishy).
Into the house! Shut the door!
Up the steps! Under the covers!
We won't go on a wolf hunt again!
(Whew!)

ADDITIONAL SUGGESTIONS

Storytelling

"How the Bat Came to Be," an Anishinabe folktale found in *Keepers of the Night: Native American Stories and Nocturnal Activities for Children* by Michael J. Caduto and Joseph Bruchac. Golden, CO: Fulcrum, 1994.

CRAFTS

Owl Paper Plate Craft

MATERIALS: paper plate for each child, 2 muffin-tin liners for each child, precut black circles or googly eyes, precut yellow triangles for beaks, feathers, glue, crayons

DIRECTIONS:
1. Flatten out the muffin-tin liners and glue them onto the top half of the paper plate, to form the circles around the owl's eyes.
2. Glue the circles or googly eyes into the center of the muffin-tin liners.
3. Decorate the owl with a beak and feathers, and color as desired.

Flying Bat Craft

MATERIALS: black construction paper, paper fasteners, white crayons

DIRECTIONS:
1. Cut the shape of the bat's body and head from black construction paper. Cut the wings as a separate piece.
2. Place the wings over the body and attach the two pieces with a paper fastener.
3. Draw the bat's face using a white crayon.

Antlered Antics

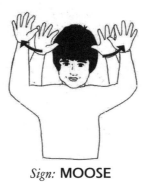

Sign: **MOOSE**

BOOKS

Mucky Moose by Jonathan Allen. New York: Macmillan, 1990.

*Beaver Pond, Moose Pond by Jim Arnosky. Washington, DC: National Geographic Society, 2000.

Elliot Gets Stuck by Andrea Beck. Toronto, ON: Kids Can Press, 2002.

The Trial of Cardigan Jones by Tim Egan. New York: Houghton Mifflin, 2004.

*Mooses Come Walking by Arlo Guthrie. New York: Chronicle, 1995.

The Rooster's Antlers: A Story of the Chinese Zodiac by Eric A. Kimmel. New York: Holiday House, 1999.

How the Reindeer Got Their Antlers by Geraldine McCaughrean. New York: Holiday House, 2000.

*If You Give a Moose a Muffin by Laura Joffe Numeroff. New York: HarperCollins, 1991.

Moosekitos: A Moose Family Reunion by Margie Palatini. New York: Hyperion, 2004.

Moosetache by Margie Palatini. New York: Hyperion, 1997.

Silver Morning by Susan Pearson. San Diego: Harcourt Brace, 1990.

*Moose, Of Course! by Lynn Plourde. Rockport, ME: Down East Books, 1999.

*Looking for a Moose by Phyllis Root. Cambridge, MA: Candlewick, 2006.

Lost in the Woods by Carl R. Sams II. Milford, MI: Carl R. Sams II Photography, 2004.

Thidwick the Big-Hearted Moose by Dr. Seuss. New York: Random House, 1948.

Imogene's Antlers by David Small. New York: Crown, 1985.

Uses for Mooses and Other Popular Pets by Mike Thaler. Mahwah, NJ: Troll, 1994.

*What Use Is a Moose? by Martin Waddell. Cambridge, MA: Candlewick, 1996.

Uncles and Antlers by Lisa Wheeler. New York: Atheneum, 2004.

*Moose Tracks! by Karma Wilson. New York: Simon and Schuster, 2006.

RECORDED MUSIC

"Doin' the Moose" from *If You Give a Moose a Muffin/Doin' the Moose/The Muffin Game* by Laura Numeroff (audiobook). New York: HarperCollins, 1997.

FINGERPLAYS/SONGS

"If I Were a Moose"

If I were a moose, I'd have antlers.
Imagine that!
But if I had antlers,
I couldn't wear a hat.

PROPS

Flannelboard Song

"M-O-O-S-E"
(to the tune of "BINGO")

PIECES NEEDED: *letters of the word MOOSE*

In the woods there lives a creature
And Moose is its name, oh.
M-O-O-S-E, M-O-O-S-E, M-O-O-S-E
And Moose is its name, oh.

Repeat, gradually replacing letters with claps and removing letters from the flannelboard.

*Flannelboard Rhyme

"Five Little Deer"

PIECES NEEDED: *5 deer*

5 little deer going out to explore,
1 found a salt lick, and then there were 4.
4 little deer with so much to see,
1 stopped for a drink, and then there were 3.
3 little deer with so much to do,
1 chased a butterfly, and then there were 2.
2 little deer, playing in the sun,
1 stopped to graze, and then there was 1.
1 little deer, playing all alone
He went home, and then there were none.

CRAFTS

Moose Antlers

MATERIALS: precut paper headband for each child, 2 precut antlers for each child, gluesticks, stickers, crayons

DIRECTIONS:
1. Glue the antlers to the headband.
2. Decorate with stickers and crayons.
3. Glue the ends of the headband together.

Antlers Coloring Sheet

MATERIALS: coloring sheet with forest background, die-cut shapes of deer or moose, glue, crayons

DIRECTIONS:
1. Glue the animal shapes to the coloring sheet.
2. Color as desired.

Bells Are Ringing

Sign: **BELL**

BOOKS

Prancing, Dancing Lily by Marsha Diane Arnold. New York: Dial, 2004.

Jingle Bells by Nick Butterworth. New York: Orchard Books, 1997.

*Ting-a-ling! by Siobhan Dodds. New York: DK, 1999.

She Did It! by Jennifer A. Ericsson. New York: Farrar, Straus and Giroux, 2002.

*General Store by Rachel Field. New York: Greenwillow, 1988.

Lilly's Big Day by Kevin Henkes. New York: Greenwillow, 2006.

*The Doorbell Rang by Pat Hutchins. New York: Greenwillow, 1986.

The Liberty Bell by Judith Jango-Cohen. Minneapolis: Lerner, 2004.

Daisy Dare by Anita Jeram. Cambridge, MA: Candlewick, 1995.

Jingle Bells by Maryann Kovalski. New York: Little, Brown, 1988.

*Jingle Bells by Michael Scott. New York: Hyperion, 2003.

Jingle Dancer by Cynthia Leitich Smith. New York: Morrow, 2000.

*Mouse's First Christmas by Lauren Thompson. New York: Simon and Schuster, 1999.

*Goodnight, Country by Susan Verlander. San Francisco: Chronicle, 2004.

*Wake Up, City by Susan Verlander. San Francisco: Chronicle, 2004.

Tell-a-bunny by Nancy Elizabeth Wallace. New York: Winslow Press, 2000.

RECORDED MUSIC

*"Jingle Bells, Samba Style" from *Baby Einstein: Baby Santa.* Disney, 2006. *(Use with jingle bells.)*

*"Telephone" from *Buzz Buzz* by Laurie Berkner. Two Tomatoes, 2001.

Christmas with Sonos Handbell Ensemble. Well-Tempered Productions, 1995.

FINGERPLAYS/SONGS

"When the Cat Goes Walking"

When the cat goes walking, her feet
make no sound. *(tiptoe)*
But the bell around her neck warns all
the mice around. *(do the sign for
BELL)*
If they don't hear the bell, then mice
come out to play. *(jump and dance)*
But when they hear a "ring-a-ling," then
they run away! *(run in place)*

*Play the freeze game with a bell. When the
bell is silent, the children are the mice playing,
dancing, and jumping. When they hear the
bell, they must freeze.*

"Are You Sleeping?"
(traditional)

Are you sleeping, are you sleeping?
Brother John, Brother John?
Morning bells are ringing.
Morning bells are ringing.
Ding dang dong.
Ding dang dong.

"Alarm Clock"

I was oh-so-tired at 1 o'clock
    (yawn and stretch)
When I heard the clock tick-tock.
    (cup ear with hand)
I was just settling down into my bed
    (mime sleep)
When RING RING the alarm clock said.
    (jump up)

Repeat with times up to 12 o'clock.

PROPS

*Flannelboard or Prop Rhyme

"Five Little Telephones"

PIECES NEEDED: *5 telephones*

5 little telephones, ringing by the door.
Mommy answered one, and then there
    were 4.
4 little telephones, ringing so loudly.
Daddy answered one, and then there
    were 3.
3 little telephones, ringing right on cue.
My brother answered one, and then there
    were 2.
2 little telephones, ringing just for fun.
My sister answered one, and then there
    was 1.
1 little telephone, and I knew what to do.
I answered that one, and—Oh! It's for
    you!

*Prop Rhyme

"Jingle Bell Moves"

PIECES NEEDED: *enough jingle bells or bell
bracelets for each child to have one*

Shake those bells up high!
Shake those bells down low!
Shake those bells in a circle just so.
Shake them up and down.
Shake them all around.
Now shake them down to touch the
    ground.
Shake them left and right.
Now shake them out of sight.
Now shake those bells with all your
    might!

*Prop Song

"There's a Bell on My Head"
(to the tune of "Spider on the Floor")

PIECES NEEDED: *enough jingle bells or bell bracelets for each child to have one*

There's a bell on my head, on my head.
There's a bell on my head, on my head.
Oh, let it be said there's a bell on my
    head.
There's a bell on my head, on my head.
There's a bell on my arm . . . It's not
    doing any harm, but . . .
There's a bell on my hand . . . Oh, isn't
    it grand . . .
There's a bell on my leg . . . Oh, help me,
    I beg . . .
There's a bell on my knee . . . Oh, can't
    you see . . .
There's a bell on my toe . . . Oh, don't
    you know . . .

*Prop Song

"Ring the Bells"
(to the tune of "Row, Row, Row Your Boat")

PIECES NEEDED: *enough jingle bells or bell bracelets for each child to have one*

Ring ring ring the bells,
Happy as can be.
Ring them high,
Ring them low,
Ring along with me.

*Prop Story   *The Doorbell Rang* by Pat Hutchins. New York: Greenwillow, 1986.
    PIECES NEEDED: *12 cookies*

CRAFTS

Liberty Bell Favor

From *Star-Spangled Crafts* by Kathy Ross (Brookfield, CT: Millbrook Press, 2003).

Jingle Bell Bracelet

MATERIALS: 2 chenille stems for each child, 1 jingle bell for each child

DIRECTIONS:
1. Thread the jingle bell onto one of the chenille stems.
2. Twine the two chenille stems together.
3. Twist the ends together to form a bracelet.

Best Buds

Sign: **FRIEND**

📖 **BOOKS**

That's What Friends Do by Kathryn Cave. New York: Hyperion, 2004.

Best Best Friends by Margaret Chodos-Irvine. New York: Harcourt, 2006.

Bud and Gabby by Anne Davis. New York: HarperCollins, 2006.

Zinnia and Dot by Lisa Campbell Ernst. New York: Viking, 1992.

That's What Friends Are For by Valeri Gorbachev. New York: Philomel, 2005.

*Four Friends Together by Sue Heap. Cambridge, MA: Candlewick, 2003.

*What Shall We Play? by Sue Heap. Cambridge, MA: Candlewick, 2002.

That's What Friends Are For by Florence Perry Heide and Sylvia Can Clief. Cambridge, MA: Candlewick, 2003.

*What a Treasure! by Jane and Will Hillenbrand. New York: Holiday House, 2006.

Horace and Morris but Mostly Dolores by James Howe. New York: Atheneum, 1999.

*Titch and Daisy by Pat Hutchins. New York: Greenwillow, 1996.

My Friend and I by Lisa Jahn-Clough. New York: Houghton Mifflin, 1999.

*Henry and Amy (Right-way-round and Upside-down) by Stephen Michael King. New York: Walker, 1998.

*My Bear and Me by Barbara Maitland. New York: Simon and Schuster, 1999.

Too Close Friends by Shen Roddie. New York: Dial, 1997.

*What about Me? by Helen Stephens. New York: DK, 1999.

*Will You Be My Friend? by Nancy Tafuri. New York: Scholastic, 2000.

*Little Quack's New Friend by Lauren Thompson. New York: Simon and Schuster, 2006.

Unlovable by Dan Yaccarino. New York: Henry Holt, 2001.

RECORDED MUSIC

*"I Had a Friend" from *Buzz Buzz* by Laurie Berkner. Two Tomatoes, 2001.

"With Our Friends" from *Rockin' Reading Readiness* by Pam Schiller and RONNO. Kimbo Educational, 2005.

"Hey Little Friend" from *Sing It! Say It! Stamp It! Sway It! Volume 3* by Peter and Ellen Allard. 80-Z Music, 2002.

*"The More We Get Together" from *Singable Songs for the Very Young* by Raffi. Rounder/UMGD, 1976.

FINGERPLAYS/SONGS

"Hello/Goodbye Friends"
(to the tune of "Twinkle Twinkle")

Hello, hello, all my friends.
It's so nice to see you again.
Hello Sarah, Hello Tom, Hello Bobby,
    Hello Abigail. *(repeat this line until
    you have said all the children's names)*
Hello, hello, all my friends.
It's so nice to see you again.

Goodbye, goodbye, all my friends
I can't wait to see you again.
Goodbye Sarah, Goodbye Tom, Goodbye
    Bobby, Goodbye Abigail. *(repeat this
    line until you have said all the children's
    names)*
Goodbye, goodbye, all my friends.
I can't wait to see you again.

"Knock Knock"

Knock knock at the door of my
    friend Jill.
"Will you come out to play?"
"I will!"

"Silver and Gold"
(traditional)

Make new friends, but keep the old.
One is silver, the other is gold.
A circle is round, it has no end.
That's how long I will be your friend.
A fire burns bright, it warms the heart.
We've been friends, from the very start.
You have one hand, I have the other.
Put them together, we have each other.

"Sign of Friendship"
(to the tune of "Row, Row, Row Your Boat")

Here's the sign for you. *(point to someone
    else)*
Here's the sign for me. *(point to yourself)*
I put my fingers together like this, *(do the
    sign for FRIEND)*
'Cause friends we'll always be.

"Ten Little Friends"
(to the tune of "Ten Little Indians")

1 little, 2 little, 3 little friends,
4 little, 5 little, 6 little friends,
7 little, 8 little, 9 little friends,
10 friends come to play.

"Rig-a-Jig-Jig"
(traditional)

As I was walking down the street, down the street, down the street,
A very good friend I chanced to meet, hi ho hi ho hi ho.
Rig-a-jig-jig and away we go, away we go, away we go,
Rig-a-jig-jig and away we go, hi ho hi ho hi ho.
We clapped our hands and stomped our feet, stomped our feet, stomped our feet,
We clapped our hands and stomped our feet, hi ho hi ho hi ho.
We jumped up high and came back down, came back down, came back down,
We jumped up high and came back down, hi ho hi ho hi ho.
Rig-a-jig-jig and away we go, away we go, away we go;
Rig-a-jig-jig and away we go, hi ho hi ho hi ho.

"Suzy's Friends"

Once there was a little girl named Suzy. She said, "I only want to be friends with people who DANCE." Can you dance?

But then she changed her mind. She said, "I only want to be friends with people who JUMP." Can you jump?

Then she changed her mind again. She said, "I only want to be friends with people who SPIN." Can you spin?

Then she changed her mind again. She said, "I only want to be friends with people who WAVE." Can you wave?

Then all her friends said, "We want to do what we feel like doing, but we still want to be your friends!" And Suzy said, "OK!" So some of them DANCED, and some of them JUMPED, and some of them SPUN, and some of them WAVED, but they all had lots of fun!

PROPS

*Flannelboard Rhyme

"Five Friends"

PIECES NEEDED: *5 children*

1 little friend wondering what to do.
Along came another, and then there were 2.
2 little friends with so much to see.
Along came another, and then there were 3.
3 little friends, off to explore.
Along came another, and then there were 4.
4 little friends, glad to be alive.
Along came another, and then there were 5.
5 little friends no longer alone.
Their mothers called them then, so they ran on home.

Flannelboard Matching Game: Friends Playing

Make flannelboard pieces of pairs of friends, each holding or wearing something related to a specific activity. The children must match the friends by figuring out which pieces go together. Some suggested pairings:

Bat/baseball
Pail/shovel
Paper/crayons
Dump truck/digger
Tutu/ballet slippers
Toy firetruck/firefighter's hat
Books/library card
Apron/mixing bowl

*Flannelboard or Puppet Story   *Thank You Bear* by Greg Foley. New York: Viking, 2007.

PIECES NEEDED: *bear, mouse, small box that mouse can fit into, monkey, owl, fox, elephant, squirrel, rabbit*

*Flannelboard or Prop Story   *Can't You Sleep, Dotty?* by Tim Warnes. Wilton, CT: Tiger Tales, 2001.

PIECES NEEDED: *dog, mouse, bird, bowl, rabbit, blanket, tortoise, flashlight, basket*

CRAFTS

Friendship Magnets

MATERIALS: construction paper, scissors, crayons or markers, stickers or other decorating materials, adhesive magnet strips

DIRECTIONS:
1. Trace two hands and cut them out. (May be precut.)
2. Overlap the hand shapes to look like the two hands are holding each other.
3. Decorate with stickers, glue, crayons, etc.
4. Place two strips of adhesive magnets on the back of the shapes.

Friendship Chains

MATERIALS: precut strips of construction paper (about 6 inches by 2 inches), glue, markers or crayons

DIRECTIONS:
1. On each strip of paper, write or draw something you like about your friend.
2. Form one strip of paper into a circle by gluing the ends together. Continue with the other strips, linking the strips together to form a chain.
3. Give the chain to your friend!

Books Are Magic

Sign: **BOOK**

BOOKS

Too Many Books! by Caroline Feller Bauer. New York: Puffin, 1986.

Wolf! by Becky Bloom. New York: Orchard, 1999.

More Than Anything Else by Marie Bradby. New York: Scholastic, 1995.

The Big White Book with Almost Nothing in It by Mike Brownlow. Wincanton, England: Ragged Bears Publishing, 2001.

*Book! Book! Book! by Deborah Bruss. New York: Scholastic, 2001.

*B Is for Books! by Annie Cobb. New York: Random House, 1996.

The Library Dragon by Carmen Agra Deedy. Atlanta, GA: Peachtree, 1994.

Charlie Cook's Favorite Book by Julia Donaldson. New York: Dial, 2005.

Stella Louella's Runaway Book by Lisa Campbell Ernst. New York: Simon and Schuster, 1998.

Miss Smith's Incredible Storybook by Michael Garland. New York: Dutton, 2003.

*Book! by Kristine O'Connell George. New York: Clarion, 2001.

Walter's Magic Wand by Eric Houghton. New York: Orchard, 1989.

I Love My Little Storybook by Anita Jeram. Cambridge, MA: Candlewick, 2002.

*I Took My Frog to the Library by Eric A. Kimmel. New York: Puffin, 1990.

The Frog Princess? by Pamela Mann. Strongsville, OH: Gareth Stevens, 1995.

Winston the Book Wolf by Marni McGee. New York: Walker, 2006.

Edward and the Pirates by David McPhail. New York: Little, Brown, 1997.

*Lola at the Library by Anna McQuinn. Watertown, MA: Charlesbridge, 2006.

Beverly Billingsly Borrows a Book by Alexander Stadler. San Diego: Harcourt, 2002.

Library Lil by Suzanne Williams. New York: Dial, 1997.

The Old Woman Who Loved to Read by John Winch. New York: Scholastic, 1996.

Can You Guess Where We're Going? by Elvira Woodruff. New York: Holiday House, 1998.

*Baby Bear's Books by Jane Yolen. San Diego: Harcourt, 2006.

RECORDED MUSIC

"These Are My Glasses" from *Whaddaya Think of That?* by Laurie Berkner. Two Tomatoes, 2001.

FINGERPLAYS/SONGS

"It's Magic"

I have something magical, it's very plain
    to see.
It can take me to strange places, like the
    mountains and the sea.
It helps me meet strange creatures, like
    fairies, trolls, and dragons,
And it helps me learn new things, like
    how to build red wagons.
What is this amazing thing? Would you
    like to take a look?
I found all this magic in the pages of a
    book!

"This Is the Way We . . ."
(to the tune of "Here We Go 'Round
the Mulberry Bush")

This is the way we go to the library,
go to the library, go to the library.
This is the way we go to the library, all
    through the day.
This is the way we read our books . . .
This is the way we turn the pages . . .
This is the way we look at pictures . . .
This is the way we listen to stories . . .

"Library Storytime"

When I am going to storytime
    (point to self)
I jump right off out of bed. *(jump)*
I wash my face, *(scrub face)*
And brush my teeth, *(brush teeth)*
And pull on clothes over my head.
    (arms up and down)
I run downstairs, *(run in place)*
And drink my milk, *(pretend to drink)*
And eat my breakfast just so.
    (pretend to chew)
I wave good-bye as I go out the door.
    (wave)
I'm so happy that I can go! *(smile)*

"Here Is My Book"

Here is my book. *(hold hands together and
    open, like a book)*
I open it wide,
To see all the pictures that are inside.

PROPS

*Flannelboard Song

"Ten Little Books"

PIECES NEEDED: *10 books*

1 little, 2 little, 3 little books,
4 little, 5 little, 6 little books,
7 little, 8 little, 9 little books,
10 little books to read!

*Matching Game: Book Matching

Using a website like Amazon.com or your library's online catalog, print out large pictures of book covers and laminate them. Be sure to print out 2 copies of each book cover. Give one set of covers to the children, one cover to each child. Hold up the remaining set one by one and sing this song to the children (to the tune of "Do You Know the Muffin Man?") to invite them to match the covers.

> Oh, do you have this book, this book, this book?
> If you have this book, bring it here to me.

*Prop Story
"The Library" from *Poppleton* by Cynthia Rylant. New York: Scholastic, 1997.

PIECES NEEDED: *duffel bag with eyeglasses, tissues, lip balm, pocket watch, bookmark, book*

ADDITIONAL SUGGESTIONS

Poetry

"I Met a Dragon Face to Face" by Jack Prelutsky or other poems in *Good Books, Good Times!* selected by Lee Bennett Hopkins. New York: HarperCollins, 1990.

CRAFTS

Magic Folder

From *The Magic Book* by Jane Bull (New York: DK, 2002).

Bookmarks

MATERIALS: 1 precut strip of cardstock (6 inches by 2 inches) for each child, hole punch, 8-inch strip of ribbon for each child, crayons or markers, stickers

DIRECTIONS:
1. Decorate your bookmark with stickers, crayons, etc.
2. Punch a hole on the top, about ½ inch from the edge.
3. Fold the ribbon in half, and push the folded end through the hole. Push the loose ends through the loop formed by the folded end, and pull them tight.

Brothers and Sisters

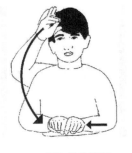

Sign: **BROTHER**

Sign: **SISTER**

BOOKS

It's All about Me! by Nancy Cote. New York: G. P. Putnam's Sons, 2005.

*When Will Sarah Come? by Nina Crews. New York: Greenwillow, 1999.

Big Brother, Little Brother by Marci Curtis. New York: Dial, 2004.

*Big Brother, Little Brother by Penny Dale. Cambridge, MA: Candlewick, 1997.

The Wildest Brother by Cornelia Funke. New York: Scholastic, 2004.

My Little Sister Ate One Hare by Bill Grossman. New York: Crown, 1996.

If I Were Queen of the World by Fred Hiatt. New York: Simon and Schuster, 1997.

*Spot's Baby Sister by Eric Hill. New York: Puffin, 1989.

You'll Soon Grow Into Them, Titch by Pat Hutchins. New York: Greenwillow, 1983.

*Do Like Kyla by Angela Johnson. New York: Orchard, 1990.

*Peter's Chair by Ezra Jack Keats. New York: Viking, 1967.

The Younger Brother's Survival Guide by Lisa Kopelke. New York: Simon and Schuster, 1996.

*My Baby Brother Has Ten Tiny Toes by Laura Leuck. Morton Grove, IL: Albert Whitman, 1997.

Who Shares? by Ewa Lipniacka. New York: Dial, 2003.

*Oh, Brother by Kathy Mallat. New York: Walker, 2003.

Stripe's Naughty Sister by Joanne Partis. Minneapolis: Carolrhoda, 2001.

*Baby Says by John Steptoe. New York: Lothrop, Lee, and Shepard, 1988.

*Oonga Boonga by Frieda Wishinsky. New York: Dutton, 1998.

Brothers Are for Making Mud Pies by Harriet Ziefert. New York: Puffin, 2001.

RECORDED MUSIC

"Brother, Come and Dance with Me" from *A Tisket, A Tasket.* Kimbo Educational, 2004.

"Sisters and Brothers" from *Free to Be You and Me* by Marlo Thomas and Friends. Arista Records, 2006.

FINGERPLAYS/SONGS

"Brothers and Sisters"

We have the same mommy,
Or we have the same daddy,
Or maybe both, you know.
We are brothers.
We are sisters.
Aren't you glad it's so?

"My Sister Has a Nose"

My sister has a nose, and I do too!
*(point to each body part as you say the
fingerplay)*
My sister has ten toes, and I do too!
My sister has elbows, and I do too!
My sister has 2 eyes, and I do too!
My sister has a tummy, and I do too!
My sister has 2 feet, and I do too!

"I've Got a Family"
(to the tune of "My Darling Clementine")

I've got a mommy,
Got a daddy,
Got a sister and a brother.
Altogether we're a family,
And we all love one another.

"Are You Sleeping?"
(traditional)

Are you sleeping, are you sleeping?
Brother John, Brother John?
Morning bells are ringing.
Morning bells are ringing.
Ding dang dong.
Ding dang dong.

PROPS

*Flannelboard Rhyme

"Jack and Jill"

PIECES NEEDED: *girl, boy, hill, well, pail*

Jack and Jill went up the hill to fetch a pail of water.
Jack fell down and broke his crown and Jill came
    tumbling after.

*Flannelboard Matching Game: Brothers and Sisters Matching

PIECES NEEDED: *pairs of simple boy and girl shapes in various colors*

If additional pairs are needed, try making some striped, some polka-dotted, etc., or, for very
large groups, mark each pair with a letter of the alphabet. Give one set out to the children
and hold up the other set piece by piece to play the matching game.

I am looking for my (brother/sister). Can you help me please?
My sister (is red/has polka-dots/is wearing an *A*), just like me.

ADDITIONAL SUGGESTIONS

Memory Game: My Little Brother Ate a Pie

Have everyone sit in a circle. Start by saying "My little brother ate a pie." The next person in the circle says "My little brother ate a pie AND a _____." Continue around the circle, adding on to the list.

"Brother Says" or "Sister Says" Game

Play this twist on "Simon Says" by replacing "Simon" with "brother" or "sister."

CRAFTS

Craft Stick Picture Frame

MATERIALS: 8 craft sticks for each child, glue, markers, crayons, stickers, glitter and other decorating materials

DIRECTIONS:
1. Place 2 craft sticks side by side and glue them together. Put them aside to dry and repeat this process by gluing the remaining craft sticks into side-by-side pairs.
2. Place 2 sets of craft sticks vertically to form the right and left sides of the frame.
3. Place the remaining 2 sets of craft sticks at the top and bottom edges of the frame, making sure the sticks overlap with the sides. Glue the frame together.
4. Decorate the front of the frame as desired.
5. Tape a picture to the back of the frame so that it shows through the front.

Jack and Jill Pictures

MATERIALS: a simple coloring sheet showing a hill and a well for each child, 2 craft sticks for each child, Jack and Jill shapes for each child (patterns can be found in *The Complete Resource Book for Toddlers and Twos* by Pamela Byrne Schiller, Beltsville, MD: Gryphon House, 2003), glue, crayons or markers

DIRECTIONS:
1. Cut a slit in the coloring sheets leading up the hill.
2. Decorate the Jack and Jill shapes, then glue them to the craft sticks to make stick puppets.
3. Decorate the coloring sheet.
4. Poke the sticks through the slit in the paper to act out the rhyme.

Bubbles

Sign: **BUBBLE**

BOOKS

Pop! A Book about Bubbles by Kimberly Brubaker Bradley. New York: HarperCollins, 2001.

*Maisy Takes a Bath by Lucy Cousins. Cambridge, MA: Candlewick, 2000.

*Mrs. Wishy-Washy by Joy Cowley. Bothell, WA: Wright Group, 1990.

Strega Nona Takes a Vacation by Tomie dePaola. New York: G. P. Putnam's Sons, 2000.

*Dog's Colorful Day by Emma Dodd. New York: Dutton, 2000.

*Pet Wash by Dayle Ann Dodds. Cambridge, MA: Candlewick, 2001.

*Elephant Small and the Splashy Bath by Sally Grindley. Hauppauge, NY: Barron's, 1998.

Big Red Tub by Julia Jarman. New York: Scholastic, 2004.

Bubble Trouble by Stephen Krensky. New York: Aladdin, 2004.

Bubble Bath Pirates by Jarrett J. Krosoczka. New York: Viking, 2003.

Squeaky Clean by Simon Puttock. New York: Little, Brown, 2002.

*Curious George at the Laundromat by Margret Rey. New York: Houghton Mifflin, 1987.

Wash Your Hands! by Tony Ross. Brooklyn, NY: Kane/Miller, 2000.

Splish! Splash! Animal Baths by April Pulley Sayre. Brookfield, CT: Millbrook Press, 2000.

The Bubble Gum Kid by Stu Smith. Philadelphia: Running Press Kids, 2006.

*Bath Time by Eileen Spinelli. New York: Marshall Cavendish, 2003.

Dad's Car Wash by Harry A. Sutherland. New York: Atheneum, 1988.

Scrubba Dub by Nancy Van Laan. New York: Atheneum, 2003.

No Bath! No Way! by Brigitte Weninger. New York: Penguin, 2004.

King Bidgood's in the Bathtub by Audrey Wood. San Diego: Harcourt, 1985.

Harry the Dirty Dog by Gene Zion. New York: HarperCollins, 1956.

RECORDED MUSIC

*"Bubbles" from *Bubbles* by Erick Traplin. Erick Traplin Music, www.ericktraplin.com.

*"I Took a Bath in a Washing Machine" from *Jim Gill Sings The Sneezing Song and Other Contagious Tunes* by Jim Gill. Jim Gill Music, 1993.

*"Everybody Wash" and other songs from *Splish Splash: Bath Time Fun* (Sesame Street). Sony Wonder, 1995.

*"The Bathtub Song" from *Tiny Tunes: Music for Very Young Children* by Carole Peterson. Macaroni Soup, 2005.

FINGERPLAYS/SONGS

*"Let's Make a Bubble"

Can you pretend to be a bubble? It's easy, you will see.
Let's all join hands in a great big circle and listen carefully.
We start our bubble very small and then it grows without a stop. *(encourage children to move outward, increasing the bubble's size)*
Bigger, bigger, bigger, bigger . . .
Oh, no! It's going to POP! *(raise hands over head and clap loudly)*

"If I Were a Bubble"

If I were a bubble *(make arms into a circle and dance and sway throughout the following lines)*
I would float and fly all day.
I would dance and I would shimmer,
And I would gently float away.
I would rise up to the ceiling
Until I reached the top.
And do you know what I'd do then?
I'd leave with a POP! (jump up)

*"Blowing Bubbles"
(to the tune of "Frère Jacques")

Blowing bubbles, blowing bubbles
All day long, all day long.
See them float and fly, see them float and fly
Then they POP. Then they POP.

"Bubble Bath"

I love bubbles in my tub.
They help me to scrub-a-dub.
Bubbles on my elbows,
Bubbles on my toes,
Bubbles on my tummy,
Bubbles are so funny.
But when a bubble tickles my nose
I say AH-CHOO! and away that bubble goes.

*"Found Some Bubblegum"
(to the tune of "Found a Peanut")

Found some bubblegum, found some bubblegum,
Found some bubblegum just now.
Just now I found some bubblegum,
Found some bubblegum just now.
So I chewed it . . .
I blew a bubble . . .
It got bigger . . .
Then it popped . . .

"POP! Go the Bubbles"
(to the tune of "Pop Goes the Weasel")

All around the storytime room
The children chase the bubbles.
The bubbles float up and away,
POP! go the bubbles.

PROPS

*Flannelboard Story   *Clifford Counts Bubbles* by Norman Bridwell. New York: Scholastic, 1992.

> PIECES NEEDED: *Little Clifford, 10 bubbles, cat, rabbit, bee, butterfly, 5 brown mice*

*Flannelboard Poem   "Trouble Bubble Bath" by Douglas Florian. From *The Fish Is Me: Bathtime Rhymes* selected by Neil Philip. New York: Clarion, 2002.

> PIECES NEEDED: *shark, bathtub. Hide the shark behind the bathtub piece, then lift the bathtub away to reveal the shark at the end of the poem.*

*Flannelboard Story   *Dog's Colorful Day* by Emma Dodd. New York: Dutton, 2000.

> PIECES NEEDED: *white dog with black spot on left ear; 9 dots in red, blue, green, brown, yellow, pink, gray, orange, purple; bathtub; small scrubber for each child made from netting material tied together in a bunch. At the end of the story, invite the children to scrub the air with their scrubbers as you remove the dots from the dog. This also makes a nice tie-in to the song "Everybody Wash" from* Splish Splash: Bath Time Fun.

*Prop Story   *Sam's Bath* by Barbro Lindgren. New York: Morrow, 1983.

> PIECES NEEDED: *bathtub, little boy doll, dog, ball, truck, cookie, spray bottle of water for splashes*

ADDITIONAL SUGGESTIONS

*Poems to Act Out

"After a Bath" by Aileen Fisher. From *The Fish Is Me: Bathtime Rhymes* selected by Neil Philip. New York: Clarion, 2002.

"Blowing Bubbles" by Margaret Hillert. From *Read-Aloud Rhymes for the Very Young* edited by Jack Prelutsky. New York: Knopf, 1986.

*Blowing Bubbles Games

Get small bubble bottles, enough for each child. (Check out the No-Spill Bubble Tumbler Minis from Little Kids, www.littlekidsinc.com. These refillable bottles lock to prevent spilling, are small and easy enough for toddlers to use, and are inexpensive enough to purchase one for every child in storytime.) Pass out the bubble bottles, and invite the children to follow your directions as they blow bubbles.

1. Can you blow 3 bubbles in a row?
2. Can you blow bubbles up high?
3. Can you stand on one foot and blow a bubble?
4. Play "Musical Bubbles"—when the children hear the music, they blow bubbles, but when the music stops, they must freeze.

Bubble Experiment: Are Bubbles Always Round?

Purchase different-shaped bubble wands or make them yourself by bending coat hangers into assorted shapes (triangle, square, circle, etc.). Use a pie tin filled with bubble soap, and experiment with each shape to show that bubbles are always round. Find additional bubble facts and experiments in *Soap Bubble Magic* by Seymour Simon (New York: Lothrop, Lee, and Shepard, 1985).

CRAFTS

*Bubble Bath Picture

MATERIALS: 1 piece of paper for each child, 1 bathtub shape for each child, various animal shapes, precut circles of waxed paper or iridescent wrapping paper for bubbles, glue, crayons or markers. (This craft is a good tie-in to *Big Red Tub* and *Mrs. Wishy-Washy.*)

DIRECTIONS:
1. Glue the bathtub onto the paper.
2. Glue the animals into the tub.
3. Glue on the circles to represent bubbles.
4. Decorate as desired.

Bubble Blowing Picture

MATERIALS: 1 piece of construction paper for each child, tempera paint, bubble solution and wands, plastic covering or newspaper for your storytime table and floor

DIRECTIONS:
1. Add some tempera paint to your bubble mixture.
2. Have children dip their bubble wands into the solution and blow bubbles onto the paper.
3. The bubbles will form designs on the paper as they pop.

Castle Tales

Sign: **KING**   *Sign:* **QUEEN**

BOOKS

Princess Smartypants by Babette Cole. New York: G. P. Putnam's Sons, 1986.

The Knight and the Dragon by Tomie dePaola. New York: Putnam and Grosset, 1980.

If I Had a Dragon by Tom and Amanda Ellery. New York: Simon and Schuster, 2006.

The Knight Who Was Afraid of the Dark by Barbara Shook Hazen. New York: Dial, 1989.

*The Missing Tarts by B. G. Hennessy. New York: Viking, 1989.

Serious Trouble by Arthur Howard. New York: Harcourt, 2003.

The Best Pet of All by David LaRochelle. New York: Dutton, 2004.

A Number of Dragons by Loreen Leedy. New York: Holiday House, 1985.

*Who Wants a Dragon? by James Mayhew. New York: Orchard, 2004.

Good Night, Princess Pruney Toes by Lisa McCourt. Mahwah, NJ: Troll, 2001.

Good Knight, Sleep Tight by David Melling. Hauppauge, New York: Barron's, 2005.

The Kiss That Missed by David Melling. Hauppauge, New York: Barron's, 2002.

The Paper Bag Princess by Robert Munsch. Toronto, ON: Annick Press, 2003.

Custard the Dragon and the Wicked Knight by Ogden Nash. New York: Little, Brown, 1961.

I Am Really a Princess by Carol Diggory Shields. New York: Dutton, 1993.

*The Popcorn Dragon by Jane Thayer. New York: Morrow, 1989.

Do Knights Take Naps? by Kathy Tucker. New York: Albert Whitman, 2000.

*There's a Dragon at My School by Jenny Tyler and Philip Hawthorn. Tulsa, OK: Usborne, 1996.

*King Bidgood's in the Bathtub by Audrey Wood. San Diego: Harcourt, 1985.

George and the Dragon by Chris Wormell. New York: Knopf, 2002.

RECORDED MUSIC

*"The Noble Duke of York" from *I Love to Sing with Barney.* Koch Records, 2003.

"Up Goes the Castle" from *Bert and Ernie's Greatest Hits.* Sony Wonder, 1996.

*"Queen of Tarts" from *Toddler Favorites Too.* Music for Little People, 2002.

FINGERPLAYS/SONGS

"This Is the Way"
(adapted traditional)

This is the way the queen rides—
Trit trot trit trot.
This is the way the king rides—
Gallop-a-trot, gallop-a-trot.
This is the way the knight rides—
Hobbledy-hoy, hobbledy-hoy.

"The King/Queen Commands"

The King/Queen commands you to stand
  on one foot.
The King/Queen commands you to stand
  on the other foot.
Now jump up and down.
Wait! The King/Queen did not command!

Repeat with other actions.

"Old King Cole"
(adapted traditional)

Old King Cole was a merry old soul,
A merry old soul was he.
He called for his pipe, and he called for
  his bowl,
And he called for his fiddlers three.
Old King Cole was a merry old soul,
A merry old soul was he.
He DANCED for his pipe, and he
  DANCED for his bowl,
And he DANCED for his fiddlers three.

Repeat with CLAPPED, JUMPED, and TURNED.

PROPS

*Flannelboard Rhyme

"Five Little Dragons"

PIECES NEEDED: *5 dragons, knight*

1 little dragon feeling kind of blue,
Another dragon comes along, and now there are 2.
2 little dragons happy as can be,
Another dragon comes along, and now there are 3.
3 little dragons letting out a roar,
Another dragon comes along, and now there are 4.
4 little dragons, see them dip and dive,
Another dragon comes along, and now there are 5.
5 little dragons, looking for some fun,
A knight comes along, the dragons run away, and now
  there are none.

*Flannelboard Rhyme

"Counting Tarts"

PIECES NEEDED: *5 tarts or pies*

5 royal tarts waiting by the door,
The jester ate one, and then there were 4.
4 royal tarts, so beautiful to see,
The knight ate one, and then there were 3.
3 royal tarts for the king, it's true,
The maid ate one, and then there were 2.
2 royal tarts, oh, isn't it fun,
The queen ate one, and then there was 1.
1 royal tart, and we are almost done,
The king ate that one, and then there were none.
Yum!

*Mask Story: "The Royal Pumpkin Pie"

PIECES NEEDED: *simple masks for the characters of the king, queen, prince, princess, wizard, jester, cat, dog, mouse, dragon. For each mask, cut a basic masquerade mask shape out of black posterboard and cut out holes for the eyes. Attach a craft stick to one side of the mask for a handle, then decorate each mask with simple shapes to go with the character, such as a crown, a star-studded wizard's hat, a jester's hat, cat ears, etc. Invite the children to become characters in the story and help you act it out. If desired, add enough animal characters so that everyone can take part in the story.*

One day the king went walking in the royal garden, and he saw a pumpkin so big that it made his mouth water. He wanted some pumpkin pie! He pulled and pulled, but that pumpkin just wouldn't let go of its vine. He called on the queen to come help him. The queen pulled on the king, and the king pulled on the pumpkin, but that pumpkin just wouldn't let go of its vine!

Continue in this pattern, adding the other characters.

Then finally, the pumpkin came loose! They all carried it together back to the royal kitchens, and made a yummy pumpkin pie. And they ate up every piece. Yum!

*Flannelboard Story   *Klippity Klop* by Ed Emberley. Boston: Little, Brown, 1974.

PIECES NEEDED: *stick puppet of knight on horse, dragon, bridge, stream, field, hill, cave, dragon, castle*

*Flannelboard Story   *Prince Peter and the Teddy Bear* by David McKee. New York: Farrar, Straus and Giroux, 1997.

PIECES NEEDED: *prince, king, queen, sword, crown, horse, throne, suit of armor, coach, golden teddy bear*

ADDITIONAL SUGGESTIONS

Knighting Ceremony

Dub each child a "Library Knight." Have each child come forward and kneel on a special pillow, then read a proclamation from a special scroll: "For worthy deeds in the pursuit of reading, and for constant kindness to books, I hereby dub thee Sir/Lady _____." Use a yardstick to tap the child on each shoulder.

CRAFTS

Dragon Pop-Up Cup

MATERIALS: one Styrofoam or paper cup for each child with a hole poked in the bottom, one craft stick for each child, glue, precut picture of a dragon, crayons or markers

DIRECTIONS:
1. Color the dragon.
2. Glue the dragon to the craft stick.
3. Place the dragon in the cup so that the stick goes through the hole in the bottom. Move the stick to make the dragon pop out of its "cave."

Bulletin Board Border Crowns

MATERIALS: wavy-edged bulletin board border cut to 22-inch lengths, crayons or markers, stickers, glue, glitter, feathers, fake gemstones and other decorating materials, stapler or tape

DIRECTIONS:
1. Decorate the crowns.
2. Measure to head and staple or tape the ends of the crown together.

Cats and Kittens

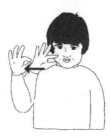

Sign: **CAT**

BOOKS

Kitty Princess and the Newspaper Dress by Emma Carlow. Cambridge, MA: Candlewick, 2003.

Storm Cats by Malachy Doyle. New York: Margaret K. McElderry Books, 2002.

I Walk at Night by Lois Duncan. New York: Viking, 2000.

*Feathers for Lunch by Lois Ehlert. San Diego: Harcourt Brace Jovanovich, 1990.

Top Cat by Lois Ehlert. San Diego: Harcourt Brace, 1998.

*Mama Cat Has Three Kittens by Denise Fleming. New York: Henry Holt, 1998.

*Kitten's First Full Moon by Kevin Henkes. New York: Greenwillow, 2004.

I Like Cats by Patricia Hubbell. New York: North-South, 2003.

Cleo on the Move by Caroline Mockford. Cambridge, MA: Barefoot Books, 2002.

Cleo's Counting Book by Caroline Mockford. Cambridge, MA: Barefoot Books, 2006.

Black Cat by Christopher Myers. New York: Scholastic, 1999.

Who Said Meow? by Maria Polushkin. New York: Bradbury Press, 1988.

Meow: A Day in the Life of Cats by Judy Reinen. New York: Little, Brown, 2001.

Cat Skidoo by Bethany Roberts. New York: Henry Holt, 2004.

*Three Little Kittens by Lorriane Siomades. Honesdale, PA: Boyds Mills Press, 2000.

*Cookie's Week by Cindy Ward. New York: Putnam, 1988.

*Have You Got My Purr? by Judy West. New York: Dutton, 1999.

RECORDED MUSIC

"The Cat Came Back" from *Whaddaya Think of That?* by Laurie Berkner. Two Tomatoes, 2001.

FINGERPLAYS/SONGS

"Five Little Kittens All in a Row"
(traditional)

Five little kittens all in a row.
(hold up five fingers)
They nod their heads just so.
(wiggle fingers)
They run left and they run right.
(move fingers to left and right)
Then stand and stretch in the bright
sunlight. (hold fingers up high)
Along comes a dog who wants some fun.
(bring thumb from other hand over)
MEOW! See how the kittens run!
(hide fingers behind back)

"I'm a Little Kitten"

I'm a little kitten, fluffy and sweet.
I have a long tail, (swish bottom)
And I have four feet. (stamp feet)
When I am angry, up goes my fur.
(arch back)
When I'm happy, hear me purrrrrr.

"My Kitten Fluff"
(to the tune of "My Dog Rags")

I've got a kitten and his name is Fluff.
He likes to get into lots of stuff.
He likes to meow and meow all day,
And when he meows, he does it in a
high way.
Meow, meow, meow, meow, meow,
meow, meow.
Meow, meow, meow, meow, meow,
meow, meow.
That's my kitten, good old Fluff.
. . . a low way.
. . . a fast way.
. . . a slow way.

"I'm a Little Kitty-Cat"
(to the tune of "I'm a Little Teapot")

I'm a little kitty-cat, covered in fur.
When I am happy hear me purr.
When I am angry, hear me hiss.
Then I'll wave my tail like this.

PROPS

*Flannelboard Rhyme

"Five Little Cats"

PIECES NEEDED: 5 cats

1 little cat wondering what to do,
Along came another, and then there were 2.
2 little cats climbing up a tree,
Along came another, and then there were 3.
3 little cats scratching at the door,
Along came another, and then there were 4.
4 little cats, glad to be alive,
Along came another, and then there were 5.
5 little cats, having so much fun,
Along came a dog! The cats ran away, and then there
were none.

*File Folder Story: "Scat the Cat"

Cut a simple cat shape out of one side of a file folder. Copy the following story and tape it to the other outer side of the folder. Tape the top and bottom edges of the folder together. Place pieces of construction paper in various colors in the folder, with white pieces on the top and bottom. Each time Scat changes colors, remove the top piece of paper.

Once upon a time, there was a little white kitten named Scat. But one day he decided he was tired of being a little white kitten. He looked at the beautiful brown tree trunks and decided brown was the color he wanted to be. So he said, "I am Scat the Cat, I am sleek and fat, and I can change colors just like THAT!"

Now he was a brown kitten. But pretty soon he saw a pretty orange flower and decided that the color he really wanted to be was orange. So he said, "I am Scat the Cat, I am sleek and fat, and I can change colors just like THAT!"

Repeat the pattern with blue—blueberries; red—strawberries; yellow—sun; black—night sky; green—grass; purple—grapes.

Then he saw the white fluffy clouds in the sky and decided that what he really REALLY wanted to be was a little white kitten. So he said, "I am Scat the Cat, I am sleek and fat, and I can change colors just like THAT!"

And that was that.

*Flannelboard Story   *Kitten's First Full Moon* by Kevin Henkes. New York: Greenwillow, 2004.

PIECES NEEDED: *kitten, moon, bug, tree, pond with reflection of moon in it, bowl of milk*

*Flannelboard or Stick Puppet Story   *Have You Got My Purr?* by Judy West. New York: Dutton, 1999.

PIECES NEEDED: *kitten, mama cat, dog, cow, pig, duck, mouse, sheep, owl*

CRAFTS

Cat Puppet

MATERIALS: 1 lunch bag for each child; precut eyes, noses, ears, and mouths; glue; crayons or markers; white chenille stems for whiskers

DIRECTIONS:
1. Glue the ears, eyes, nose, mouth, and whiskers onto the bottom of the bag to create a face.
2. Decorate as desired.
3. Place hand inside bag and fold the bottom of the bag down in order to use your puppet.

Cat Ears

MATERIALS: 1 strip of paper for each child for headband, precut ears, tape or stapler, decorating materials

DIRECTIONS:
1. Tape the ears to the headband and decorate as desired.
2. Size to head and tape or staple ends of the headband together.

Chinese Stories

Sign: **CHINA**

![book icon] **BOOKS**

Cleversticks by Bernard Ashley. New York: Crown, 1991.

The Runaway Rice Cake by Ying Chang Compestine. New York: Simon and Schuster, 2001.

The Empty Pot by Demi. New York: Henry Holt, 1990.

The Greatest Treasure by Demi. New York: Scholastic, 1998.

How the Ox Star Fell from Heaven by Lily Toy Hong. Morton Grove, IL: Albert Whitman, 1991.

*Two of Everything by Lily Toy Hong. Morton Grove, IL: Albert Whitman, 1993.

*My First Chinese New Year by Karen Katz. New York: Henry Holt, 2004.

The Rooster's Antlers: A Story of the Chinese Zodiac by Eric A. Kimmel. New York: Holiday House, 1999.

In the Snow by Huy Voun Lee. New York: Henry Holt, 1995.

1, 2, 3, Go! by Huy Voun Lee. New York: Henry Holt, 2000.

Big Jimmy's Kum Kau Chinese Take Out by Ted Lewin. New York: HarperCollins, 2002.

*Dim Sum for Everyone by Grace Lin. New York: Knopf, 2001.

*Fortune Cookie Fortunes by Grace Lin. New York: Knopf, 2004.

The Seven Chinese Brothers by Margaret Mahy. New York: Scholastic, 1990.

Tikki Tikki Tembo by Arlene Mosel. New York: Henry Holt, 1968.

C Is for China by Sungwan So. Parsippany, NJ: Silver Press, 1997.

*Red Is a Dragon: A Book of Colors by Roseanne Thong. New York: Chronicle, 2001.

The Seven Chinese Sisters by Kathy Tucker. Morton Grove, IL: Albert Whitman, 2003.

Beyond the Great Mountains: A Visual Poem about China by Ed Young. San Francisco: Chronicle, 2005.

Lon Po Po: A Red-Riding Hood Story from China by Ed Young. New York: Philomel, 1989.

RECORDED MUSIC

Chinese Lullabies by Beijing Angelic Choir. Wind Records, 1996.

"In the People's Republic of China" and "A Train Ride to the Great Wall" from *I Know the Colors in the Rainbow* by Ella Jenkins. Educational Activities, Inc., 1994.

*"China (Show Ha Mo)" from *Multicultural Rhythm Stick Fun* by Georgiana Stewart. Kimbo Educational, 2006.

*"Chinese New Year: Dancing Dragon" from *A World of Parachute Play* by Georgiana Stewart. Kimbo Educational, 1997.

FINGERPLAYS/SONGS

"Chopsticks"

I have two little chopsticks.
I got them at the store.
I use them to eat my rice,
And then I eat some more!

"Chinese 1, 2, 3"

1, 2, 3, can you count with me?
In Chinese we say
yi, er, san.
That is 1, 2, 3.

"Hello"

As I was walking down the street, down
    the street, down the street,
My little friend I chanced to meet, and so
    I said "Hello."
But in China, walking down the street,
    down the street, down the street,
In China, walking down the street, people
    say "Ni hao." *(pronounced "nee haw")*

"The Senses"
(traditional Chinese nursery rhyme)

Little eyes see pretty things,
Little nose smells what is sweet,
Little ears hear pleasant sounds,
Mouth likes delicious things to eat.

"Five Fingers"
(traditional Chinese nursery rhyme)

This one is old, *(hold up each finger as you
    say the lines)*
This one is young,
This one has no meat,
This one has gone to buy some hay,
And this one is on the street.

"The Cow"
(traditional Chinese nursery rhyme)

A cow is on the mountain,
The old saying goes,
On her legs are four feet;
On her feet are eight toes.
Her tail is behind
On the end of her back,
And her head is in front
On the end of her neck.

"Good Morning Song"
(to the tune of "Happy Birthday")

Good morning to you, good morning
    to you,
Good morning everybody, good morning
    to you.
Ni hao *(nee haw)* to you, ni hao to you,
Ni hao everybody, ni hao to you.

PROPS

*Flannelboard Rhyme

"Five Fortune Cookies"

PIECES NEEDED: *5 fortune cookies*

5 fortune cookies waiting by the door,
My mother ate one, and then there were 4.
4 fortune cookies—what's inside? We'll see!
My father ate one, and then there were 3.
3 little fortune cookies, with messages, it's true,
My sister ate one, and then there were 2.
2 little fortune cookies, isn't this fun?
My brother ate one, and then there was 1.
1 little fortune cookie, yum yum yum,
I ate that one, and then there were none.
Let's count those cookies in Chinese:
Yi, er, san, si, wu!

Flannelboard Story   "The Rat's Tale" from *The Dragon's Tale and Other Animal Fables of the Chinese Zodiac* by Demi. New York: Henry Holt, 1996.

PIECES NEEDED: *rat, sun, cloud, wind, rock*

ADDITIONAL SUGGESTIONS

Chinese Character Cards

Using the books of Huy Voun Lee listed above, copy the Chinese characters onto large pieces of posterboard and laminate. Use these cards to introduce the concept of Chinese characters while sharing Lee's stories. Have the children draw the characters in the air with their fingers.

Chopstick Pickup Game

PIECES NEEDED: *a pair of chopsticks and a pom-pom for each child*

Have the children put the pom-poms on a floor or table and practice using the chopsticks to pick them up. For older children, you could have a "chopstick relay race," where they have to carry the pom-pom across the room with the chopsticks.

CRAFTS

Paper Lantern

MATERIALS: 1 piece of construction paper for each child, a strip of construction paper about 7 inches by 1 inch for each child, scissors, tape, decorating materials

DIRECTIONS:
1. Fold the construction paper in half the long way.
2. Starting from the folded edge, cut slits in the paper at 1-inch intervals, stopping about 2 inches from the opposite edge of the paper.
3. Unfold the paper.
4. Wrap the shorter edges of the paper around, overlap, and tape them together.
5. Tape the strip of construction paper to the top of the lantern to form a handle.
6. Decorate as desired.

Chinese Dragon Stick Puppet

MATERIALS: 2 craft sticks for each child, precut dragon head and tail pieces, construction paper precut into 4½-by-6-inch strips, tape or glue, crayons or markers

DIRECTIONS:
1. Decorate the head and tail pieces as desired.
2. Accordion-fold a strip of construction paper so that it forms a long wavy strip.
3. Tape or glue the dragon's head to one end of the construction paper, and the tail to the other end.
4. Glue or tape the craft sticks to the head and tail pieces.
5. Hold the dragon puppet by the sticks and make it dance like the dragon in the Chinese New Year parade.

Dinosaur Daze

Sign: **DINOSAUR**

BOOKS

Dinosaur Days by Liza Baker. New York: HarperCollins, 2003.

*Bones, Bones, Dinosaur Bones by Byron Barton. New York: HarperCollins, 1990.

*Dinosaurs, Dinosaurs by Byron Barton. New York: HarperCollins, 1989.

Little Grunt and the Big Egg by Tomie dePaola. New York: Holiday House, 1990.

Dinorella: A Prehistoric Fairy Tale by Pamela Duncan Edwards. New York: Hyperion, 1997.

Dinosaurs by Gail Gibbons. New York: Holiday House, 1987.

Can I Have a Stegosaurus, Mom? Can I? Please? by Lois G. Grambling. Mahwah, NJ: BridgeWater, 1995.

*Curious George's Dinosaur Discovery by Catherine Hapka. New York: Houghton Mifflin, 2006.

*Dad's Dinosaur Day by Diane Dawson Hearn. New York: Simon and Schuster, 1993.

Princess Dinosaur by Jill Kastner. New York: Greenwillow, 2001.

*Dinosaur Dinosaur by Kevin Lewis. New York: Scholastic, 2006.

Dinosaurumpus! by Tony Mitton. New York: Orchard Books, 2002.

*If the Dinosaurs Came Back by Bernard Most. San Diego: Harcourt, 1978.

Saturday Night at the Dinosaur Stomp by Carol Diggory Shields. Cambridge, MA: Candlewick, 1997.

*Dinosaur Roar! by Paul and Henrietta Stickland. New York: Puffin, 1994.

*Ten Terrible Dinosaurs by Paul Stickland. New York: Puffin, 1997.

Edwina, the Dinosaur Who Didn't Know She Was Extinct by Mo Willems. New York: Hyperion, 2006.

*How Do Dinosaurs Say Good Night? by Jane Yolen. New York: Scholastic, 2000.

RECORDED MUSIC

**"Dinosaur Rock and Roll" from *Dancin' Magic* by Joanie Bartels. BMG Special Products, 1991.

"Dinosaur Tap" from *Rhythm Sticks Rock* by Georgiana Stewart. Kimbo Educational, 2006.

*"We Are the Dinosaurs" from *Whaddaya Think of That?* by Laurie Berkner. Two Tomatoes, 2001.

FINGERPLAYS/SONGS

"Dinosaur, Dinosaur"

Dinosaur, Dinosaur turn around.
Dinosaur, Dinosaur, stomp on the
    ground.
Dinosaur, Dinosaur, swing your tail.
Dinosaur, Dinosaur, let out a wail!

"I Am a T. Rex"
(to the tune of "I'm a Little Teapot")

I am a T. Rex on the hunt.
I've got a tail in back and sharp claws up
    front.
When I am hungry, hear me roar.
I'm a ferocious dinosaur!

"Five Green Dinosaurs"
(to the tune of "10 Green Bottles")

5 green dinosaurs looking for their lunch.
5 green dinosaurs looking for their lunch.
And if one green dinosaur finds
    something good to munch,
There'll be 4 green dinosaurs looking for
    their lunch.
4 green dinosaurs . . .
3 green dinosaurs . . .
2 green dinosaurs . . .
1 green dinosaur . . .

"Have You Seen the Dinosaur?"
(to the tune of "Do You Know
    the Muffin Man?")

Have you seen the dinosaur,
The dinosaur, the dinosaur?
Have you seen the dinosaur,
That lives in my backyard?

"If You're a Dinosaur"
(to the tune of "If You're Happy
    and You Know It")

If you're a dinosaur and you know it,
    stomp your feet.
If you're a dinosaur and you know it,
    stomp your feet.
If you're a dinosaur and you know it, then
    your actions will show it.
If you're a dinosaur and you know it,
    stomp your feet.
. . . swing your tail.
. . . show your teeth.
. . . let out a roar.

"Dinosaurs Lived Long, Long Ago"

Dinosaurs lived long, long ago,
Even before mommy and daddy, you
    know.
Some dinosaurs ate plants,
And some ate meat,
But now you'll never see a dinosaur
    walking down the street!

"Did You Ever See a Dinosaur?"
(to the tune of "Did You Ever See a Lassie?")

Did you ever see a dinosaur, a dinosaur, a
    dinosaur?
Did you ever see a dinosaur go this way
    and that?
Go this way and that way, and that way
    and this way.
Did you ever see a dinosaur go this way
    and that?

PROPS

*Flannelboard Song

"Five Dinosaurs"
(to the tune of "One Elephant
Went Out to Play")

PIECES NEEDED: *5 dinosaurs*

1 dinosaur went out to play,
Over the hills and far away.
He had such enormous fun, he called for
    another dinosaur to come.
2 dinosaurs . . .
3 dinosaurs . . .
4 dinosaurs . . .
5 dinosaurs . . . they had such enormous
    fun, and then went home when the
    day was done.

*Flannelboard Rhyme

"Color Dinosaurs"

PIECES NEEDED: *simple dinosaur shapes in
red, blue, yellow, green, and black, enough for
each child to hold one*

If your dinosaur is red, put it on
    your head.
If your dinosaur is blue, put it on
    your shoe.
If your dinosaur is yellow, put it on
    your elbow.
If your dinosaur is green, put it on
    your knee.
If your dinosaur is black, put it on
    your back.
Now use your ears, use your ears, and
    listen carefully:
If your dinosaur is _____, bring it up
    to me.

*Repeat with each color and invite the children
to place their dinosaurs on the flannelboard.*

CRAFTS

T. Rex Finger Puppet

Instructions and a template are available at http://www.enchantedlearning.com/crafts/
puppets/twofinger/.

Dinosaur Egg Craft

MATERIALS: construction paper, paper fastener for each child, crayons, decorating materials

DIRECTIONS:
1. Before the program, cut out a small dinosaur shape and an egg for each child from
   construction paper. Cut the egg in half with a zigzag line to make it look as if it has
   cracked open.
2. Have the children decorate their dinosaurs.
3. Glue the dinosaur to the bottom half of the egg, so that it looks like it is sitting in
   the egg.
4. Using the paper fastener, fasten the top half of the egg to the bottom half at the
   corner, so that the top of the egg can flip open and closed.

Elephant Jamboree

Sign: **ELEPHANT**

BOOKS

Elephants Can Paint Too! by Katya Arnold. New York: Atheneum, 2005.

*Nellie's Knot by Ken Brown. New York: Four Winds Press, 1993.

*Mommy, What If . . . ? by Carla Dijs. New York: Simon and Schuster, 2002.

*Little Elephant by Miela Ford. New York: Greenwillow, 1994.

I've Got an Elephant by Anne Ginkel. Atlanta, GA: Peachtree, 2006.

Big Little Elephant by Valeri Gorbachev. San Diego: Harcourt, 2005.

*Elephant Small and the Splashy Bath by Sally Grindley. Hauppauge, NY: Barron's, 1998.

Never Ride Your Elephant to School by Doug Johnson. New York: Henry Holt, 1995.

*When the Elephant Walks by Keiko Kasza. New York: Putnam and Grosset, 1990.

*Splash! by Flora McDonnell. Cambridge, MA: Candlewick, 1999. (with a spray bottle)

Elmer by David McKee. New York: Lothrop, Lee, and Shepard, 1968.

Emma Kate by Patricia Polacco. New York: Philomel, 2005.

Bashi, Elephant Baby by Theresa Radcliffe. New York: Viking, 1997.

The Trouble with Elephants by Chris Riddell. New York: J. B. Lippincott, 1988.

The Obvious Elephant by Bruce Robinson. New York: Bloomsbury, 2000.

*A Nose Like a Hose by Jenny Samuels. New York: Scholastic, 2003.

"Stand Back," Said the Elephant. "I'm Going to Sneeze!" by Patricia Thomas. New York: Lothrop, Lee, and Shepard, 1990.

*Just a Little Bit by Ann Tompert. New York: Houghton Mifflin, 1993.

*Seven Blind Mice by Ed Young. New York: Philomel, 1992.

RECORDED MUSIC

*"Elephant Swing" from *Animal Walks* by Georgiana Stewart. Kimbo Educational, 1987.

*"Elephant Rock" from *Baby Class Favorites*. Kimbo Educational, 2000.

"Elephant Party Jam" from *Let's Dance!* by Sharon, Lois, and Bram. Drive Entertainment, 1995.

*"The Elephant" from *Early Childhood Classics: Old Favorites with a New Twist* by Hap Palmer. Hap-Pal Music, Inc., 2000.

"One Elephant, Deux Elephants" from *One Elephant Went Out to Play* by Sharon, Lois, and Bram. A&M, 1978.

"Elephant Train" from *Wiggles, Jiggles, and Giggles* by Stephen Fite. Melody House, 2000.

FINGERPLAYS/SONGS

"The Elephant Goes Like This and That"
(traditional)

The elephant goes like this and that.
He's terribly huge and terribly fat.
He has no fingers, he has no toes,
But goodness gracious, what a nose!

"Walking Down the Street"

Walking down the street
We saw an elephant.
We will never have to wonder
Which way he went!

"Elephant, Elephant"

Elephant, Elephant, stomp stomp stomp.
Elephant, Elephant, chomp chomp
     chomp. *(mime bringing food to mouth
     with trunk)*
Elephant, Elephant, turn around.
Elephant, Elephant, make a sound!
     (trumpet like an elephant)

"If You're a Happy Elephant"
(to the tune of "If You're Happy and You Know It")

If you're a happy elephant, wave your
     trunk.
If you're a happy elephant, wave your
     trunk.
If you're a happy elephant, then your
     trunk will surely show it.
If you're a happy elephant, wave your
     trunk.

If you're a sad elephant, droop your ears.
If you're a sad elephant, droop your ears.
If you're a sad elephant, then your ears
     will surely show it,
If you're a sad elephant, droop your ears.

If you got scared by a mouse, run away.
If you got scared by a mouse, run away.
If you got scared by a mouse, then your
     run will surely show it.
If you got scared by a mouse, run away.

PROPS

Prop Song

"Willaby Wallaby Woo"
(traditional)

Piece needed: elephant puppet

Willaby wallaby woo,
An elephant sat on you.
Willaby wallaby wee,
An elephant sat on me.
Willaby wallaby wara,
An elephant sat on Sarah . . . *(continue with other children's names)*

*Flannelboard Song

"Five Elephants"

PIECES NEEDED: *5 elephants*

1 elephant went out to play
Underneath the sun one day.
She had such enormous fun,
She called for another elephant to come.
2 elephants . . .
3 elephants . . .
4 elephants . . .
5 elephants went out to play
Underneath the sun one day.
When the sun set and the day was done,
5 little elephants headed home.

Prop Story   *How to Catch an Elephant* by Amy Schwartz. New York: DK, 1999.

PIECES NEEDED: *3 cakes, raisins, telescope, tweezers, elephant puppet*

*Flannelboard Story   *Just a Little Bit* by Ann Tompert. New York: Houghton Mifflin, 1993.

PIECES NEEDED: *seesaw, elephant, mouse, giraffe, zebra, lion, bear, crocodile, mongoose, monkey, ostrich, beetle*

ADDITIONAL SUGGESTIONS

Poetry

"It's Hard to Be an Elephant" from *A Pizza the Size of the Sun* by Jack Prelutsky. New York: Greenwillow, 1994.

 **CRAFTS**

Paper Plate Elephant

MATERIALS: 1 paper plate for each child, ear shapes precut from gray construction paper, 1 precut strip of gray construction paper (12 by 2 inches) for each child, glue, decorating materials

DIRECTIONS:
1. Glue the ears to the sides of the paper plate.
2. Accordion-fold the long strip of construction paper. Attach one end of it to the paper plate to form the trunk.
3. Draw in eyes and decorate as desired.

Unforgettable Elephant Craft from FamilyFun.com

This clever craft elephant actually squirts water from its trunk. Directions and templates can be found at http://jas.familyfun.go.com/arts-and-crafts?page=CraftDisplay&craftid=11129.

Fall Fest

Sign: **AUTUMN**

BOOKS

Every Autumn Comes the Bear by Jim Arnosky. New York: Putnam and Grosset, 1993.

Leaf Baby by Mary Brigid Barrett. San Diego: Harcourt, 1998.

Clifford's First Autumn by Norman Bridwell. New York: Scholastic, 1997.

The Little Scarecrow Boy by Margaret Wise Brown. New York: HarperCollins, 1998.

Dappled Apples by Jan Carr. New York: Holiday House, 2001.

Pumpkin Soup by Helen Cooper. New York: Farrar, Straus and Giroux, 1998.

Nuts to You! by Lois Ehlert. San Diego: Harcourt, 1993.

Red Leaf, Yellow Leaf by Lois Ehlert. San Diego: Harcourt, 1991.

It's Fall! by Linda Glaser. Brookfield, CT: Millbrook, 2001.

Fall Leaves Fall by Zoe Hall. New York: Scholastic, 2000.

It's Pumpkin Time! by Zoe Hall. New York: Scholastic, 1994.

In the Leaves by Huy Voun Lee. New York: Henry Holt, 2005.

Moon Glowing by Elizabeth Partridge. New York: Dutton, 2002.

Apples and Pumpkins by Anne Rockwell. New York: Macmillan, 1989.

Scarecrow by Cynthia Rylant. San Diego: Harcourt, 1998.

Patty's Pumpkin Patch by Teri Sloan. New York: G. P. Putnam's Sons, 1999.

Fall Is for Friends by Suzy Spafford. New York: Scholastic, 2003.

Pumpkin Day! by Nancy Elizabeth Wallace. New York: Marshall Cavendish, 2002.

Do Cows Turn Colors in the Fall? by Viki Woodworth. New York: Child's World, 1998.

Pumpkin Time by Kathleen Weidner Zoehfeld. New York: HarperCollins, 2004.

RECORDED MUSIC

"Squirrel, Squirrel" from *Wee Sing: Animals Animals Animals* by Pamela Conn Beall and Susan Hagen Nipp. Price Stern Sloan, 2006.

"What Falls in the Fall?" from *Whaddaya Think of That?* by Laurie Berkner. Two Tomatoes, 2001.

FINGERPLAYS/SONGS

"Leaves Are Falling"
(to the tune of "Frère Jacques")

Leaves are falling, leaves are falling,
On the ground, on the ground.
Rake them up into a pile.
Rake them up into a pile.
Then jump in.
Then jump in.

"Way Up High"
(traditional)

Way up high in the apple tree,
3 little apples smiled at me.
I shook that tree as hard as I could.
Down fell the apples and MMMM, they
    were good!

"I Am Popcorn"

I am popcorn in the pot. *(hunch down)*
Now the oil is getting hot.
I start small, as you can see,
But I am getting hotter, 1, 2, 3.
I sizzle on without a stop, *(rise gradually)*
Till suddenly I start to POP! *(jump up)*

"Autumn Leaves"
(to the tune of "London Bridge")

Autumn leaves are falling down,
Falling down, falling down.
Autumn leaves are falling down,
Red, yellow, orange, and brown.

"Rake the Leaves"
(to the tune of "Row, Row, Row Your Boat")

Rake, rake, rake the leaves,
Raking in our yard.
Then we put them in the bags.
We are working hard.

"Gray Squirrel"
(traditional)

Gray squirrel, gray squirrel, shake your
    bushy tail.
Gray squirrel, gray squirrel, shake your
    bushy tail.
Wrinkle up your little nose,
Hold a nut between your toes,
Gray squirrel, gray squirrel, shake your
    bushy tail.

"The Pumpkin Song"
(improvise a tune or chant)

I had a little pumpkin,
I put it down just so,
And then I waved my magic wand
And it began to grow . . . and grow . . .
    and grow . . . and grow . . . and
    grow! *(use arms to show size)*

I had a giant pumpkin *(use large movements
    and sing in a big booming voice)*
And quick as you can blink,
I waved my magic wand
And it began to shrink . . . and shrink . . .
    and shrink . . . and shrink . . . and
    shrink!

I had a tiny pumpkin, *(use tiny movements
    and sing in a small voice)*
I put it down just so,
And then I waved my magic wand
And it began to grow . . . and grow . . .
    and grow . . . and grow . . .
Till I said STOP!

"Did You Ever See a Scarecrow?"
(to the tune of "Did You Ever See a Lassie?")

Did you ever see a scarecrow, a scarecrow, a scarecrow?
(use a floppy-armed scarecrow movement throughout the song)
Did you ever see a scarecrow go this way and that?
Go this way and that way,
And that way and this way?
Did you ever see a scarecrow go this way and that?

Props

*Flannelboard Rhyme

"Leaf Colors"

PIECES NEEDED: *red, yellow, brown, and orange baskets, and enough leaves of these four colors that each child can hold one. Place the baskets on the flannelboard and give the leaves out to the children. Then invite them to place their leaves in the correct basket during this rhyme.*

So many leaves are on the trees,
But they start shaking in the breeze.
Then the wind really starts to blow,
And the leaves start to let go!
Use your eyes now, look and see.
If you have a red leaf, bring it to me.

Repeat with other colors.

*Flannelboard Song

"Five Brown Acorns"
(to the tune of "10 Green Bottles")

PIECES NEEDED: *5 acorns, tree*

5 brown acorns hanging on the tree,
5 brown acorns hanging on the tree,
And if one brown acorn should fall down
    to me,
There'll be 4 brown acorns hanging on
    the tree.
4 brown acorns . . .
3 brown acorns . . .
2 brown acorns . . .
1 brown acorn . . .

*Leaf Streamers

Cut out leaf shapes from orange, yellow, red, and brown construction paper. Attach a length of curling ribbon to each shape. To make your streamers more durable, laminate the leaf shapes before attaching the ribbon. Pass out one leaf streamer to each child and play your favorite freeze dance.

CRAFTS

Leaf Rubbings

MATERIALS: 1 piece of white paper for each child, 1 leaf for each child, crayons

DIRECTIONS:
1. Place the leaf on the table.
2. Place the paper over the leaf.
3. Rub the crayon over the paper and the impression of the leaf will appear.

Leaf People

MATERIALS: construction paper, leaves, googly eyes, glue, crayons or markers

DIRECTIONS:
1. Glue 1–2 leaves onto a piece of paper.
2. Use crayons or markers to add legs, ears, arms, etc.
3. Glue googly eyes onto the leaf to form a face.

Family Fun

Sign: **FAMILY**

BOOKS

Grandma According to Me by Karen Magnuson Beil. New York: Doubleday, 1992.

Are You Going to Be Good? by Cari Best. New York: Farrar, Straus and Giroux, 2005.

*I Love Daddy by Lizi Boyd. Cambridge, MA: Candlewick, 2004.

*I Love My Daddy by Sebastian Braun. New York: HarperCollins, 2004.

*I Love My Mommy by Sebastian Braun. New York: HarperCollins, 2004.

*Mommy, Carry Me Please! by Jane Cabrera. New York: Holiday House, 2004.

Day Out with Daddy by Stephen Cook. New York: Walker, 2006.

*Feast for Ten by Cathryn Falwell. New York: Clarion, 1993.

We Have a Baby by Cathryn Falwell. New York: Clarion, 1993.

I Love You, Grandpa by Vivian French. Cambridge, MA: Candlewick, 2004.

*Spot Visits His Grandparents by Eric Hill. New York: Penguin, 1996.

What Aunts Do Best/What Uncles Do Best by Laura Numeroff. New York: Simon and Schuster, 2004.

Families Are Different by Nina Pellegrini. New York: Holiday House, 1991.

Truman's Aunt Farm by Jama Kim Rattigan. New York: Houghton Mifflin, 1994.

Cherry Pies and Lullabies by Lynn Reiser. New York: Greenwillow, 1998.

The Relatives Came by Cynthia Rylant. New York: Bradbury Press, 1985.

*On Mother's Lap by Ann Herbert Scott. New York: Clarion, 1992.

Lucky Pennies and Hot Chocolate by Carol Diggory Shields. New York: Dutton, 2000.

*Noisy Nora by Rosemary Wells. New York: Dial, 1997.

*Cousins Are for Holiday Visits by Harriet Ziefert. New York: Penguin, 2002.

RECORDED MUSIC

*"Family Goodbyes" from *Jim Gill Sings Moving Rhymes for Modern Times* by Jim Gill. Jim Gill Music, 2006.

A Celebration of Family by various artists. Music for Little People, 2001.

FINGERPLAYS/SONGS

"This Is My Family"

This is the mommy kind and dear.
   (point to thumb)
This is the daddy sitting near.
   (point to index finger)
This is the sister tall and strong.
   (point to middle finger)
This is the brother singing a song.
   (point to ring finger)
This is the baby sweet as can be.
   (point to pinkie finger)
All together they are a family!

"Here Are Grandma's Glasses"
(traditional)

Here are grandma's glasses,
Here is grandma's hat.
Here is how she folds her hands
And lays them in her lap.

"When My Cousins Come to Stay"

When my cousins come to stay,
We always have such fun.
We run and jump and laugh and play
Outside in the sun.
But when the day is done and we
Go in and shut the door,
There are so many of us now,
I must sleep on the floor!

"I've Got a Family"
(to the tune of "My Darling Clementine")

I've got a mommy, got a daddy,
Got a sister and a brother.
All together we're a family
And we all love one another.

"The Family"
(to the tune of "The Wheels on the Bus")

The sisters in the family go ha ha ha,
Ha ha ha, ha ha ha.
The sisters in the family go ha ha ha,
All through the day.

The brothers in the family go hee hee hee,
Hee hee hee, hee hee hee.
The brothers in the family go hee hee hee,
All through the day.

The babies in the family go wah wah wah,
Wah wah wah, wah wah wah.
The babies in the family go wah wah wah,
All through the day.

The daddy in the family goes shh shh shh,
Shh shh shh, shh shh shh.
The daddy in the family goes shh shh shh,
All through the day.

The mommy in the family says "I love
      you,"
"I love you," "I love you."
The mommy in the family says "I love
      you,"
All through the day.

"Jack and Jill"

From Wee Sing Children's Songs and Fingerplays *by Pamela Conn Beall and Susan Hagen Nipp (Price Stern Sloan, 2002).*

PROPS

"Five in My Family"

PIECES NEEDED: *mother, father, sister, brother, baby*

Let's count the people in the family:
Number 1 is the mother, you see.
2 is the father, big and tall.
3 is the brother, but that's not all!
4 is the sister, pretty as can be.
5 is the littlest, just a baby.
And every day, when home they arrive,
They count 1, 2, 3, 4, and 5!

*Flannelboard or Stick Puppet Story: "The Giant Pumpkin"

PIECES NEEDED: *pumpkin, mother, father, sister, brother, baby, aunt, uncle, cousin, grandmother, grandfather*

One day the father went out to his vegetable garden to check on his prize pumpkin. Wasn't he surprised when he saw that it was ENORMOUS! "Perfect!" he thought to himself. "I will pick this pumpkin and take it home to make a giant pumpkin pie for our family dinner tonight." And he grabbed that pumpkin and PULLED and PULLED, but that pumpkin wouldn't let go of its vine. So he called for his wife, the mother in the family. The mother PULLED on the father, and the father PULLED on the pumpkin, but that pumpkin wouldn't let go of its vine.

Repeat pattern with sister, brother, baby, aunt, uncle, cousin, grandmother, grandfather.

And finally the pumpkin came loose! They all worked together to roll that pumpkin back to the house. They cut it up and mixed up a pie, and put it in the oven. And then after their dinner, they each had a big helping of pumpkin pie with ice cream—even the baby! Yum, yum!

*Prop Story: "Mommy's Briefcase"

PIECES NEEDED: *briefcase, papers, pens, calculator, toy or old cell phone, toy money, granola bar or other snack, picture of a family, calendar or datebook, and other items that one might carry to work in a briefcase*

Every morning my mother gets ready to go to work. She packs all the things she needs in her briefcase. Would you like to see what's inside?

Remove each item and talk about its purpose, saving the picture for last.

But the most important thing she puts in her briefcase is a picture of our family, so she won't miss us too much while she is at work!

*Flannelboard Story   *The Napping House* by Audrey Wood. San Diego: Harcourt Brace, 1984.

PIECES NEEDED: *bed, house, granny, child, dog, cat, mouse, flea*

ADDITIONAL SUGGESTIONS

"Mommy Says" Game

This game is a variation on "Simon Says." Repeat with Daddy, Grandma, Grandpa, etc., giving directions.

CRAFTS

Family Portraits

MATERIALS: 1 sheet of construction paper for each child; craft sticks; glue; crayons or markers; decorating materials; die-cuts or printed pictures of mothers, fathers, sisters, brothers, babies, and grandparents (printable pictures are available at DLTK's craft site: http://www.dltk-bible.com/genesis/family_puppets.htm)

DIRECTIONS:
1. Invite each child to find pictures representing the people who live in her or his home.
2. Glue the pictures to the construction paper.
3. Draw a frame around the edge of the paper and decorate as desired.

Family Dinner Napkin Rings

MATERIALS: toilet paper and paper towel rolls cut into 2-inch rings, 2-inch-long strips of wrapping paper, tape, scissors, decorating materials

DIRECTIONS:
1. Tape one end of the wrapping paper strip to the inside of a ring.
2. Wrap the strip of wrapping paper around and around the ring until all the cardboard is covered.
3. Tape the other end inside the ring and trim the excess paper.
4. Decorate as desired.

Fast and Slow

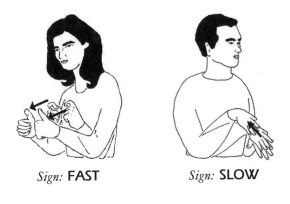

Sign: **FAST**   *Sign:* **SLOW**

BOOKS

Zoom! by Diane Adams. Atlanta, GA: Peachtree, 2005.

Slow Days, Fast Friends by Erik Brooks. Morton Grove, IL: Albert Whitman, 2005.

*Snail Trail by Ruth Brown. New York: Crown, 2000.

Raccoon's Last Race by Joseph Bruchac and James Bruchac. New York: Dial, 2004.

*Turtle's Race with Beaver by Joseph Bruchac and James Bruchac. New York: Dial, 2004.

*Bertie and Small and the Fast Bike Ride by Vanessa Cabban. Cambridge, MA: Candlewick, 1999.

*"Slowly, Slowly, Slowly," Said the Sloth by Eric Carle. New York: Philomel, 2002.

Slippers Loves to Run by Andrew Clements. New York: Dutton, 2006.

Hare and Tortoise Race to the Moon by Oliver J. Corwin. New York: Abrams, 2002.

Ruby in Her Own Time by Jonathan Emmett. New York: Scholastic, 2003.

Leo the Late Bloomer by Robert Kraus. New York: HarperCollins, 1971.

Tortoise Brings the Mail by Dee Lillegard. New York: Dutton, 1997.

The Tortoise and the Jackrabbit by Susan Lowell. Flagstaff, AZ: Rising Moon, 1994.

The Very Sleepy Sloth by Andrew Murray. Wilton, CT: Tiger Tales, 2003.

Axle Annie and the Speed Grump by Robin Pulver. New York: Dial, 2005.

The Race by Caroline Repchuck. New York: Chronicle, 2001.

*Blue Tortoise by Alan Rogers. Chicago: Two-Can Publishing, 1998.

*Come Back, Hannah! by Marisabina Russo. New York: Greenwillow, 2001.

So Slow! by Dave and Julie Saunders. New York: Marshall Cavendish, 2001.

The Tortoise and the Hare by Janet Stevens. New York: Holiday House, 1984.

Turtle Time: A Bedtime Story by Sandol Stoddard. New York: Houghton Mifflin, 1995.

That's Not Fair, Hare! by Julie Sykes. Hauppauge, NY: Barron's, 2001.

Fast Food! Gulp! Gulp! by Bernard Waber. New York: Houghton Mifflin, 2001.

*Hi, Harry! by Martin Waddell. Cambridge, MA: Candlewick, 2003.

*Stella and Roy by Ashley Wolff. New York: Dutton, 1993.

RECORDED MUSIC

*"Shakey Shakey" from *Yummy Yummy* by The Wiggles. Koch Records, 2000.

*"The Tempo Marches On" from *Jim Gill Sings Do Re Mi on His Toe Leg Knee* by Jim Gill. Jim Gill Music, Inc., 1999.

*"Slow and Fast" from *Rhythms on Parade (Revised Expanded Version)* by Hap Palmer. Hap-Pal Music, Inc., 1995.

"Song about Slow, Song about Fast" from *Walter the Waltzing Worm* by Hap Palmer. Educational Activities, Inc., 1983.

*"Clap Your Hands" from *Wee Sing Children's Songs and Fingerplays* by Pamela Conn Beall and Susan Hagen Nipp. Price Stern Sloan, 2002.

*"The Snail" from *Wee Sing: Games, Games, Games* by Pamela Conn Beall and Susan Hagen Nipp. Price Stern Sloan, 2006.

*"The Airplane Song" from *Whaddaya Think of That?* by Laurie Berkner. Two Tomatoes, 2001.

FINGERPLAYS/SONGS

"Fast and Slow"

Running, running, running fast,
We're really moving, but it won't last.
Now running, running, running slow,
Go as slowly as you can go.
Clapping . . .
Jumping . . .
Turning . . .
Dancing . . .

"Five Green Turtles"
(to the tune of "10 Green Bottles")

5 green turtles sitting on the grass.
They move slowly, they don't move
    very fast.
But if one green turtle should decide to
    swim away,
There'll be 4 green turtles left there
    to play.
4 green turtles . . .
3 green turtles . . .
2 green turtles . . .
1 green turtle . . .

"My Kitten Fluff"
(to the tune of "My Dog Rags")

I've got a kitten and his name is Fluff.
He likes to get into lots of stuff.
He likes to meow and meow all day,
And when he meows, he does it in a
    fast way.
Meow, meow, meow, meow, meow,
    meow, meow,
Meow, meow, meow, meow, meow,
    meow, meow.
That's my kitten, good old Fluff.
. . . a slow way.

PROPS

*Flannelboard Rhyme

"Turtle Colors"

PIECES NEEDED: *5 large felt turtles, each with a circular eye of a different color; enough small circles in the colors of the turtles' eyes for each child to hold one*

This little turtle was so slow
That one day even his dots decided to go.
Help him find them if you can—
Do you have a red dot in your hand?

Repeat with other colors, inviting the children to place their dots on the turtles as you call out the colors.

Flannelboard Story   *The Donkey That Went Too Fast: A Philippine Folktale* by David Orme. Columbus, OH: Gingham Dog Press, 2005.

PIECES NEEDED: *2 donkeys carrying baskets of coconuts, man, boy*

*Puppet Story   "The Hare and the Tortoise" from *One-Person Puppetry Streamlined and Simplified* by Yvonne Awar Frey. Chicago: American Library Association, 2005.

PIECES NEEDED: *rabbit puppet, turtle or tortoise puppet*

*Prop Song   "Shakey Shakey" from *Yummy Yummy* by The Wiggles. Koch Records, 2000.

PIECES NEEDED: *shaker eggs or scarves*

ADDITIONAL SUGGESTIONS

Poetry

"Snail's Pace" by Aileen Fisher. From *Read-Aloud Rhymes for the Very Young* edited by Jack Prelutsky. New York: Knopf, 1986.

CRAFTS

Tortoise and Hare Stick Puppet Race

MATERIALS: 1 sheet of construction paper for each child, scissors, tortoise/turtle and hare/rabbit die-cut shapes, 2 craft sticks for each child, glue or tape, crayons or markers, scissors

DIRECTIONS:
1. Fold the construction paper as if you are making a greeting card. Starting from the folded side, make two cuts in the page. Stop about 2 inches from the edge of the paper.
2. Unfold the paper and lay it so that the cuts run lengthwise across it.
3. Decorate the hare and tortoise shapes and glue or tape them to the craft sticks.
4. Place the sticks in the slots and make the two animals race.
5. Decorate the paper with trees, other animals, a finish line, etc.

Shaker Eggs

MATERIALS: plastic Easter eggs, colored masking tape, stickers, medium-sized jingle bells

DIRECTIONS:
1. Open an egg and place 1–2 jingle bells inside.
2. Close the egg and run a strip of colored masking tape over the seam.
3. Decorate with stickers and shake fast or slow!

Giant Veggies

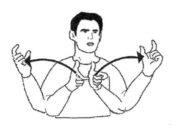

Sign: **GIANT**

BOOKS

The Tale of the Turnip by Brian Alderson. Cambridge, MA: Candlewick, 1999.

The Trouble with Grandad by Babette Cole. New York: G. P. Putnam's Sons, 1988.

Jamie O'Rourke and the Big Potato: An Irish Folktale by Tomie dePaola. New York: G. P. Putnam's Sons, 1992.

Sing, Henrietta, Sing by Lynn Downey. Nashville, TN: Ideals Children's Books, 1997.

Growing Vegetable Soup by Lois Ehlert. San Diego: Harcourt Brace, 1987.

Lunch by Denise Fleming. New York: Henry Holt, 1992.

Vegetable Garden by Douglas Florian. San Diego: Harcourt Brace Jovanovich, 1991.

Mrs. Rose's Garden by Elaine Greenstein. New York: Simon and Schuster, 1996.

Grandma Lena's Big Ol' Turnip by Denia Lewis Hester. Morton Grove, IL: Albert Whitman, 2005.

Bear and Bunny Grow Tomatoes by Bruce Koscielniak. New York: Knopf, 1993.

The Carrot Seed by Ruth Krauss. New York: Harper and Row, 1945.

The Turnip by Pierr Morgan. New York: Philomel, 1990.

The Giant Carrot by Jan Peck. New York: Dial, 1998.

Big Pumpkin by Erica Silverman. New York: Simon and Schuster, 1992.

Pumpkin, Pumpkin by Jeanne Titherington. New York: Greenwillow, 1986.

The Gigantic Turnip by Aleksei Tolstoy. Cambridge, MA: Barefoot Books, 1998.

The Enormous Carrot by Vladimir Vagin. New York: Scholastic, 1998.

Scarlette Beane by Karen Wallace. New York: Dial, 1999.

A Little Story about a Big Turnip by Tatiana Zunshine. Columbus, OH: Pumpkin House, 2003.

RECORDED MUSIC

"The Valley of Vegetables" from *Buzz Buzz* by Laurie Berkner. Two Tomatoes, 2001.

*"Lettuce Sing (Fresh Fruit and Veggies)" from *Top of the Tots* by The Wiggles. HIT Entertainment, 2004. *(use with streamers)*

FINGERPLAYS/SONGS

"Five Fat Peas"
(traditional)

5 fat peas in the peapod pressed,
(curl fingers of one hand together, cover with other hand)
1 grew, 2 grew, and so did all the rest.
(pop fingers out one by one)
They grew, and they grew,
(move hands apart)
And they grew, and they never stopped
Until they grew so big that the peapod
POPPED! *(clap)*

"Watermelon, Watermelon"

Watermelon, watermelon, big and round,
Watermelon, watermelon, touch the ground.
Watermelon, watermelon, pink and yummy,
Watermelon, watermelon in my tummy.

"I'm a Little Carrot"
(to the tune of "I'm a Little Teapot")

I'm a little carrot underneath the ground.
(huddle down)
I stay in the soil and I don't make a sound.
If the rain falls and the sun shines just so,
I push my leaves up to say hello!
(raise arms above head and wave)

"Celery and Carrots"
(to the tune of "Apples and Bananas")

I like to eat eat eat celery and carrots.
I like to eat eat eat celery and carrots.

Repeat, replacing the vowel sound in each word with a long a sound, then a long e, a long i, a long o, and a long u.

"The Pumpkin Song"
(improvise a tune or chant)

I had a little pumpkin,
I put it down just so,
And then I waved my magic wand
And it began to grow . . . and grow . . .
    and grow . . . and grow . . . and
    grow! *(use arms to show size)*

I had a giant pumpkin, *(use large movements and sing in a big booming voice)*
And quick as you can blink,
I waved my magic wand
And it began to shrink . . . and shrink . . .
    and shrink . . . and shrink . . . and
    shrink!

I had a tiny pumpkin, *(use tiny movements and sing in a small voice)*
I put it down just so,
And then I waved my magic wand
And it began to grow . . . and grow . . .
    and grow . . . and grow . . .
Till I said STOP!

"This Is the Way"
(to the tune of "Here We Go 'Round the Mulberry Bush")

This is the way we dig the dirt,
Dig the dirt, dig the dirt.
This is the way we dig the dirt,
So early in the morning.
. . . we plant the seeds
. . . we water the seeds
. . . the sun does shine
. . . the sprouts come up
. . . we pick the veggies
. . . we wash them off
. . . we crunch crunch crunch

PROPS

*Flannelboard Rhyme

"Five Giant Pumpkins"

PIECES NEEDED: *5 large pumpkins, pumpkin pie, jack o'lantern, pumpkin carriage, blue ribbon*

5 giant pumpkins sitting on the floor,
1 became a pumpkin pie, and then there were 4.
4 giant pumpkins, orange as can be,
1 became a jack o'lantern, and then there were 3.
3 giant pumpkins, enormous, it's true,
1 became a carriage for Cinderella, and then
     there were 2.
2 giant pumpkins underneath the sun,
1 got first prize at the fair, and then there was 1.
1 giant pumpkin sitting all alone.
I picked that one up, and carried it home.

*Flannelboard or Stick Puppet Story: "The Giant Watermelon"

PIECES NEEDED: *watermelon, mother, father, sister, brother, baby, aunt, uncle, cousin, grandmother, grandfather*

One day the father went out to his vegetable garden to check on his prize watermelon. Wasn't he surprised when he saw that it was ENORMOUS! "Perfect!" he thought to himself. "I will pick this watermelon and take it home and cut it up for our family dinner tonight." And he grabbed that watermelon and PULLED and PULLED, but that watermelon wouldn't let go of its vine. So he called for his wife, the mother in the family. The mother PULLED on the father, and the father PULLED on the watermelon, but that watermelon wouldn't let go of its vine.

Repeat pattern with sister, brother, baby, aunt, uncle, cousin, grandmother, grandfather.

And finally the watermelon came loose! They all worked together to roll that watermelon back to the house. They cut it up and after their dinner, they each had a big slice—even the baby! Yum, yum!

Prop Game: Pin the Vine to the Giant Pumpkin

PIECES NEEDED: *a large, laminated poster with a picture of a pumpkin on it; vine cut from green construction paper for each child; a blindfold*

Give each child a vine with a loop of tape attached to it. Have the children take turns being blindfolded and trying to attach the vine to the pumpkin's stem.

*Flannelboard Story   *The Carrot Seed* by Ruth Krauss. New York: Harper and Row, 1945.

PIECES NEEDED: *mother, father, boy, seed, watering can, big brother, giant carrot, a patch of earth*

CRAFTS

Paper Bag Pumpkin

MATERIALS: 1 white paper bag for each child, tissue paper, green yarn, markers or crayons, vines cut from green construction paper, glue

DIRECTIONS:
1. Color the paper bag orange.
2. Open the paper bag all the way.
3. Stuff the bag about half full with crumpled tissue paper.
4. Gather the top of the bag together and tie it shut with green yarn.
5. Push the "stem" downward to make the bag fluff out into more of a pumpkin shape.
6. Decorate with crayons, markers, etc., and glue on vines.

Vegetable Stamping

MATERIALS: Raw vegetables such as corn on the cob, potatoes, carrots, and celery (leave some vegetables whole and cut some crosswise to create different shapes); paper; paint; plastic or newspaper to cover table and floor

DIRECTIONS:
1. Give each child a large piece of paper. Let the children paint designs on their paper by dipping the vegetables in the paint and stamping or rolling them on the paper.
2. For more designs, cut the potatoes into shapes such as circles, squares, and hearts.

Give Me a Hand

Sign: **HANDS**

BOOKS

Busy Fingers by C. W. Bowie. Watertown, MA: Charlesbridge, 2003.

Clap Your Hands by Lorinda Bryan Cauley. New York: G. P. Putnam's Sons, 1992.

The Story of Chopsticks by Ying Chang Compestine. New York: Holiday House, 2001.

Hands by Lois Ehlert. San Diego: Harcourt Brace, 1997.

Ticklemonster and Me: A Play-Along Book by Max Haynes. New York: Doubleday, 1999.

My Hands Can by Jean Holzenthaler. New York: Dutton, 1978.

Hands Can by Cheryl Willis Hudson. Cambridge, MA: Candlewick, 2003.

Peekaboo Morning by Rachel Isadora. New York: G. P. Putnam's Sons, 2002.

Hands! by Virginia L. Kroll. Honesdale, PA: Boyds Mills Press, 1997.

Hand Games by Mario Mariotti. Brooklyn, NY: Kane/Miller, 1992.

Here Are My Hands by Bill Martin Jr. and John Archambault. New York: Henry Holt, 1985.

Moses Sees a Play by Isaac Millman. New York: Farrar, Straus and Giroux, 2004.

Lucy's Picture by Nicola Moon. New York: Dial, 1994.

Clap Hands by Helen Oxenbury. New York: Simon and Schuster, 1987.

The Kissing Hand by Audrey Penn. Washington, DC: Child and Family Press, 1993.

The Handmade Alphabet by Laura Rankin. New York: Dial, 1991.

A Book of Hugs by Dave Ross. New York: HarperCollins, 1999.

Wash Your Hands! by Tony Ross. Brooklyn, NY: Kane/Miller, 2000.

Let's Look at Hands by Simona Sideri. Slough, UK: Zero to Ten Ltd., 2001.

My Two Hands, My Two Feet by Rick Walton. New York: G. P. Putnam's Sons, 2000.

Bear Wants More by Karma Wilson. New York: Simon and Schuster, 2003.

RECORDED MUSIC

*"Put Your Finger On" from *Feel the Music* by Parachute Express. Walt Disney Records, 1991.

*"I Have Ten Little Fingers" from *Fingerplays and Footplays for Fun and Learning* by Rosemary Hallum and Henry "Buzz" Glass. Educational Activities, Inc., 1994.

*"Hands Are for Clapping" from *Jim Gill Sings The Sneezing Song and Other Contagious Tunes* by Jim Gill. Jim Gill Music, 1993.

*"One Day a Hand Went Walking" from *Jollity Farm* by various artists. Big Blue Dog Records, 2001.

*"Put Your Hands Up in the Air" from *Learning Basic Skills through Music, Volume 1* by Hap Palmer. Educational Activities, 1969.

*"Where Is Thumbkin?" from *Preschool Action Time* by Carol Hammett. Kimbo Educational, 1988.

*"Fishin' for a Ticklin'" from *Sing Me a Story* by Bob McGrath. Bob's Kids Music, 1997.

"Look at My Hands" from *Signing Time Songs, Volumes 1–3* by Rachel de Azevedo Coleman. Two Little Hands Productions, 2002.

FINGERPLAYS/SONGS

More fingerplays can be found in Clap Your Hands: Finger Rhymes *by Sarah Hayes (New York: Lothrop, Lee, and Shepard, 1988). This book includes multiple rhymes with bright, child-friendly illustrations of finger motions to go with them.*

"Ten Little Fingers"

Ten little fingers to wiggle,
One little mouth to giggle,
Two little hands to wave around,
One little bottom to sit right down.

"On My Head"
(traditional)

On my head my hands I place,
On my shoulders, on my face,
On my hips and at my side,
Then behind me they will hide.
I raise my hands way up high,
I can make my fingers fly.
I hold them out in front of me,
Then I clap them 1, 2, 3!

"Open, Shut Them"
(traditional)

Open, shut them,
Open, shut them,
Give a little clap, clap, clap.
Open, shut them,
Open, shut them,
Lay them in your lap, lap, lap.
Creep them, creep them,
Creep them, creep them,
Right up to your chin.
Open wide your little mouth,
But do not let them in!

"My Drum"

My knees can be a drum: rum tum tum.
The floor can be a drum: rum tum tum.
My head can be a drum: rum tum tum.

"Our Hands Say Thank You"
(traditional)

Our hands say thank you with a clap,
   clap, clap.
Our feet say thank you with a tap,
   tap, tap.
Clap, clap, clap, tap, tap, tap.
We roll our hands around
And say goodbye!

"Ten Little Fingers"
(to the tune of "10 Little Indians")

1 little, 2 little, 3 little fingers,
4 little, 5 little, 6 little fingers,
7 little, 8 little, 9 little fingers,
10 fingers on my hands.

PROPS

*Flannelboard Rhyme

"Color Mittens"

PIECES NEEDED: *pairs of mitten shapes in felt, 2 of each color or pattern. Place one of each pair on the flannelboard and give the others to the children.*

I have two little mittens,
I wear them on my hands.
But I have lost a mitten,
Please help me if you can.
Look at your mitten, what do you see?
If your mitten is _____, please bring it
   to me.

Repeat with other colors, inviting the children to place their mittens on the flannelboard as you call out the colors.

*Stick Puppet Rhyme

"Hands Can"

PIECES NEEDED: *4 large hands cut out of posterboard. Attach each hand to a paint stirrer. Leave hands #1 and #2 as they are. On hand #3, glue down the thumb, middle, ring, and pinky fingers. On hand #4, glue down the middle and ring fingers.*

Hands can say STOP. *(hold up hand #1)*
Hands can say GO. *(wave #1 toward you)*
Hands can say SHHH. *(hold #3 to
   your lips)*
Hands can wave to and fro. *(wave #1 and
   #2 above your head)*
But of all the things that hands can do,
The best is when they say I LOVE YOU.
   (hold up #4)

ADDITIONAL SUGGESTIONS

Storytelling

Tell simple stories using some basic American Sign Language from *Beyond Words: Great Stories for Hand and Voice* by Valerie Marsh (Fort Atkinson, WI: Alleyside Press, 1995).

String Games

Demonstrate string games and tricks from *Super String Games* by Camilla Gryski (New York: Beech Tree, 1987).

Activity: Shadow Puppets

Using the book *Shadowplay* by George Mendoza (New York: Holt, Rinehart, and Winston, 1974), invite kids to imitate the shadow puppets and create their own. Use an overhead projector and a blank wall to re-create the shadow puppets.

A Story to Act Out

Use a variety of stuffed animals to act out the different kinds of hugs in *A Book of Hugs* by Dave Ross. If desired, invite volunteers to demonstrate each hug on a stuffed animal.

*Activity: Things We Do with Our Hands

Use *Bear Wants More* by Karma Wilson to discuss the many things we do with our hands. (In the story, Bear eats and catches fish with his hands.) You could also teach the sign MORE to go with this story and invite children to sign it each time the word appears in the story. Whether by design or coincidence, the illustration on the cover looks as if the animals are signing MORE.

Activity: Signing

When reading *Moses Sees a Play* by Isaac Millman, pause to teach the signs shown in the illustrations. Discuss how to applaud in sign language (by waving hands in the air), and show how Moses and his classmates do this after the play in the story.

CRAFTS

I LOVE YOU Sign Language Stick Puppets

MATERIALS: construction paper, scissors, craft sticks, glue, decorating materials

DIRECTIONS:
1. Have each child trace his or her hand onto construction paper and cut out the shape. (You may wish to provide precut handshapes instead.)
2. Have the children glue down the middle and ring fingers to make the I LOVE YOU sign.
3. Attach a craft stick and decorate.

Textured Collages

Building on the concepts found in *Lucy's Picture* by Nicola Moon in which a young girl creates a textured picture for her blind grandfather, provide children with a variety of textured materials such as feathers, sequins, fabric, wallpaper scraps, felt, sand, and foam shapes, and invite them to create their own pictures.

Good Morning

Sign: **GOOD**   *Sign:* **MORNING**

BOOKS

Happy Healthy Monsters: Elmo's Breakfast Bingo. New York: Random House, 2005.

Pig, Horse, or Cow, Don't Wake Me Now by Arlene Alda. New York: Doubleday, 1994.

*Wakey-Wakey by Dawn Apperly. New York: Little, Brown, 1999.

Just Another Morning by Linda Ashman. New York: HarperCollins, 2004.

Good Morning, Garden by Barbara Brenner. Chanhassen, MN: NorthWord Press, 2004.

Giggle-Wiggle Wake-Up! by Nancy White Carlstrom. New York: Knopf, 2003.

Who Gets the Sun Out of Bed? by Nancy White Carlstrom. New York: Little, Brown, 1992.

Nothing at All by Denys Cazet. New York: Orchard Books, 1994.

*The Grumpy Morning by Pamela Duncan Edwards. New York: Scholastic, 1998.

*Wake-Up Kisses by Pamela Duncan Edwards. New York: HarperCollins, 2002.

*What's in Baby's Morning? by Judy Hindley. Cambridge, MA: Candlewick, 2004.

*Peekaboo Morning by Rachel Isadora. New York: G. P. Putnam's Sons, 2002.

*Milton the Early Riser by Robert Kraus. New York: Simon and Schuster, 1972.

*Wake Up, Me! by Marni McGee. New York: Simon and Schuster, 2002.

Bedhead by Margie Palatini. New York: Simon and Schuster, 2000.

*Morning Song by Mary McKenna Siddals. New York: Henry Holt, 2001.

Day Breaks by Bethea verDorn. New York: Arcade, 1992.

"Mom, Wake Up and Play!" by Brigitte Weninger. New York: Penguin, 2004.

*Hey, Pancakes! by Tamson Weston. San Diego: Harcourt, 2003.

*Now It Is Morning by Candace Whitman. New York: Farrar, Straus and Giroux, 1999.

RECORDED MUSIC

"Good Morning, Mr. Sun" from *The Bird Is the Word: Big Bird's Favorite Songs.* Sony Wonder, 1995.

*"Carolina in the Morning" and "Red Red Robin" from *Good Morning Exercises for Kids* by Georgiana Stewart. Kimbo Educational, 2006.

*"Wake Up Toes" and other songs from *Morning Magic* by Joanie Bartels. BMG, 2003.

"What Did You Eat?" from *Patriotic and Morning Time Songs* by Hap Palmer. Educational Activities, Inc., 1997.

"Wake Up and Clap" from *Makin' Music: Come Outside to Play*. Makin' Music Rockin' Rhythms, 2002.

*"Brush Your Teeth" from *Singable Songs for the Very Young* by Raffi. Rounder/UMGD, 1976.

"Say Good Day!" from *Tiny Tunes: Music for Very Young Children* by Carole Peterson. Macaroni Soup, 2005.

FINGERPLAYS/SONGS

"Knock on the Door"

Knock on the door at the start of the day.
Wake up! Wake up! It's time to play!
Get out of bed and don't be slow.
It's time to tell the world hello!

"Eggs for Breakfast"

Mix up the eggs with a whisk whisk whisk.
Pour them in the pan with a hiss hiss hiss.
Cook up the eggs with a zum zum zum.
Eat up the eggs with a yum yum yum.

"Good Morning to You"
(to the tune of "Happy Birthday")

Good morning to you,
Good morning to you,
Good morning everybody,
Good morning to you.

"Animals Wake Up"

Bunnies wake up with a hop hop hop.
Horses wake up with a clop clop clop.
Cows wake up with a moo moo moo.
Roosters wake up with a cock-a-doodle-doo.
Monkeys wake up with a scratch scratch scratch.
But I wake up with a yaaaaaaaawn and a stretch.

"In the Morning"
(to the tune of "For He's a Jolly Good Fellow")

The sun comes up in the morning,
The moon goes down in the morning,
The sun comes up in the morning,
It's time to say good day!

PROPS

*Flannelboard or Prop Rhyme

"Five Toothbrushes"

PIECES NEEDED: *5 toothbrushes in red, orange, green, blue, and yellow*

5 little toothbrushes hanging in a row,
Red, orange, green, blue, and yellow.
Along comes Mommy to the bathroom door,
She brushes her teeth, and now there are 4.
4 little toothbrushes, such a sight to see,
Daddy's here to brush his teeth, and now there are 3.
3 little toothbrushes, we know what to do,
Sister's here to brush her teeth, and now there are 2.
2 little toothbrushes having so much fun,
Brother comes to brush his teeth, and now there is 1.
1 little toothbrush, and we are almost done,
That one's mine, I'll brush my teeth, and now there are none.

*Flannelboard Story: "Pancake Man"

PIECES NEEDED: *pancake man, woman, man, little girl, little boy, dog, cat, fox, river*

One day a lady was making pancakes. Her little girl asked her to make a special pancake shaped like a little man, so she did. But as soon as she flipped it over in the pan, that pancake jumped right up out of the pan and started dancing around the kitchen. The Pancake Man said, "Run, run, as fast as you can! You can't catch me, I'm the Pancake Man!" The Pancake Man ran out of the house. The lady chased the Pancake Man out the door. She ran into her husband, and said "Help!" So the man chased the lady, and the lady chased the Pancake Man, and the Pancake Man said, "Run, run, as fast as you can! You can't catch me, I'm the Pancake Man!"

Continue pattern, adding all characters except the fox and the river.

Then the Pancake Man came to a wide river. There was a fox there, and as the Pancake Man stood by the water trying to figure out how to cross the river, the fox said, "Hop on my back! I will carry you across!" So the Pancake Man jumped onto the fox's back, and the fox started swimming across the river. But soon the Pancake Man said, "I'm getting wet!" So the fox said, "Climb up onto my head." The Pancake Man climbed up onto the fox's head. Soon the Pancake Man said again, "I'm getting wet!" So the fox said, "Poor Pancake Man, climb up onto my snout, and you will stay dry." And just as the Pancake Man climbed up to the fox's snout, the fox opened up his mouth and SNAP, ate the Pancake Man in one big bite.

*Flannelboard Story   *Wake Up, Sun!* by David L. Harrison. New York: Random House, 1986.

PIECES NEEDED: *dog, pig, well, cow, barn, chicken, farmer and wife, baby, sun*

*Puppet Rhyme   "Good-Morning" by Muriel Sipe. From *Read-Aloud Rhymes for the Very Young* edited by Jack Prelutsky. New York: Knopf, 1986.

PIECES NEEDED: *duck puppet, mouse puppet, dog puppet, bird puppet*

CRAFTS

Wake Up Puppet

From *Crafts from Your Favorite Fairy Tales* by Kathy Ross (Brookfield, CT: Millbrook, 1997).

Rising Sun Pop-Up Cup

MATERIALS: 1 Styrofoam or paper cup with a hole poked in the bottom for each child, 1 craft stick for each child, glue, 1 precut sun shape for each child, crayons or markers

DIRECTIONS:
1. Decorate the sun as desired.
2. Glue the sun to the craft stick.
3. Place the sun in the cup so that the stick goes through the hole in the bottom. Move the stick to make the sun rise.

Happy New Year!

Sign: **HAPPY** *Sign:* **NEW YEAR**

BOOKS

The Noisemakers by Judith Caseley. New York: Greenwillow, 1992.

*A Kitten's Year by Nancy Raines Day. New York: HarperCollins, 2000.

*All Year Long by Kathleen W. Deady. Minneapolis: Carolrhoda, 2004.

*Pajamas Anytime by Marsha Hayles. New York: G. P. Putnam's Sons, 2005.

A Year in the City by Kathy Henderson. Cambridge, MA: Candlewick, 1996.

Moo in the Morning by Barbara Maitland. New York: Farrar, Straus and Giroux, 2000.

The Turning of the Year by Bill Martin Jr. San Diego: Harcourt Brace, 1998.

Goodbye Old Year, Hello New Year by Frank Modell. New York: Greenwillow, 1984.

*Here Comes Spring and Summer and Fall and Winter by Mary Murphy. New York: DK, 1999.

*My Love for You All Year Round by Susan L. Roth. New York: Dial, 2003.

Long Night Moon by Cynthia Rylant. New York: Simon and Schuster, 2004.

*Month by Month a Year Goes Round by Carol Diggory Shields. New York: Dutton, 1998.

*All Year Long by Nancy Tafuri. New York: Greenwillow, 1983.

*Snowy Flowy Blowy: A Twelve Months Rhyme by Nancy Tafuri. New York: Scholastic, 1999.

*Midnight Babies by Margaret Wild. New York: Clarion, 1999.

RECORDED MUSIC

*"The Hokey Pokey" from *Dancin' Magic* by Joanie Bartels. BMG Special Products, 1991.

"Feliz Ano Nuevo" from *Holiday Songs for All Occasions.* Kimbo Educational, 1978.

*"Happy Little New Year" from *Merry, Merry Christmas* by Captain Kangaroo. Drive Entertainment, 2002. *(use with streamers)*

FINGERPLAYS/SONGS

"On January 1st"

On January 1st I open my eyes.
The same old sun is in the sky.
I stretch my arms out just this way.
A whole new year has come to stay.

"Happy New Year"
(to the tune of "Frère Jacques")

Happy New Year, Happy New Year.
Celebrate, Celebrate.
Goodbye to the old year,
Hello to the new year.
It will be great, it will be great.

PROPS

Prop Fingerplay

"Noisemakers"

PIECES NEEDED: *noisemakers*

All year long the night time
Is a time for quiet.
But when New Year's Eve comes
It sounds like a riot!
When it's midnight, girls and boys
Take their noisemakers and make some
    NOISE!

*Flannelboard Rhyme

"Five Little Noisemakers"

PIECES NEEDED: *5 noisemakers*

5 little noisemakers sitting by the door,
My aunt took one, and then there were 4.
4 little noisemakers, ready for a spree,
My uncle took one, and then there were 3.
3 little noisemakers, shiny and new,
My cousin took one, and then there were 2.
2 little noisemakers, won't this be fun?
My sister took one, and then there was 1.
1 little noisemaker sitting all alone,
I took that one, and then there were none.
On New Year's Eve when the clock struck
    midnight
We blew on our noisemakers with all
    our might.

*Prop Fingerplay

"Countdown Rhyme"

PIECES NEEDED: *confetti*

On New Year's Eve we wait and wait
For the New Year to celebrate.
Is it midnight yet? No, not quite.
It seems we've been waiting all through
    the night.
At 11:59, here we go—
Everybody counts down to zero.
10 . . . 9 . . . 8 . . . 7 . . . 6 . . . 5 . . . 4 . . .
    3 . . . 2 . . . 1 . . . 0
Happy New Year! *(throw confetti)*

*Flannelboard Song

"Our New Year"
(to the tune of "Happy Birthday")

PIECES NEEDED: *felt cutouts or magnets
showing the numbers of the old and new years*

(Current year), (Current year),
Goodbye, goodbye, goodbye (Current
    year).
(New year), (New year),
Hello, hello, hello (New year).

(*Example: 2008, 2008,
    Goodbye, goodbye, goodbye 2008.
    2009, 2009,
    Hello, hello, hello 2009.*)

*Streamers

Make enough simple streamers for each child to have one. Use them during a streamer dance with your favorite freeze dance song or with the New Year's music listed above. To make the streamers, simply tape a length of crepe streamer to a straw.

CRAFTS

Midnight Fireworks

MATERIALS: 1 piece of white construction paper for each child, glitter crayons in various colors, several thick black crayons, craft sticks

DIRECTIONS:
1. Cover the paper with desired colors using the glitter crayons in any color except black.
2. Completely cover the glitter crayon designs with black crayon.
3. Using the craft stick, etch away the black crayon in fireworks designs to reveal the colors underneath. The finished picture will look like fireworks against the night sky.

Countdown Clock

MATERIALS: 1 paper plate for each child, precut numbers 1–12, 1 paper fastener for each child, 2 clock hands precut from black construction paper for each child, glue, decorating materials

DIRECTIONS:
1. Glue the numbers around the outside of the paper plate to form the clock face.
2. Punch a hole in the center of the plate. Punch a hole in the end of each of the hands, then fasten the hands to the plate using the paper fastener.
3. Decorate as desired.

I See the Moon

Sign: **MOON**

BOOKS

Moongame by Frank Asch. New York: Simon and Schuster, 1984.

And If the Moon Could Talk by Kate Banks. New York: Farrar, Straus and Giroux, 1998.

Goodnight Moon by Margaret Wise Brown. New York: Harper, 1947.

Papa, Please Get the Moon for Me by Eric Carle. New York: Simon and Schuster, 1986.

See You Soon Moon by Donna Conrad. New York: Knopf, 2001.

I'll Catch the Moon by Nina Crews. New York: Greenwillow, 1996.

Bringing Down the Moon by Jonathan Emmett. Cambridge, MA: Candlewick, 2001.

Kitten's First Full Moon by Kevin Henkes. New York: Greenwillow, 2004.

Moondogs by Daniel Kirk. New York: G. P. Putnam's Sons, 1999.

Tom and Pippo See the Moon by Helen Oxenbury. New York: Aladdin, 1988.

Can't Sleep by Chris Raschka. New York: Orchard, 1995.

Moonbathing by Liz Rosenberg. San Diego: Harcourt Brace, 1996.

Long Night Moon by Cynthia Rylant. New York: Simon and Schuster, 2004.

New Moon by Pegi Deitz Shea. Honesdale, PA: Boyds Mills Press, 1996.

What the Sun Sees, What the Moon Sees by Nancy Tafuri. New York: Greenwillow, 1997.

Over the Moon by Rachel Vail. New York: Orchard, 1998.

Moon Glows by Bethea verDorn. New York: Arcade, 1990.

Zoom! Zoom! Zoom! I'm Off to the Moon! by Dan Yaccarino. New York: Scholastic, 1997.

Owl Moon by Jane Yolen. New York: Scholastic, 1987.

Moonride by Harriet Ziefert. New York: Houghton Mifflin, 2000.

RECORDED MUSIC

*"The Martian Hop" from *Dancin' Magic* by Joanie Bartels. BMG Special Products, 1991.

Dancing on the Moon by John and David. Youngheart Music, 1998.

Space Songs for Children: Fun Songs and Activities about Outer Space by Tonja Weimer. Pearce-
   Evetts, 1993.

FINGERPLAYS/SONGS

*"The Man in the Moon"
(traditional)

The man in the moon looked out of
   the moon
And what do you think he said?
"Now that I am getting up,
It's time for children to go to bed!"

*"Let's Go to the Moon"

Zoom! Let's go to the moon!
Let's take a trip
In my rocket ship!
Get ready for the countdown!
10-9-8-7-6-5-4-3-2-1! Blastoff!

"I'm a Little Rocket"
(to the tune of "I'm a Little Teapot")

I'm a little rocket going to the moon.
I'm getting fueled up and I'll leave soon.
Hear my boosters fire, with loud sounds.
I'm all ready to start the countdown.
5 . . . 4 . . . 3 . . . 2 . . . 1 . . . Blastoff!

*"I See the Moon"
(traditional)

I see the moon, the moon sees me
   (make circle over head with arms)
Down through the branch of the old oak
   tree. (wave arms like tree branches)
Please let the light that shines on me
   (wiggle fingers to show moon's light)
Shine on the one I love. (hug self)

*"If I Were"
(to the tune of "I'm Glad I'm Me [Sammy]"
by Hap Palmer, Early Childhood Classics,
Hap-Pal Music, 2000)

If I were a wolf then I would howl at
   the moon,
Howl at the moon, howl at the moon.
If I were a wolf then I would howl at
   the moon—
Arooooooooo!

If I were an alien I'd fly to the moon,
Fly to the moon, fly to the moon.
If I were an alien I'd fly to the moon—
Vrooooooommm!

If I were a star I'd blow a kiss to
   the moon,
Kiss to the moon, kiss to the moon.
If I were a star I'd blow a kiss to
   the moon—
Mwa!

But I'm glad I'm me and I can wave to
   the moon,
Wave to the moon, wave to the moon.
I'm glad I'm me and I can wave to
   the moon—
Hi moon!

*"Reach for the Moon"

Reach up high, reach for the moon,
Maybe we will reach it soon.
Make a circle over your head,
We have made our own moon instead!

PROPS

*Flannelboard or Stick Puppet Rhyme

"Hey Diddle Diddle"

Patterns can be found in The Flannelboard Storytelling Book *by Judy Sierra (New York: H. W. Wilson, 1997).*

Hey Diddle Diddle,
The cat and the fiddle,
The cow jumped over the moon.
The little dog laughed to see such sport,
And the dish ran away with the spoon.

*Flannelboard Rhyme

"Five Little Stars (and the Moon Too)"

PIECES NEEDED: *5 stars, moon*

5 little stars in the nighttime sky.
The first one said, "What a pretty night, oh my!"
The second one said, "Let's twinkle all night long."
The third one said, "Let's sing a starry song."
The fourth one said, "The moon is on the rise."
The fifth one said, "It's time to close our eyes."
Then up went the moon and out went the light,
And the 5 little stars twinkled through the night.

*Flannelboard Story   *Moongame* by Frank Asch. New York: Simon and Schuster, 1984.

PIECES NEEDED: *bear, bird, tree, moon, cloud, flower, rock, house with window, cheese wheel, yellow balloon, forest animals as desired*

*Flannelboard Story   *Kitten's First Full Moon* by Kevin Henkes. New York: Greenwillow, 2004.

PIECES NEEDED: *kitten, moon, bug, tree, pond with reflection of moon in it, bowl of milk*

*Flannelboard Story   *The Moon Might Be Milk* by Lisa Shulman. New York: Dutton, 2007.

PIECES NEEDED: *moon, cat, milk, hen, egg, butterfly, sugar, dog, butter, mouse, flour, grandmother, cookies, girl*

ADDITIONAL SUGGESTIONS

Storytelling

"The Night the Moon Fell Into the Well" retold by Martha Hamilton and Mitch Weiss in *Stories in My Pocket: Tales Kids Can Tell.* Golden, CO: Fulcrum, 1996.

Activity: Over the Moon

Make a large paper moon and act out the various directions (or invite volunteers to do so) in *Over the Moon* by Rachel Vail (New York: Orchard, 1998). For a fun, surprising twist at the end, use the "Magic Door to Books" trick found in *Leading Kids to Books through Magic* by Carolyn Feller Bauer (Chicago: American Library Association, 1996) to actually walk *through* your moon.

CRAFTS

Moon and Stars

MATERIALS: 1 coloring sheet with a picture of the moon on it for each child, star stickers, crayons or markers

DIRECTIONS:
1. Place star stickers on coloring sheet.
2. Color as desired.

Moon Masks

MATERIALS: 1 paper plate with eyeholes cut out for each child, crayons, star stickers, star shapes cut from aluminum foil, chenille stems, craft sticks, glue or tape

DIRECTIONS:
1. Decorate the mask with star stickers and crayons.
2. For a 3-D effect, coil chenille stems around a pencil to make a spiral, then attach them to the mask. Attach aluminum foil stars to the ends of the chenille stems.
3. Attach a craft stick to the bottom of the mask for a handle.

Join the Parade

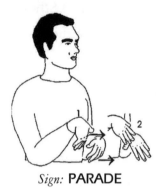

Sign: **PARADE**

BOOKS

Monsieur Saguette and His Baguette by Frank Asch. Toronto, ON: Kids Can Press, 2004.

*Thump, Thump, Rat-a-Tat-Tat by Gene Baer. New York: HarperCollins, 1989.

Parade Day: Marching through the Calendar Year by Bob Barner. New York: Holiday House, 2003.

Easter Parade by Irving Berlin, illustrated by Lisa McCue. New York: HarperCollins, 2003.

*Clifford and the Big Parade by Norman Bridwell. New York: Scholastic, 1998.

Follow the Leader! by Emma Chichester Clark. New York: Simon and Schuster, 1999.

Milly and the Macy's Parade by Shana Corey. New York: Scholastic, 2002.

*Parade by Donald Crews. New York: Greenwillow, 1983.

Meet the Marching Smithereens by Ann Hayes. San Diego: Harcourt Brace, 1995.

*My First Chinese New Year by Karen Katz. New York: Henry Holt, 2004.

Humpty Dumpty by Daniel Kirk. New York: G. P. Putnam's Sons, 2000.

Froggy Plays in the Band by Jonathan London. New York: Viking, 2002.

The Aunts Go Marching by Maurie J. Manning. Honesdale, PA: Boyds Mills Press, 2003.

Spunky Monkeys on Parade by Stuart J. Murphy. New York: HarperCollins, 1999.

*Curious George at the Parade by H. A. Rey. New York: Houghton Mifflin, 1999.

*Fourth of July Mice by Bethany Roberts. New York: Clarion, 2004.

On the Morn of Mayfest by Erica Silverman. New York: Simon and Schuster, 1998.

The Biggest Parade by Elizabeth Winthrop. New York: Henry Holt, 2006.

Animal Music by Harriet Ziefert. New York: Houghton Mifflin, 1999.

First Night by Harriet Ziefert. New York: G. P. Putnam's Sons, 1999.

RECORDED MUSIC

"The Animal Parade" from *Animal Walks* by Georgiana Stewart. Kimbo Educational, 1987.

*"Our Fancy Dance Parade" from *Choo Choo to the Zoo: Creative Movement and Play* by Georgiana Stewart. Kimbo Educational, 2006.

"Circus Parade" from *Circus Magic* by Linda Arnold. Rounder/UMGD, 1998.

"The Parade Came Marching" from *Great Big Fun* by Tom Chapin. Music for Little People, 2001.

"The Alphabet Parade" from *A Great Day for Learning* by Barney. Lyons/HIT Entertainment, 1999. (*give kids letters to carry and make a parade*)

"Walkin'" from *Makin' Music: Come Outside to Play.* Makin' Music Rockin' Rhythms, 2002.

*"You're a Grand Old Flag" from *Musical Scarves and Activities* by Georgiana Stewart. Kimbo Educational, 2002. (*use scarves or flags*)

*"Marching Song" from *Run, Jump, Skip, and Sing* by Barney. Koch Records, 2003.

*"The Animal Parade" from *Wee Sing: Animals Animals Animals* by Pamela Conn Beall and Susan Hagen Nipp. Price Stern Sloan, 2006.

FINGERPLAYS/SONGS

"Left Foot, Right Foot"

Left foot, right foot,
Here we go,
Marching in the parade like so.
Wave a flag or ring a bell,
The parade thing is just swell!

"I'm a Big Parade Balloon"
(to the tune of "I'm a Little Teapot")

I'm a big parade balloon
Up in the sky.
See me float and see me fly.
If the day is windy, hear me say,
Hold on tight or I'll float away.

"March Along"
(to the tune of "Row, Row, Row Your Boat")

March march march along,
March in the parade.
Wave your flag and march along,
Join in the parade.

"The Parade Car"

Riding in the parade car down the street
I wave and wave to everyone I meet!

"The Marching Band"

I want to play in the marching band!
It will be the best band in the land.
First I'll play the slide trombone,
        (*mime playing a trombone*)
Then I'll bang the big bass drum.
        (*mime playing the drum*)
I'll play the tuba, oompa-pa,
        (*mime playing the tuba*)
Then the flute, tra-la-la.
        (*mime playing the flute*)
I'll march until the parade is done.
Being in the marching band is such fun!

"First Me, Then You"

First me, then you,
Say what I say, and do what I do.
Stand on tiptoes way up high,
Reach your arms into the sky.
Turn yourself around and round,
Now sit right down on the ground.

PROPS

*Flannelboard Rhyme

"Five Clowns in the Parade"

PIECES NEEDED: *5 clowns*

5 happy clowns in the circus parade.
The first one said, "Oh! I'm so glad you stayed!"
The second one said, "Let's tumble through the streets."
The third one said, "Let's get something to eat."
The fourth one said, "Here comes the marching band!"
The fifth one said, "The elephants are close at hand."
Then "TA DA" went the music and on came the spotlight,
And 5 little clowns tumbled out of sight.

*Parade

PIECES NEEDED: *streamers, scarves, or flags to wave while marching in a parade (enough for each child to have one), musical instruments to play while marching in a parade (enough for each child to have one)*

*Prop Story   *I Went Walking* by Sue Williams. San Diego: Harcourt Brace Jovanovich, 1990.

Flannelboard patterns can be found in 2's Experience Felt Board Fun *by Liz and Dick Wilmes (Elgin, IL: Building Blocks, 1994).*

CRAFTS

Popping Firecracker Puppet

From *Star-Spangled Crafts* by Kathy Ross (Brookfield, CT: Millbrook Press, 2003).

Parade Flags

MATERIALS: 4-by-6-inch piece of white construction paper for each child, 2-by-2-inch square of blue construction paper for each child, 1 straw for each child, tape, glue, star stickers, red crayons

DIRECTIONS:
1. Glue the blue construction paper to the upper left-hand corner of the white construction paper.
2. Decorate the blue square with star stickers.
3. Draw red stripes on the flag.
4. Tape the flag to the straw and wave.

Just Ducky

Sign: **DUCK**

BOOKS

Duck in the Truck by Jez Alborough. New York: HarperCollins, 1999.

Baby Duck's New Friend by Frank Asch. San Diego: Harcourt, 2001.

Five Little Ducks by Ivan Bates. New York: Orchard, 2006.

Ready or Not, Dawdle Duckling by Toni Buzzeo. New York: Dial, 2005.

This Way, Ruby! by Jonathan Emmett. New York: Scholastic, 2006.

Across the Stream by Mirra Ginsburg. New York: Greenwillow, 1982.

Silly Goose and Dizzy Duck Play Hide-and-Seek by Sally Grindley. New York: DK, 1999.

The Littlest Duckling by Gail Herman. New York: Viking, 1996.

In the Rain with Baby Duck by Amy Hest. Cambridge, MA: Candlewick, 1995.

Do Like a Duck Does! by Judy Hindley. Cambridge, MA: Candlewick, 2002.

Just Ducky by Kathy Mallat. New York: Walker, 2002.

Ducks, Ducks, Ducks by Carolyn Otto. New York: HarperCollins, 1991.

One Cold Little Duck, Duck, Duck by Lisa Westberg Peters. New York: Greenwillow, 2000.

Duck Stuck by Phyllis Root. Cambridge, MA: Candlewick, 1998.

Duck on a Bike by David Shannon. New York: Scholastic, 2002.

Quack, Daisy, QUACK! by Jane Simmons. New York: Little, Brown, 2002.

Waddle, Waddle, Quack, Quack, Quack by Barbara Anne Skalak. San Francisco: Chronicle, 2005.

Little Quack by Lauren Thompson. New York: Simon and Schuster, 2003.

Come On, Baby Duck! by Nick Ward. Intercourse, PA: Good Books, 2004.

RECORDED MUSIC

*"Six Little Ducks" from *More Singable Songs* by Raffi. Rounder/UMGD, 1977.

*"Mama Duck" from *Sing It! Say It! Stamp It! Sway It! Volume 3* by Peter and Ellen Allard. 80-Z Music, 2002.

"Ducky Duddle" from *Tiny Tunes: Music for Very Young Children* by Carole Peterson. Macaroni Soup, 2005.

*"Little White Duck" from *Toddlers on Parade* by Carol Hammett and Elaine Bueffel. Kimbo Educational, 1999.

*"Five Little Ducks" from *Wee Sing: Animals Animals Animals* by Pamela Conn Beall and Susan Hagen Nipp. Price Stern Sloan, 2006.

FINGERPLAYS/SONGS

"Duck Hokey Pokey"
(to the tune of "The Hokey Pokey")

You put your right wing in, you put your
    right wing out,
You put your right wing in and you shake
    it all about.
You do the Duck Hokey Pokey and you
    waddle all around.
Quack quack quack quack quack!
. . . left wing
. . . right webbed foot
. . . left webbed foot
. . . beak
. . . tail feather
. . . whole duck self

"Duckling Do"

Duckling do, duckling see,
Duckling do it just like me.
Duckling open your little beak,
Duckling jump on your duckling feet.
Duckling paddle, duckling flap,
Waddle around with a quack quack quack!

"Duckling Parade"

It's a duckling parade!
They are lined up behind their mama,
10 little ducklings, quacking like they
    wanna.
Mama Duck goes left and right,
10 little ducklings follow, what a sight!
Ducklings going fast and slow,
10 little ducklings ready to go.
1, 2, 3, 4, 5, 6, 7, 8, 9, 10!

"The Ducks on the Pond"
(to the tune of "The Wheels on the Bus")

The ducks on the pond go quack quack
    quack,
Quack quack quack, quack quack quack.
The ducks on the pond go quack quack
    quack,
All through the day.

The ducklings in the eggs go hatch hatch
    hatch,
Hatch hatch hatch, hatch hatch hatch.
The ducklings in the eggs go hatch hatch
    hatch,
All through the day.

The little baby ducklings go flap flap flap,
Flap flap flap, flap flap flap.
The little baby ducklings go flap flap flap,
All through the day

The ducks on the pond go quack quack
    quack,
Quack quack quack, quack quack quack.
The ducks on the pond go quack quack
    quack,
All through the day.

"I'm a Little Duckling"
(to the tune of "I'm a Little Teapot")

I'm a little duckling,
Yellow and fat.
I've got a little beak and feathers on my
    back.
When the sun is shining, watch me play.
I paddle through the water and quack all day.

"Waddle Duck"

Waddle waddle waddle duck, *(waddle)*
Paddle paddle paddle duck. *(move hands as if paddling in a circle)*
Tail up, tail down, *(overlap hands behind you to make a tail and move
    it up and down)*
Quack quack quack.

PROPS

*Flannelboard Rhyme

"Five Little Ducks"

PIECES NEEDED: *5 ducks*

5 little ducks swimming by the shore,
1 dove under the water, and then there
    were 4.
4 little ducks so pretty to see,
1 chased a dragonfly and then there were 3.
3 little ducks on the water so blue,
1 stopped to eat some bread, and then
    there were 2.
2 little ducks, swimming in the sun,
1 stopped to take a nap, and then there
    was 1.
1 little duck, swimming all alone,
He quacked and paddled and swam toward
    home.

*Flannelboard Song

"Color Ducks"
(to the tune of "The Farmer in the Dell")

PIECES NEEDED: *enough duck shapes in various
colors for each child to hold one, pond*

The ducks are in the pond, the ducks are in
    the pond.
Quack quack quack quack quack quack,
    the ducks are in the pond.
Red ducks are in the pond . . .

*Repeat with other colors, inviting the children
to place their ducks in the pond as you call their
colors.*

*Flannelboard Story   *Webster J. Duck* by Martin Waddell. Cambridge, MA:
Candlewick, 2001.

PIECES NEEDED: *egg, baby duck, dog, cow, sheep, mama duck*

CRAFTS

Duck Feet

MATERIALS: 2 duck feet shapes (large enough to fit over a child's shoe) cut from orange construction paper for each child, hole punch, yarn, crayons

DIRECTIONS:
1. Punch holes in the two back corners of each duck foot.
2. Tie a length of yarn to each hole.
3. Decorate the duck feet.
4. Tie the duck feet around each child's ankles so the feet fit over his or her shoes.

Fluffy Ducks

MATERIALS: 1 duck shape cut from construction paper for each child, yellow cotton balls, googly eyes, glue

DIRECTIONS:
1. Pull the cotton balls apart to make yellow fuzz.
2. Glue the fuzz onto the duck shape.
3. Glue a googly eye onto the duck's face.

Let's Make Music

Sign: **MUSIC**

BOOKS

Zoo Song by Barbara Bottner. New York: Scholastic, 1987.

My Family Plays Music by Judy Cox. New York: Holiday House, 2003.

**If You're Happy and You Know It* by Penny Dann. Hauppauge, NY: Barron's, 2000.

The Song of Six Birds by Rene Deetlefs. New York: Dutton, 1999.

Gabriella's Song by Candace Fleming. New York: Atheneum, 1997.

Manuelo the Playing Mantis by Don Freeman. New York: Viking, 2004.

**When Uncle Took the Fiddle* by Libba Moore Gray. New York: Orchard, 1999.

**The Wheels on the Bus* by Maryann Kovalski. Toronto, ON: Kids Can Press, 1987.

Mole Music by David McPhail. New York: Henry Holt, 1999.

We All Sing with the Same Voice by J. Philip Miller and Sheppard M. Greene. New York: HarperCollins, 1982.

Moses Goes to a Concert by Isaac Millman. New York: Farrar, Straus and Giroux, 1998.

Zin! Zin! Zin! A Violin by Lloyd Moss. New York: Simon and Schuster, 1995.

**Take Me Out to the Ballgame* by Jack Norworth. New York: Aladdin, 1999.

Snake Alley Band by Elizabeth Nygaard. New York: Doubleday, 1998.

Ten Monkey Jamboree by Dianne Ochiltree. New York: Simon and Schuster, 2001.

**Doing the Animal Bop* by Jan Ormerod. Hauppauge, NY: Barron's, 2005.

How Much Is That Doggie in the Window? by Iza Trapani. Boston: Whispering Coyote Press, 1997.

*Skip to My Lou by Nadine Bernard Westcott. New York: Little, Brown, 1989.

Animal Music by Harriet Ziefert. New York: Houghton Mifflin, 1999.

RECORDED MUSIC

"Follow the Band" from *Jim Gill's Irrational Anthem* by Jim Gill. Jim Gill Music, Inc., 2001.

*"Old Mac Donald's Band" from *Rhythms on Parade (Revised Expanded Version)* by Hap Palmer. Hap-Pal Music, 1995.

*"Tap Your Sticks" from *Rhythms on Parade (Revised Expanded Version)* by Hap Palmer. Hap-Pal Music, 1995.

*"Old MacDonald Had a Band" from *Singable Songs for the Very Young* by Raffi. Rounder/UMGD, 1976.

*"Play the Band" from *Tiny Tunes: Music for Very Young Children* by Carole Peterson. Macaroni Soup, 2005.

*"I Know a Chicken" from *Whaddaya Think of That?* by Laurie Berkner. Two Tomatoes, 2001. *(use with shaker eggs)*

FINGERPLAYS/SONGS

"My Drum"

My knees can be a drum: rum tum rum.
The floor can be a drum: rum tum rum.
My head can be a drum: rum tum rum.

"The Marching Band"

I want to play in the marching band!
It will be the best band in the land.
First I'll play the slide trombone,
   (mime playing the trombone)
Then I'll bang the big bass drum.
   (mime playing the drum)
I'll play the tuba, oompa-pa,
   (mime playing the tuba)
Then the flute, tra-la-la.
   (mime playing the flute)
I'll march until the parade is done.
Being in the marching band is such fun!

"The Drum Says"

When the drum says walk, we walk walk walk.
When the drum says run, we run run run.
When the drum says gallop, we gallop gallop gallop.
When the drum says stop, we STOP!

"Singing, Singing"
(to the tune of "A Bicycle Built for Two")

Singing, singing. It's what I love to do.
There's nothing better than making music with you.
You can say la la la la, or even say da da da da.
Just lend an ear and listen here,
And sing a song with me.

PROPS

*Flannelboard Rhyme

"Five Little Instruments"

PIECES NEEDED: *tuba, violin, bass drum, oboe, triangle*

5 little instruments waiting by the door,
My brother chose the tuba, and then
    there were 4.
4 little instruments as you can see,
My sister chose a violin, and then there
    were 3.
3 little instruments shiny and new,
My mother chose a big bass drum, and
    then there were 2.
2 little instruments, isn't this fun?
My father chose an oboe, and then there
    was 1.
1 little instrument, sitting all alone,
I picked up the triangle, and then there
    were none.

Prop Song

"Shake Those Eggs"
(to the tune of "Skip to My Lou")

PIECES NEEDED: *shaker eggs, enough for each child to have one*

Shake those eggs and shake them high.
Shake those eggs and shake them low.
Shake those eggs off to the side.
Now shake them in a circle like so.

*Prop Game: Radio Sing-Along

Make a large circle out of posterboard. From another piece of posterboard, cut out a large arrow. Attach the arrow to the center of the circle with a paper fastener. Write "LOUD" at the top of the circle, and "SOFT" at the bottom. During the program, have the children sing along to a song that everyone knows, such as "Twinkle Twinkle Little Star." As you move the arrow around the circle, the children must change the volume of the song.

Prop Song   "Follow the Band" from *Jim Gill's Irrational Anthem* by Jim Gill.

*Prop Song   "Old Mac Donald's Band" from *Rhythms on Parade (Revised Expanded Version)* by Hap Palmer.

*Prop Song   "Old MacDonald Had a Band" from *Singable Songs for the Very Young* by Raffi.

*Prop Song   "Play the Band" from *Tiny Tunes: Music for Very Young Children* by Carole Peterson.

    PIECES NEEDED: *enough musical instruments for each child to have one. Pass out the instruments and invite children to play along with one of the above songs.*

*Prop Song   "Tap Your Sticks" from *Rhythms on Parade (Revised Expanded Version)* by Hap Palmer.

PIECES NEEDED: *enough rhythm sticks for each child to have two*

Flannelboard Story   "The Bremen Town Musicians"

Patterns can be found in The Flannelboard Storytelling Book *by Judy Sierra (New York: H. W. Wilson, 1997).*

ADDITIONAL SUGGESTIONS

Feel the Beat

After reading the book *Moses Goes to a Concert* by Isaac Millman (New York: Farrar, Straus and Giroux, 1998), give each child a balloon to hold in his or her lap as you play music. Discuss how even people who cannot hear can feel the music.

Poetry

"Pickety Fence" by David McPhail. From *Knock at a Star: A Child's Introduction to Poetry,* edited by X. J. Kennedy and Dorothy M. Kennedy. New York: Little, Brown, 1999.

PIECES NEEDED: *enough rhythm sticks for each child to have two*

CRAFTS

Instrument Crafts

From *Child's Play: 200 Instant Crafts and Activities for Preschoolers* by Leslie Hamilton (New York: Crown, 1989).

Shaker Eggs

MATERIALS: plastic Easter eggs, colored masking tape, stickers, medium-sized jingle bells

DIRECTIONS:
1. Open an egg and place 1–2 jingle bells inside.
2. Close the egg and run a strip of colored masking tape over the seam.
3. Decorate with stickers and shake.

Let's Talk Turkey

Sign: **TURKEY**

BOOKS

Over the River: A Turkey's Tale by Derek Anderson. New York: Simon and Schuster, 2005.

Sometimes It's Turkey, Sometimes It's Feathers by Lorna Balian. Watertown, WI: Star Bright Books, 2004.

A Plump and Perky Turkey by Teresa Bateman. New York: Marshall Cavendish, 2001.

The Firefighters' Thanksgiving by Maribeth Boelts. New York: G. P. Putnam's Sons, 2004.

Clifford's Thanksgiving Visit by Norman Bridwell. New York: Scholastic, 1993.

A Turkey for Thanksgiving by Eve Bunting. New York: Clarion, 1991.

Over the River and Through the Wood by Lydia Marie Child. Illustrated by David Catrow. New York: Henry Holt, 1996.

Look Who's in the Thanksgiving Play! A Lift-the-Flap Story by Andrew Clements. New York: Simon and Schuster, 1999.

Thanksgiving Day by Gail Gibbons. New York: Holiday House, 1983.

One Little, Two Little, Three Little Pilgrims by B. G. Hennessey. New York: Viking, 1999.

I Know an Old Lady Who Swallowed a Pie by Alison Jackson. New York: Dutton, 1997.

Giving Thanks by Jonathan London. Cambridge, MA: Candlewick, 2003.

Thanks for Thanksgiving by Julie Markes. New York: HarperCollins, 2004.

This First Thanksgiving Day: A Counting Story by Laura Krauss Melmed. New York: HarperCollins, 2001.

1, 2, 3 Thanksgiving! by W. Nikola-Lisa. Morton Grove, IL: Albert Whitman, 1991.

Setting the Turkeys Free by W. Nikola-Lisa. New York: Hyperion, 2004.

Thanksgiving Mice! by Bethany Roberts. New York: Clarion, 2001.

Thanksgiving Day by Anne Rockwell. New York: HarperCollins, 1999.

Thanksgiving Treat by Catherine Stock. New York: Macmillan, 1990.

Turk and Runt by Lisa Wheeler. New York: Atheneum, 2002.

Turkey on the Loose! by Sylvie Wickstrom. New York: Dial, 1990.

RECORDED MUSIC

*"The Turkey Wobble" from *Holiday Songs for All Occasions.* Kimbo Educational, 1978.

*"The Little Pilgrim" from *Toddlers on Parade* by Carol Hammett and Elaine Bueffel. Kimbo Educational, 1999.

"(I'm Gonna Eat) On Thanksgiving Day" from *Whaddaya Think of That?* by Laurie Berkner. Two Tomatoes, 2001.

FINGERPLAYS/SONGS

"Did You Ever See a Turkey?"
(to the tune of "Did You Ever See a Lassie?")

Did you ever see a turkey, a turkey, a turkey,
Did you ever see a turkey go this way and that?
Go this way and that way, and that way and this way.
Did you ever see a turkey go this way and that?

"Thanksgiving Time"

Thanksgiving time comes once a year
On Thanksgiving we give a cheer!
Turkey and stuffing, corn and pies
Mashed potatoes before our eyes!
We'll laugh laugh laugh,
And we'll eat eat eat,
And when we're done we'll go to sleep sleep sleep!

"If You're a Turkey and You Know It"
(to the tune of "If You're Happy and You Know It")

If you're a turkey and you know it, give a gobble.
If you're a turkey and you know it, give a gobble.
If you're a turkey and you know it, then you really ought to show it.
If you're a turkey and you know it, give a gobble.
. . . shake your tail feathers
. . . wag your wattle

"The Turkey"
(traditional)

The turkey is a funny bird.
Its head goes wobble, wobble.
And all it knows is just one word:
"Gobble, gobble, gobble!"

"I'm a Little Turkey"
(to the tune of "I'm a Little Teapot")

I'm a little turkey, gobble gobble gobble,
Here is my tail and here is my wattle.
Most of the year I stay and play.
When Thanksgiving comes, I run away.

"The Twelve Hours of Thanksgiving"
(to the tune of "The Twelve Days of Christmas")

In the first hour of Thanksgiving, my mama made for me
One delicious turkey.
In the second hour of Thanksgiving, my mama made for me
Corn on the cob and one delicious turkey.
. . . third hour: lovely green beans
. . . fourth hour: mashed potatoes
. . . fifth hour: cranberry sauce
. . . sixth hour: big bowl of stuffing
. . . seventh hour: big yummy biscuits
. . . eighth hour: a big bowl of gravy
. . . ninth hour: cornbread
. . . tenth hour: yummy orange carrots
. . . eleventh hour: slice of pumpkin pie
. . . twelfth hour: big bowl of ice cream

PROPS

*Flannelboard Rhyme

"Five Fat Turkeys"

PIECES NEEDED: *5 turkeys*

5 fat turkeys standing by the door,
1 hid in the barn, and then there were 4.
4 fat turkeys under the tree,
1 hid in its branches, and then there
    were 3.
3 fat turkeys who didn't know what to do,
1 hid in the pig pen, and then there
    were 2.
2 fat turkeys sitting in the sun,
1 hid in the bushes, and then there was 1.
1 fat turkey, sitting all alone,
He ran away, and then there were none.

*Flannelboard Rhyme

"Turkey Feathers"

PIECES NEEDED: *turkey body, enough large feathers in various colors that each child can hold one*

There was a little turkey
Who was looking for his tail,
And when he couldn't find it
He started to weep and wail.
He said "Woe is me!
Please tell me whether
You can help me find
My RED tail feather."

Repeat with each color, inviting the kids to place their feathers on the flannelboard as you call their color. As an additional activity, you may invite the children to name something of each color that they are thankful for.

*Flannelboard Story: "Mama's Magic Table"

PIECES NEEDED: *table with 3 leaf extensions, mother, father, 3 girls, 2 boys, 1 grandmother, 2 grandfathers, 3 aunts, 3 uncles, turkey, bowl of stuffing, bowl of sweet potatoes, bowl of carrots, bowl of green beans, plate of biscuits, bowl of gravy, bowl of mashed potatoes, bowl of cranberry sauce, pumpkin pie*

My mama has a magic table. When we sit at the table for dinner each night, it's just the right size for me and my sister and my mama and daddy. But every year when my family comes to visit, she can make it bigger. *(Insert one leaf.)* There, now we'll have enough room for the turkey and the stuffing. DING DONG. My grandma and grandpa are here, and look, they've brought sweet potatoes. Lucky we have room on the table. DING DONG. Now Aunt Sarah and Uncle Jim are here, and they've brought carrots and green beans. Uh-oh, looks like we'll have to make the table bigger again. *(Insert second leaf.)* DING DONG. Uncle Bobby and Aunt Jenny are here, with my cousins Annie, Joe, and Fred. And look! They brought my favorite biscuits, and mashed potatoes. DING DONG. Now here come Aunt Sue and Uncle Tony, and they have cranberry sauce and gravy. We're going to need to make that table even bigger! *(Insert third leaf.)* Now there's enough room for everybody. But wait—somebody's missing! DING DONG. There he is! It's Grandpa

Jeff, and he brought the pumpkin pie. Now we can sit down and eat at our magic table. But you know what? I think it's magic not because it can get bigger, but because all the people I love are gathered around it. Happy Thanksgiving!

*File Folder Story: "Tough Tom Turkey"

Cut a simple turkey shape out of one side of a file folder. Copy the story below and tape it to the uncut outer side of the folder. Tape the top and bottom edges of the folder together. Place pieces of construction paper in various colors in the folder, with brown pieces on the top and bottom. Each time Tom changes colors, remove the top piece of paper.

Once upon a time, there was a brown turkey named Tom. He knew that Thanksgiving was coming though, so he decided he needed to do something to hide himself. He said, "I know! I'll change my color, and stand in front of the red barn, and then the farmer won't see me and want to eat me for his Thanksgiving dinner!" So he waggled his wattle and he said, "I am Tough Tom Turkey, I am sleek and fat, and I can change colors just like THAT!"

Now he was a red turkey, and the farmer couldn't see him when he stood in front of the red barn. That's called camouflage. But soon he got bored of just standing around outside the barn, and he wanted to sit among the pretty orange flowers. So he waggled his wattle and he said, "I am Tough Tom Turkey, I am sleek and fat, and I can change colors just like THAT!" And now he was an orange turkey.

Repeat the pattern with blue—house; white—fence; pink—pigs; green—tractor; purple—grapes.

Then he looked in the window and saw that Thanksgiving was over, and the family had gone to bed. He sighed in relief. And then he waggled his wattle and he said, "I am Tough Tom Turkey, I am sleek and fat, and I can change colors just like THAT!"

And that was that.

Prop Game: Pin the Feather on the Turkey

PIECES NEEDED: *1 large poster with a picture of a turkey's body on it, 1 feather cut from construction paper for each child, a blindfold*

Give each child a feather with a loop of tape attached to it. Have the children take turns being blindfolded and trying to attach the feather to the turkey.

CRAFTS

Handprint Turkey

MATERIALS: 1 piece of construction paper for each child, pencil, crayons, googly eyes, feathers and other decorating materials, glue

DIRECTIONS:
1. Help each child trace her or his open hand onto the construction paper.
2. Use the googly eyes, crayons, and feathers to decorate the shape as a turkey, with the thumb providing the head and the fingers providing the feathers.

Leaf-Tail Turkeys

MATERIALS: 1 turkey body cut from construction paper for each child, 1 piece of construction paper for each child, autumn leaves in various colors (4–5 per child), glue, crayons

DIRECTIONS:
1. Glue the leaves to the back of the turkey so that they stick up like a tail.
2. Place glue on the construction paper, and then glue the turkey to it, leaf side down.
3. Decorate the turkey as desired.

Lost and Found

Sign: **LOOK FOR**

 **BOOKS**

Louella Mae, She's Run Away! by Karen Beaumont Alarcon. New York: Henry Holt, 1997.

*Where's My Teddy? by Jez Alborough. Cambridge, MA: Candlewick, 1992.

*We're Going on a Lion Hunt by David Axtell. New York: Henry Holt, 1999.

*Where's My Mommy? by Jo Brown. Wilton, CT: Tiger Tales, 2002.

From Here to There by Margery Cuyler. New York: Henry Holt, 1999.

As the Crow Flies: A First Book of Maps by Gail Hartman. New York: Bradbury, 1991.

Dog Gone by Amanda Harvey. New York: Random House, 2004.

*Cowboy Baby by Sue Heap. Cambridge, MA: Candlewick, 1998.

*Spot's Treasure Hunt by Eric Hill. New York: G. P. Putnam's Sons, 2002.

*Kipper's Lost Ball by Mick Inkpen. San Diego: Harcourt, 1991.

Lost and Found by Oliver Jeffers. New York: Philomel, 2005.

Mapping Penny's World by Loreen Leedy. New York: Henry Holt, 2000.

Hansel and Gretel by James Marshall. New York: Dial, 1990.

Zigby Hunts for Treasure by Brian Paterson. New York: HarperCollins, 2002.

*Oliver Finds His Way by Phyllis Root. Cambridge, MA: Candlewick, 2002.

*We're Going on a Bear Hunt by Michael Rosen. New York: Simon and Schuster, 1989.

Sheep Take a Hike by Nancy Shaw. New York: Houghton Mifflin, 1994.

*Come Along, Daisy! by Jane Simmons. New York: Little, Brown, 1997.

*Where Are You? by Francesca Simon. Atlanta, GA: Peachtree, 1998.

From Here to There by Nancy Skultety. Honesdale, PA: Boyds Mills Press, 2005.

*Little Quack's Hide and Seek by Lauren Thompson. New York: Simon and Schuster, 2004.

RECORDED MUSIC

*"Down By the Station" from *Away We Go! 15 Tunes for Tiny Travelers*. St. Clair
Entertainment Group, Inc., 2004.

"We're Going on a Bear Hunt" from *Away We Go! 15 Tunes for Tiny Travelers*. St. Clair
Entertainment Group, Inc., 2004.

*"The Wheels on the Bus" from *Rise and Shine* by Raffi. Rounder/UMGD, 1982.

*"Where, Oh Where Has My Little Dog Gone?" from *Singable Nursery Rhymes* by Dennis
Buck. Kimbo Educational, 1986.

FINGERPLAYS/SONGS

"Lost at the Grocery Store"

If you are at the grocery store,
And suddenly you can't see your grown-
    up anymore,
Here is just what you should do:
Find someone who works at the store
And he or she will help you!

"Police Officers Cheer"

Who will help us when we're lost?
Police officers! Police officers!
Who will help us get home, whatever the
    cost?
Police officers! Police officers!
So if you're lost, look and see.
Police officers! Police officers!
Who are good friends to you and me?
Police officers! Police officers!

"Going to the Library"

I know the way to my favorite place.
When I'm going there I always race.
I hurry to get in the car.
I am glad it's not too far.
We go down the street and stop at the
    traffic light.
Then we make a left turn, then a right.
Then we drive on for awhile,
And when I see it I start to smile.
We stop our car and our books we carry.
Do you know where we're going? It's the
    LIBRARY!

"Hurry, Hurry, Drive the Fire Truck"
(adapted traditional)

Hurry, hurry, drive the fire truck.
Hurry, hurry, drive the fire truck.
Hurry, hurry, drive the fire truck.
Ding, ding, ding, ding, ding!

Hurry, hurry, turn the corner.
Hurry, hurry, turn the corner.
Hurry, hurry, turn the corner.
Ding, ding, ding, ding, ding!

Hurry, hurry, find the fire.
Hurry, hurry, find the fire.
Hurry, hurry, find the fire.
Ding, ding, ding, ding, ding!

Hurry, hurry, squirt the water.
Hurry, hurry, squirt the water.
Hurry, hurry, squirt the water.
Ding, ding, ding, ding, ding!

Slowly, slowly, back to the station.
Slowly, slowly, back to the station.
Slowly, slowly, back to the station.
Ding, ding, ding, ding, ding!

"Read a Map"
(to the tune of "Brush Your Teeth")

When you wake up in the morning, it's a quarter to one,
And you want to have a little fun.
Read a map, cha-cha-cha-cha, cha-cha-cha-cha-cha.
Read a map, cha-cha-cha-cha, cha-cha-cha-cha-cha.
. . . quarter to two, and you don't know what to do . . .
. . . quarter to three, and you don't know where to be . . .
. . . quarter to four, and you're trying to get out the door . . .
. . . quarter to five, and you're helping mom and dad drive . . .
. . . quarter to six, and you want to go to your friend Nick's . . .
. . . quarter to seven, and you want to find the 7-Eleven . . .
. . . quarter to eight, and you've got to be somewhere that just can't wait . . .
. . . quarter to nine, and there's a place you just can't find . . .
. . . quarter to ten . . . fold up your map and go to bed!

"Row, Row, Row Your Boat"
(adapted traditional)

Row, row, row your boat gently down the stream,
Merrily merrily merrily merrily, life is but a dream.

Fly, fly, fly your plane gently through the air,
Fly it up and fly it down all without a care.

Drive, drive, drive your car gently down the street,
Look around and smile at all the friends that you meet.

Ride, ride, ride your train gently down the tracks,
Reach up high, reach down low, now sit back and relax.

PROPS

*Puppet Rhyme

"My Dog Ran Away"

PIECE NEEDED: *dog puppet*

My dog ran away! My dog ran away!
Oh what can I say? My dog ran away!
I looked up high,
I looked down low,
I looked to the sides,
And in a circle like so.

I looked in the cupboards,
I looked in the drawer,
I looked under the bed,
And I looked on the floor.
I've looked in all those places I said,
But—what's this? He's on my head!

Flannelboard Story: "Lost Larry"

PIECES NEEDED: *1 head, 1 hat, 1 shirt, 2 arms, 2 legs, 1 pair of shorts, 2 socks, 2 shoes. Before storytime, hide these pieces around your storytime area.*

You know, my friend Larry was always losing things. He would leave his socks lying outside on the lawn, or his hat in the car. He could never find anything! One day his mom said to him, "Larry, if you're not careful, you're going to lose your whole self one of these days, piece by piece!" And do you know what happened? HE DID! Can you help me find him and put him back together?

Have the children search the storytime room until all the pieces are found.

Who has Larry's head? Can you bring it up to the flannelboard?

Repeat with other pieces.

Look at that! Silly Larry is all in one piece again. Thanks for your help! I bet Larry will be a lot more careful about losing things from now on!

Flannelboard Activity: Our Storytime Room

PIECES NEEDED: *felt pieces representing the tables, chairs, shelves, and other large items in your storytime room or library*

Use the pieces to introduce the concept of making a map. Tell the children to imagine they are birds looking down from the sky at the storytime room. What would they see? Help the children make a simple map of the storytime area.

String Story   *Lost! A Story in String* by Paul Fleischman. New York: Henry Holt, 2000.

*Flannelboard Story   *Buried Treasure: All about Using a Map* by Kirsten Hall. New York: Children's Press, 2003.

PIECES NEEDED: *map, 4 blue houses, 6 red flowers, store, 4 rocks, house with red door, tree*

*Flannelboard Story   *Don't Get Lost!* by Pat Hutchins. New York: Greenwillow, 2004.

PIECES NEEDED: *mother, baby cow, horse, sheep, pig, apple tree, hay bales, pond, turnips*

*Flannelboard Story   *Moongame* by Frank Asch. New York: Simon and Schuster, 1984.

PIECES NEEDED: *bear, bird, tree, moon, cloud, flower, rock, house with window, cheese wheel, yellow balloon, forest animals as desired*

ADDITIONAL SUGGESTIONS

Treasure Hunt

Make a winding path of newspaper or carpet squares on the floor. Tape large pictures of trees, houses, and other landmarks at intervals along the path. Make a large map from posterboard and help the children follow it ("Turn left at the blue house." "When you see the cow, go straight ahead."). This would be a great activity to open or close storytime, as the children could use the map to "find" the first book or their closing craft.

CRAFTS

Treasure Map

MATERIALS: 1 piece of white paper for each child, a teabag, a cup of water, markers

DIRECTIONS:
1. Tear the edges off the paper to make it look ragged.
2. Crumple the paper into a ball, and then smooth it back out (but not too smooth!)
3. Dip the teabag into the water, then squeeze out most of the water. Rub the damp teabag over the paper to give it an aged, stained appearance.
4. Use the markers to draw a treasure map.

Lost and Found Picture

MATERIALS: 2 identical ovals cut from colored construction paper for each child, 1 die-cut or printout of a dog shape for each child, 1 piece of white construction paper for each child, 1 piece of construction paper (smaller than the white piece but large enough to cover the oval) for each child, glue, crayons

DIRECTIONS:
1. Glue one of the ovals to the white piece of construction paper. The oval is the dog's rug.
2. Glue the dog onto the rug and decorate as desired.
3. Place the smaller piece of construction paper so that it covers the dog and the rug. Glue one edge down to form a flap.
4. Glue the remaining oval onto the flap, in roughly the same position as the rug below it.
5. Lift the flap to "find" the dog.

Make a Wish

Sign: **WISH**

BOOKS

Fish Wish by Bob Barner. New York: Holiday House, 2000.

Bears, Bears Everywhere by Mara Bergman. Hauppauge, NY: Barron's, 1997.

The Crunching Munching Caterpillar by Sheridan Cain. Wilton, CT: Tiger Tales, 2000.

Mordant's Wish by Valerie Coursen. New York: Henry Holt, 1997.

The Pig Who Wished by Joyce Dunbar. New York: DK, 1999.

The Youngest Fairy Godmother Ever by Stephen Krensky. New York: Simon and Schuster, 2000.

I Wish I Could Fly by Ron Maris. New York: Greenwillow, 1986.

The Witch's Walking Stick by Susan Meddaugh. New York: Houghton Mifflin, 2005.

Willa the Wonderful by Susan Milord. New York: Houghton Mifflin, 2003.

Mama, If You Had a Wish by Jeanne Modesitt. New York: Simon and Schuster, 1993.

If the Dinosaurs Came Back by Bernard Most. San Diego: Harcourt, 1978.

Pink Magic by Donna Jo Napoli. New York: Clarion, 2005.

So Few of Me by Peter H. Reynolds. Cambridge, MA: Candlewick, 2006.

Wish Come True Cat by Ragnhild Scamell. Hauppauge, NY: Barron's, 2001.

Whoosh! Went the Wish by Toby Speed. New York: G. P. Putnam's Sons, 1997.

The Fairytale Cake by Mark Sperring. New York: Scholastic, 2005.

The Fisherman and His Wife by Rosemary Wells. New York: Dial, 1998.

Max and Ruby's Midas by Rosemary Wells. New York: Penguin, 1995.

The Three Wishes by Margot Zemach. New York: Farrar, Straus and Giroux, 1986.

Three Wishes by Harriet Ziefert. New York: Penguin, 1993.

RECORDED MUSIC

"I Wish I Were" from *Laugh 'n Learn Silly Songs* by Dr. Pam Schiller. Kimbo Educational, 2004.

"Somebody's Birthday" from *Holidays and Special Times* by Greg and Steve. Youngheart Records, 1989.

*"When You Wish Upon a Star" from *Disney's Greatest, Volume 1*. Walt Disney Records, 2001. *(use with streamers or scarves)*

FINGERPLAYS/SONGS

"Three Good Wishes"
(traditional)

Wash the dishes, wipe the dishes,
Ring the bell for tea.
3 good wishes, 3 good kisses,
I will give to thee.

"Dandelion"

Dandelion, dandelion,
Pretty and yellow.
You are such a happy fellow.
But when your hair turns soft and white,
We make a wish and blow it out of sight!

"Animal Wishes"

Act out each animal.

Make a wish, make a wish, what do you
    want to be?
I wish I was a shiny fish, swimming in
    the sea.
I wish I was a great big eagle, flying
    through the air.
I wish I was a monkey, swinging without
    a care.
I wish I was an elephant, I'd swing my
    trunk like this.
I wish I was a slithery snake, I would hiss
    and hiss.
I wish I was a lion, I'd throw back my
    head and roar.
I wish I was a butterfly, I'd spread my
    wings and soar.
But of all the things that I wish to be,
The thing I like the best is . . . me!

"Magic Lamp"

I rubbed and rubbed the magic lamp,
And what do you think I saw?
The genie popped out of the lamp,
And said, "3 wishes, that's all!"
I thought and thought about my wish,
And said, "I wish I knew
What I should wish for."
"Ha!" said the genie.
"Now you only have 2!"

"Birthday Wishes"
(to the tune of "Frère Jacques")

On your birthday, on your birthday,
Close your eyes, close your eyes.
First blow out the candles,
First blow out the candles.
Then make a wish.
Make a wish.

"If You Wish"
(to the tune of "If You're Happy
and You Know It")

If you wish that you could fly, flap
    your arms.
If you wish that you could fly, flap
    your arms.
If you wish that you could fly, then
    you really ought to show it.
If you wish that you could fly, flap
    your arms.
If you wish that you could drive, drive
    your car . . .
If you wish that you could skate, move
    your feet . . .

PROPS

*Flannelboard Song

"Counting Candles"
(to the tune of "Happy Birthday")

PIECES NEEDED: *cake with 5–10 candles*

How many candles on the cake?
How many candles on the cake?
I wish you could tell me.
How many candles on the cake?
1 candle on the cake . . .

Repeat with higher numbers.

Now let's make a wish.
Now let's make a wish.
We'll blow out the candlestick,
And then make a wish.

*Flannelboard or Prop Rhyme

"The Wishing Well"

PIECES NEEDED: *wishing well flannelboard piece or well made from cardboard; felt or actual coins, enough for each child to hold one*

So many pennies in the wishing well.
Each one has a secret to tell.
Come on up and make a wish.
Let's see Sarah do it like this!

Repeat with each child's name, inviting each child to come put a coin in the well and, if desired, share his or her wish.

*File Folder Story: "Scat the Cat"

Cut a simple cat shape out of one side of a file folder. Copy the following story and tape it to the uncut outer side of the folder. Tape the top and bottom edges of the folder together. Place pieces of construction paper in various colors in the folder, with white pieces on the top and bottom. Each time Scat changes colors, remove the top piece of paper.

Once upon a time, there was a little white kitten named Scat. But one day he decided he was tired of being a little white kitten. He looked at the beautiful brown tree trunks and wished he was a brown kitten. So he said, "I am Scat the Cat, I am sleek and fat, and I can change colors just like THAT!"

Now he was a brown kitten. But pretty soon he saw a pretty orange flower and decided that the color he really wished to be was orange. So he said, "I am Scat the Cat, I am sleek and fat, and I can change colors just like THAT!"

Repeat the pattern with blue—blueberries; red—strawberries; yellow—sun; black—night sky; green—grass; purple—grapes.

Then he saw the white fluffy clouds in the sky and decided that what he really, REALLY wished to be was a little white kitten. So he said, "I am Scat the Cat, I am sleek and fat, and I can change colors just like THAT!"

And that was that.

*Flannelboard Story   *I Wish I Were* by Genevieve Laurencin. New York: G. P. Putnam's Sons, 1987.

PIECES NEEDED: *boy, sheep, monkey, cat, giraffe, porcupine, bee, mouse, fish, chameleon, bird*

Puppet Story   "The Fisherman's Three Wishes" in *One-Person Puppetry Streamlined and Simplified* by Yvonne Awar Frey. Chicago: American Library Association, 2005.

PIECES NEEDED: *fish puppet, fisherman puppet*

ADDITIONAL SUGGESTIONS

Poetry

"The Wish" by Ann Friday and "Wish" by Dorothy Brown Thompson. From *Read-Aloud Rhymes for the Very Young* edited by Jack Prelutsky. New York: Knopf, 1986.

CRAFTS

Wishing Wands

MATERIALS: 1 straw for each child, 1 star cut from posterboard for each child, lengths of curling ribbon, scissors, glitter, glue, stickers, crayons and other decorating materials

DIRECTIONS:
1. Cut 2 small slits in the top of the straw.
2. Place glue on the bottom edge of the star.
3. Slide the bottom edge of the star into the slit on the straw.
4. Tie lengths of ribbon around the base of the star.
5. Decorate the wand with glitter, stickers, and crayons.

Birthday Wishing Candles Picture

MATERIALS: 1 coloring sheet of a cake for each child, candles cut from various colors of construction paper, glue, crayons, decorating materials

DIRECTIONS:
1. Glue the candles onto the cake.
2. Draw in flames and decorate as desired.

Make Me Laugh

Sign: **LAUGH**

BOOKS

Do Cows Bark? New York: DK, 2003.

Can You Make a Piggy Giggle? by Linda Ashman. New York: Dutton, 2002.

Don't Be Silly, Mrs. Millie! by Judy Cox. New York: Marshall Cavendish, 2005.

Cock-a-Moo-Moo by Juliet Dallas-Conte. New York: Little, Brown, 2001.

Serious Farm by Tim Egan. New York: Houghton Mifflin, 2003.

Silly Goose and Dizzy Duck Play Hide-and-Seek by Sally Grindley. New York: DK, 1999.

Ticklemonster and Me by Max Haynes. New York: Doubleday, 1999.

The Seven Silly Eaters by Mary Ann Hoberman. San Diego: Harcourt, 1997.

The Two Sillies by Mary Ann Hoberman. San Diego: Harcourt, 2000.

Silly Suzy Goose by Petr Horacek. Cambridge, MA: Candlewick, 2006.

Ten Tiny Tickles by Karen Katz. New York: Simon and Schuster, 2005.

The Very Sleepy Sloth by Andrew Murray. Wilton, CT: Tiger Tales, 2003.

The Sillies by Charnan Simon. New York: The Child's World, 2007.

Don't Make Me Laugh by James Stevenson. New York: Farrar, Straus and Giroux, 1999.

Toby's Silly Faces by Cyndy Szekeres. New York: Simon and Schuster, 2000.

Tickle Tum! by Nancy Van Laan. New York: Atheneum, 2001.

Silly Fred by Karen Wagner. New York: Macmillan, 1989.

Silly Sally by Audrey Wood. San Diego: Harcourt Brace, 1992.

Not a Little Monkey by Charlotte Zolotow. New York: Harper and Row, 1989.

RECORDED MUSIC

*"Tickle Toe" from *Jim Gill Makes It Noisy in Boise, Idaho* by Jim Gill. Jim Gill Music, 1995.

*"Silly Dance Contest" from *Jim Gill Sings The Sneezing Song and Other Contagious Tunes* by Jim Gill. Jim Gill Music, 1993.

*"Wiggle in My Toe" from *Late Last Night* by Joe Scruggs. Lyons Group/Fox, 1984.

"Annie Mae" from *Laugh 'n Learn Silly Songs* by Dr. Pam Schiller. Kimbo Educational, 2004.

"Laugh With Me!" from *Run, Jump, Skip, and Sing* by Barney. Koch Records, 2003.

*"Fishin' for a Ticklin'" from *Sing Me a Story* by Bob McGrath. Bob's Kids Music, 1997.

*"Tickle Tickle Teddy" from *Teddy Bear Tunes* by Georgiana Stewart. Kimbo Educational, 2003. *(have enough small teddy bears to go around)*

"Tony Chestnut" from *Tony Chestnut and Fun Time Action Songs* by The Learning Station. Kaladon Publishing, 1997.

"Wiggles, Jiggles, and Giggles" from *Wiggles, Jiggles, and Giggles* by Stephen Fite. Melody House, 2000.

FINGERPLAYS/SONGS

"Willaby Wallaby Woo"
(traditional)

Willaby wallaby woo,
An elephant sat on you.
Willaby wallaby wee,
An elephant sat on me.
Willaby wallaby wara,
An elephant sat on Sarah . . . *(continue with other children's names)*

"Silly Style Nursery Rhymes"

Present the silly rhymes below as if you think they are the real versions, and let the children correct you after each line.

Little Miss Muffet sat on . . . an easy chair,
Eating her . . . pepperoni pizza.
Along came a . . . monkey,
And sat down beside her . . . and asked her out to dinner!

Old Mother Hubbard went to the . . . refrigerator
To get her poor dog a . . . soda.
But when she got there, the cupboard was . . . full of elephants
And so her poor dog had . . . ice cream.

"Laughing Freeze Game"

Laugh laugh laugh when my fingers say laugh, *(wiggle fingers)*
But when my fingers say stop, you must stop. *(hold palm facing out)*

Repeat these actions, and the children must watch to know when to laugh and when to stop.

"Silly Clown"

If I were a silly clown, I'd have a great big nose.
I'd wear 2 big and floppy shoes that went way past my toes.
I would wiggle, I would turn, I'd jump high as can be,
And when the people saw me, they'd say "Hee hee hee hee hee!"

"Tickle Tickle"

Tickle tickle in the air,
Tickle tickle here and there.
Tickle tickle through the night,
Tickle tickle left and right.
Tickle tickle on my toes,
Tickle tickle on my nose.
Tickle tickle on my tummy,
Tickle tickle on my mommy!

PROPS

*Flannelboard Rhyme

"Five Little Clowns"

PIECES NEEDED: *5 clowns*

5 little clowns tumbling in the door,
1 tumbled away, and then there were 4.
4 little clowns so funny to see,
1 tumbled away, and then there were 3.
3 little clowns and the silly things they do,
1 tumbled away, and then there were 2.
2 little clowns, laughing as they run,
1 tumbled away, and then there was 1.
1 little clown, having so much fun,
He tumbled away, and then there were none.

*Prop Game: Don't Make Me Laugh, Kitty!

PIECE NEEDED: *cat puppet. Take the cat puppet around the storytime room and have him approach each child in turn. The cat could jump on their heads, make pitiful meows, tickle their arms, etc. Each time a child laughs, move on to the next child.*

My little kitty loves to play a special game. He loves to make people laugh. But I told him that you all would be good at this game. I told him you wouldn't laugh, no matter what my kitty does. Do you want to try it?

CRAFTS

Clown Paper Plate Craft

MATERIALS: 1 paper plate for each child; circles, triangles, and crescents cut from various colors of construction paper; various colors of cotton balls; glue; crayons and other decorating materials; large triangles for hats

DIRECTIONS:
1. Glue the circles, triangles, and crescents into place on the paper plate to form the clown's nose, eyes, and mouth, and the apples of his cheeks.
2. Pull apart cotton balls and flatten them out, then glue them onto the plate to form the clown's hair.
3. Glue the large triangle into place for the hat.
4. Decorate as desired.

Silly Dingleboppers

MATERIALS: 1 long strip of construction paper to form a headband for each child, 2 chenille stems for each child, small shapes cut out of construction paper, glue or stapler, crayons, glitter, stickers, other decorating materials

DIRECTIONS:
1. Size the headband for each child and glue or staple the ends together.
2. Curl one end of each chenille stem around a crayon to create a silly shape, then staple the straight end of the stem to the headband.
3. Select small shapes to attach to the curled ends of the stems. If desired, color or decorate before attaching.

Monkey Business

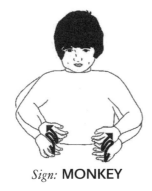

Sign: **MONKEY**

BOOKS

Monkey Do! by Allan Ahlberg. Cambridge, MA: Candlewick, 1998.

Hug by Jez Alborough. Cambridge, MA: Candlewick, 2000.

Don't Wake Up Mama! by Eileen Christelow. New York: Clarion, 1992.

Five Little Monkeys Jumping on the Bed by Eileen Christelow. New York: Clarion, 1989.

Five Little Monkeys Sitting in a Tree by Eileen Christelow. New York: Clarion, 1991.

Little Monkey Lost by Keith DuQuette. New York: G. P. Putnam's Sons, 2007.

Little Monkey's One Safe Place by Richard Edwards. London: Frances Lincoln's Children's Books, 2005.

The Boy Who Loved Bananas by George Elliott. Toronto, ON: Kids Can Press, 2005.

Can't Catch Me! by Michael Foreman. Atlanta, GA: Anderson Press, 2005.

One Monkey Too Many by Jackie French Koller. San Diego: Harcourt Brace, 1999.

Water Hole Waiting by Jane Kurtz and Christopher Kurtz. New York: Greenwillow, 2002.

Ten Monkey Jamboree by Dianne Ochiltree. New York: Simon and Schuster, 2001.

Little Monkey Says Good Night by Ann Whitford Paul. New York: Farrar, Straus and Giroux, 2003.

Curious George by H. A. Rey. New York: Houghton Mifflin, 1941.

Curious George Visits the Zoo by H. A. Rey. New York: Houghton Mifflin, 1985.

Caps for Sale by Esphyr Slobodkina. New York: Harper and Row, 1968.

RECORDED MUSIC

*"Monkey Bounce" from *Choo Choo to the Zoo: Creative Movement and Play* by Georgiana Stewart. Kimbo Educational, 2006.

"Here Sits a Monkey" from *The Corner Grocery Store* by Raffi. Rounder/UMGD, 1979.

*"This Little Monkey" from *Preschool Action Time* by Carol Hammett. Kimbo Educational, 1988.

FINGERPLAYS/SONGS

*"Monkey See, Monkey Do"

I clap my hands, monkeys do too.
Monkey see, monkey do.
I stomp my feet, monkeys do too.
Monkey see, monkey do.
I wave my arms . . .
I jump up and down . . .
I turn around . . .
I sing a song . . .
I hop on one foot . . .

"Five Little Monkeys
Jumping on the Bed"
(traditional)

5 little monkeys jumping on the bed,
1 fell off and bumped his head.
Mama called the doctor and the doctor
    said,
"No more monkeys jumping on the bed!"
4 little monkeys . . .
3 little monkeys . . .
2 little monkeys . . .
1 little monkey . . .
No little monkeys . . .

"Ten Little Monkeys"
(to the tune of "10 Little Indians")

1 little, 2 little, 3 little monkeys,
4 little, 5 little, 6 little monkeys,
7 little, 8 little, 9 little monkeys,
10 little monkeys swinging in the tree.

"Five Little Monkeys
Sitting in a Tree"
(traditional)

5 little monkeys sitting in a tree,
Teasing Mr. Crocodile: "Can't catch me!"
Along comes Mr. Crocodile, quiet as
    can be.
SNAP!
4 little monkeys . . .
3 little monkeys . . .
2 little monkeys . . .
1 little monkey . . .
No little monkeys sitting in a tree.
Away swims Mr. Crocodile, full as can be.

"I'm a Little Monkey"
(to the tune of "I'm a Little Teapot")

I'm a little monkey, small and brown.
I can reach up and then touch the
    ground.
I can swing my tail and turn around.
I can jump up and then sit down.

"Swinging"
(to the tune of "A Bicycle Built for Two")

Swinging, swinging,
Swinging through the trees.
We are monkeys swinging in the breeze.
We wave our long tails,
And giggle without fail,
And we will swing,
And do our thing,
And eat bananas for lunch!

PROPS

*Flannelboard Rhyme

"Counting Bananas"

PIECES NEEDED: *5 bananas, monkey puppet*

5 yellow bananas, and not one more.
The monkey ate one, and then there were 4.
4 yellow bananas, so yummy to see.
The monkey ate one, and then there were 3.
3 yellow bananas, and he knew what to do.
The monkey ate one, and then there were 2.
2 yellow bananas, hanging in the sun.
The monkey ate one, and then there was 1.
1 yellow banana, well, for goodness' sake!
The monkey ate that one, and he got a
    tummyache!
Now there are no little bananas hanging on
    the tree.
Monkey, your tummy wouldn't hurt, if you
    had shared them with me!

*Flannelboard Song

"Color Monkeys"
(to the tune of "Frère Jacques")

PIECES NEEDED: *5–6 monkey shapes in
various colors; banana shapes in matching
colors, with enough bananas for each child to
hold one*

I'm a red monkey, I'm a red monkey.
Look and see, look and see.
If you have a red banana,
If you have a red banana,
Please bring it to me.
Please bring it to me.

*Repeat with other colors, inviting children
to place their bananas on the flannelboard
when their colors are called.*

*Flannelboard Story *Caps for Sale* by Esphyr Slobodkina. New York: Harper and Row,
1968.

> **PIECES NEEDED:** *peddler; monkeys; large tree; 1 checkered cap for peddler; caps in blue, red, gray,
> and brown*

CRAFTS

CD Monkey

MATERIALS: 1 CD or CD-ROM for each child, 2 ear shapes cut from brown construction paper
for each child, 1 circle cut from brown construction paper for each child, googly eyes, small
round black stickers, crayons, glue

DIRECTIONS:
1. Glue the circle to the CD to form the monkey's muzzle.
2. Glue the ears to the sides of the CD.
3. Use the black stickers to form the monkey's nostrils.
4. Glue on googly eyes and decorate with crayons as desired.

5 Little Monkeys Stick Puppets

MATERIALS: precut monkey shapes, 5 per child (patterns may be found in *2's Experience Fingerplays* by Liz and Dick Wilmes, Elgin, IL: Building Blocks, 1994); craft sticks; glue; crayons

DIRECTIONS:
1. Color the monkeys as desired.
2. Glue each monkey to a craft stick.
3. Use the monkeys with the "5 Little Monkeys" rhymes.

Native Americans

Sign: **NATIVE AMERICAN**

BOOKS

The First Strawberries: A Cherokee Story by Joseph Bruchac. New York: Dial, 1993.

How Chipmunk Got His Stripes by Joseph Bruchac and James Bruchac. New York: Dial, 2001.

Raccoon's Last Race by Joseph Bruchac and James Bruchac. New York: Dial, 2004.

Turtle's Race with Beaver by Joseph Bruchac and James Bruchac. New York: Dial, 2004.

The Legend of the Bluebonnet: An Old Tale of Texas by Tomie dePaola. New York: G. P. Putnam's Sons, 1983.

The Legend of the Indian Paintbrush by Tomie dePaola. New York: G. P. Putnam's Sons, 1988.

Mole's Hill: A Woodland Tale by Lois Ehlert. San Diego: Harcourt Brace, 1994.

One Little, Two Little, Three Little Pilgrims by B. G. Hennessey. New York: Viking, 1999.

Giving Thanks by Jonathan London. Cambridge, MA: Candlewick, 2003.

The Legend of the Lady Slipper: An Ojibwe Tale by Lise Lunge-Larsen and Margi Preus. New York: Houghton Mifflin, 1999.

Grandmother's Dreamcatcher by Becky Ray McCain. Morton Grove, IL: Albert Whitman, 1998.

Coyote: A Trickster Tale from the American Southwest by Gerald McDermott. San Diego: Harcourt Brace, 1994.

Dancing with the Indians by Angela Shelf Medearis. New York: Holiday House, 1991.

Dreamcatcher by Audrey Osofsky. New York: Orchard, 1992.

Long Night Moon by Cynthia Rylant. New York: Simon and Schuster, 2004.

On Mother's Lap by Ann Herbert Scott. New York: Clarion, 1992.

Jingle Dancer by Cynthia Leitich Smith. New York: Morrow, 2000.

The Rattlesnake Who Went to School by Craig Kee Strete. New York: G. P. Putnam's Sons, 1994.

Coyote and the Laughing Butterflies by Harriet Peck Taylor. New York: Macmillan, 1995.

RECORDED MUSIC

American Indian Dances, compiled and edited by Ronnie and Stu Lipner. Smithsonian Folkways, 1958.

Authentic Music of the American Indian. Legacy International, 1994.

FINGERPLAYS/SONGS

"Mother Earth"

Mother Earth gives us all we need,
  (spread arms wide)
From the mighty tree to the tiny seed.
  *(reach high, then show tiny seed
  with fingers)*
From the little squirrel *(hold hands together
  as if eating a nut)*
To the running deer. *(run in place)*
From the soaring eagle *(pretend to fly)*
To the mighty bear. *(spread arms and roar)*
So take care of the Earth we must,
Because these things are a gift to us.

"Ten Little Indians"
(traditional)

1 little, 2 little, 3 little Indians,
4 little, 5 little, 6 little Indians,
7 little, 8 little, 9 little Indians,
10 little Indian boys.

"I'm a Little Hunter"
(to the tune of "I'm a Little Teapot")

I'm a little hunter, I'm a Navajo.
Here is my arrow and here is my bow.
When I go out hunting, I'm quiet as
  a mouse.
I'll catch a deer and bring it to my house.

"The Drum"

When the drum says pum-pum, *(use a
  drum or drum on your knees or a table)*
We dance to the drum.
We sing and we dance.
We dance to the drum.

Repeat quickly, then slowly.

PROPS

*Flannelboard Rhyme

"Five Little Teepees"

PIECES NEEDED: *5 teepees*

5 little teepees and not one more.
1 got packed up, and then there were 4.
4 little teepees underneath a tree.
1 got packed up, and then there were 3.
3 little teepees, when the day was new.
1 got packed up, and then there were 2.
2 little teepees, sitting in the sun.

1 got packed up, and then there was 1.
1 little teepee, and now we're almost done.
That 1 got packed up, and then there
  were none.
No little teepees were left there that day.
They were all packed up, and the tribe
  was on its way.

*Ribbons for Dancing

Make dancing ribbons like the ones in the story *Dancing with the Indians* by Angela Shelf Medearis (New York: Holiday House, 1991). Use large binder rings and tie on lengths of colorful ribbons. Make enough for each child to have one, and use these ribbons with the recordings suggested above.

*Flannelboard Story   *Coyote and the Laughing Butterflies* by Harriet Peck Taylor. New York: Macmillan, 1995.

PIECES NEEDED: *coyote, wife, cactus, butterflies, sun, lake, lizard, beaver, bag of salt. Put the butterfly pieces on clothespins so that you can use them to lift the coyote piece when the butterflies carry him through the air.*

ADDITIONAL SUGGESTIONS

Stick Game

From *More Than Moccasins: A Kid's Activity Guide to Traditional North American Indian Life* by Laurie Carlson (Chicago: Chicago Review Press, 1994), pp. 104–5.

Storytelling

"Coyote's Song" from *Twenty Tellable Tales* by Margaret Read MacDonald. Chicago: American Library Association, 2005.

CRAFTS

Native American Painting

MATERIALS: blackberries, blueberries, raspberries, small bowls, wooden spoons, vinegar, Indian Paintbrush or other type of grass, cotton swabs, paper

DIRECTIONS:
1. Let each child have a turn mashing some berries with a wooden spoon.
2. Add a few drops of vinegar to prevent mold growth.
3. Mash the berries some more.
4. Using cotton swabs or grasses, paint designs on the paper with this natural paint. Let the children experiment with different types of grass to create different designs.

Native American Headbands

MATERIALS: long strips of construction paper to form a headband for each child, feathers, glue, stickers, crayons and other decorating materials, stapler

DIRECTIONS:
1. Size the headband and staple the ends together.
2. Decorate as desired with feathers, stickers, crayons, and other decorating materials.

Ode to Ice Cream

Sign: **ICE CREAM**

BOOKS

Ice Cream Bear by Jez Alborough. Cambridge, MA: Candlewick, 1989.

Ice Cream by Elisha Cooper. New York: Greenwillow, 2002.

Ice Cream: The Full Scoop by Gail Gibbons. New York: Holiday House, 2006.

Wemberly's Ice-Cream Star by Kevin Henkes. New York: Greenwillow, 2003.

Sidewalk Trip by Patricia Hubbell. New York: HarperCollins, 1999.

From Cow to Ice Cream by Bertram T. Knight. New York: Children's Press, 1997.

Simply Delicious! by Margaret Mahy. New York: Orchard Books, 1999.

I Like Ice Cream by Robi Pickering. New York: Children's Press, 2000.

Garth Pig and the Icecream Lady by Mary Rayner. New York: Atheneum, 1977.

Curious George Goes to an Ice Cream Shop by H. A. Rey. New York: Houghton Mifflin, 1989.

Isaac the Ice Cream Truck by Scott Santoro. New York: Henry Holt, 1999.

RECORDED MUSIC

*"Ice Cream Cone" from *Buzz Buzz* by Laurie Berkner. Two Tomatoes, 2001.

FINGERPLAYS/SONGS

"My Favorite Treat"

Ice cream, ice cream, my favorite treat.
There are so many ways for us to eat.
In a bowl, or from a cone,
At a party, or right at home.
In an ice-cream sandwich or an ice-cream cake.
So many choices for us to make!

"I Scream"
(adapted traditional)

I scream, you scream,
We all scream for ice cream.
I jump, you jump,
We all jump for ice cream.
I turn . . .
I clap . . .
I stomp . . .
I run . . .
I hop . . .

"Ice Cream Taster"

When I grow up, I know just what I
    want to be.
An ice cream taster! Yes, that's the job
    for me!
I'll take a bit of every flavor,
And every one I will savor.
Like maybe . . . strawberry-lemon-
    fruitcake
blueberry-peppermint-birthday cake.
Or meatloaf-mashed-potato-pumpkin-pie.
What flavors of ice cream would you like
    to try?

"I Like Ice Cream"

I like ice cream, yes I do!
Not just 1 scoop, I want 2!
Not just 2 scoops, I want 3!
Ice cream's yummy as can be!
Not just 3 scoops, I want 4.
Ooops! It fell all over the floor.

"Hurry, Hurry"
(to the tune of "Hurry, Hurry,
Drive the Fire Truck")

Hurry, hurry, lick the ice cream.
Hurry, hurry, lick the ice cream.
Hurry, hurry, lick the ice cream.
Before it melts away!

"Chocolate Ice Cream Cone"
(to the tune of "Baby Bumblebee")

I'm bringing home a chocolate ice
    cream cone.
I'm so glad I've got my very own.
I'm bringing home a chocolate ice
    cream cone.
MMMM! Yummy!

I'm licking up my chocolate ice
    cream cone.
I'm so glad I've got my very own.
I'm licking up my chocolate ice
    cream cone.
Brain freeze! OW!

I'm crunching up my chocolate ice
    cream cone.
I'm so glad I've got my very own.
I'm crunching up my chocolate ice
    cream cone.
Now it's all over my hands!

I'm cleaning up my chocolate ice
    cream cone.
I'm so glad I had my very own.
I'm cleaning up my chocolate ice
    cream cone.
All gone!

"Melting Ice Cream"
(to the tune of "Frère Jacques")

Licking my ice cream, licking my
    ice cream.
It can't wait. It can't wait.
I don't want it to melt. I don't want it
    to melt.
Oops! Too late. Oops! Too late.

PROPS

*Flannelboard Song

"Silly Ice Cream Song"

(to the tune of "Silly Pizza Song," from
Signing Time Songs, Volumes 1–3 by
Rachel de Azevedo, Two Little Hands
Productions, 2002)

PIECES NEEDED: *a bowl or cone with ice cream
in it; shapes representing various kinds of foods
to go on top, some appropriate for ice cream and
some not (examples: cherries, cookies, chocolate,
bananas, nuts, whipped cream, meatloaf,
pickles, mashed potatoes). As you sing the song,
add a topping with each verse.*

I like chocolate on my ice cream.
I like chocolate ice cream please.
Give me chocolate on my ice cream.
Give to me some ice cream please.

I like bananas on my ice cream.
I like banana ice cream please.
Give me bananas on my chocolate.
Give me chocolate on my ice cream.
Give to me some ice cream please.

Repeat pattern with other toppings.

*Flannelboard Rhyme

"Ice Cream Shapes"

PIECES NEEDED: *1 large brown triangle, 1
large white circle, 1 small red circle, 5 small
rectangles for sprinkles*

Here we have a triangle.
What do you think it is?
Now let's add a circle
So it looks like this.
Another circle goes on top
But it's not yet time to stop.
Now some rectangles on will go
And what this is I think you know!
All along you've probably known
We were making an ice cream cone!

*Flannelboard Story: "Ice Cream Scoops"

PIECES NEEDED: *cone, several different color scoops of ice cream*

Once upon a time there was a little boy named Tommy. Tommy
LOVED ice cream. One day he decided to go to the corner ice
cream shop. But when he got there, he couldn't decide what flavor
to get.

"Should I get vanilla?" he asked. He decided to get one scoop
of vanilla on his ice cream cone.

But then he saw the chocolate. He decided to get a scoop of
that, too.

*Repeat with strawberry, fudge ripple, pistachio, bubblegum, etc., until the
ice cream cone is towering high on the flannelboard.*

Finally he was ready to eat his ice cream cone. Slurp! He ate the
(begin with last scoop and repeat until all the flavors are eaten). Then he
ate the cone with a crunch crunch crunch.

"Oh no! Now I have a tummyache!" said Tommy.

*Prop Story   *Wemberly's Ice-Cream Star* by Kevin Henkes. New York: Greenwillow, 2003.

PIECES NEEDED: *stuffed rabbit, ice cream star made from star shape glued to a craft stick, 2 bowls, 2 spoons*

CRAFTS

Ice Cream Magnets

MATERIALS: 1 triangle cut from brown construction paper for each child, 1 large pom-pom for each child, 1 small red pom-pom for each child, glue, adhesive magnet strips

DIRECTIONS:
1. Fold the triangle into a cone and glue the ends together.
2. Glue the large pom-pom into the cone to form the ice cream scoop.
3. Glue the small red pom-pom on top for a cherry.
4. Attach a strip of adhesive magnet to the back of the cone.

Build a Sundae

MATERIALS: 1 coloring sheet for each child with a picture of a bowl on it; paper circles in various colors to represent ice cream scoops; paper shapes representing bananas, nuts, whipped cream, sprinkles, and other toppings; glue; crayons

DIRECTIONS:
1. Select the toppings you want to make your sundae and glue them onto the coloring sheet.
2. Color as desired.

On the Water

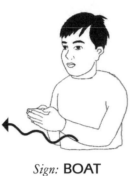

Sign: **BOAT**

BOOKS

Captain Duck by Jez Alborough. New York: HarperCollins, 2002.

Who Sank the Boat? by Pamela Allen. New York: Putnam and Grosset, 1982.

Boats by Byron Barton. New York: HarperCollins, 1986.

The Bridge Is Up! by Babs Bell. New York: HarperCollins, 2004.

Sail Away, Little Boat by Janet Buell. Minneapolis: Carolrhoda, 2006.

Little Bear's Little Boat by Eve Bunting. New York: Clarion, 2003.

This Boat by Paul Collicut. New York: Farrar, Straus and Giroux, 2001.

Row, Row, Row Your Boat by Penny Dann. Hauppauge, NY: Barron's, 2000.

My Blue Boat by Chris L. Demarest. San Diego: Harcourt Brace, 1995.

To the Island by Charlotte Egell. New York: DK, 1998.

Pirate PiggyWiggy by Christyan and Diane Fox. New York: Handprint Books, 2003.

Boat Book by Gail Gibbons. New York: Holiday House, 1983.

Ferryboat by Betsy Maestro. New York: Thomas Y. Crowell, 1986.

I Love Boats by Flora McDonnell. Cambridge, MA: Candlewick, 1995.

I'm Mighty! by Kate and Jim McMullan. New York: HarperCollins, 2003.

Busy Boats by Tony Mitton. Boston: Kingfisher, 2002.

Dory Story by Jerry Pallotta. Watertown, MA: Charlesbridge, 2000.

Blue Tortoise by Alan Rogers. Chicago: Two-Can Publishing, 1998.

Sheep on a Ship by Nancy Shaw. New York: Houghton Mifflin, 1989.

Come Along, Daisy! by Jane Simmons. New York: Little, Brown, 1997.

RECORDED MUSIC

"Sailing to the Sea" from *Great Big Fun* by Tom Chapin. Music for Little People, 2001.

*"Row Row Your Baby" from *Hunk-Ta-Bunk-Ta Funsies, Volume 2* by Katherine Dines. Hunk-Ta-Bunk-Ta Music, 2004.

"A Sailor Went to Sea" from *Sing It! Say It! Stamp It! Sway It! Volume 3* by Peter and Ellen Allard. 80-Z Music, 2002.

FINGERPLAYS/SONGS

"Dragonfly, Dragonfly"

Dragonfly, dragonfly turn around.
Dragonfly, dragonfly touch the ground.
Dragonfly, dragonfly on the water
    you stay.
Dragonfly, dragonfly fly away!

"Captain's Rhyme"

I'm the captain of the ship.
I'm going on a little trip.
I turn the wheel to the left and right.
And keep on sailing through the night.
Maybe you can join my crew.
I think sailing is fun, don't you?

"Row, Row, Row Your Boat"
(adapted traditional)

Row, row, row your boat
Gently down the stream.
Merrily merrily merrily merrily
Life is but a dream.

Sail, sail, sail your ship
Gently on the sea.
Merrily merrily merrily merrily
There's so much out there to see.

"On the Pond"
(to the tune of "The Wheels on the Bus")

The ducks on the pond go quack quack
    quack,
Quack quack quack, quack quack quack.
The ducks on the pond go quack quack
    quack,
All through the day.

The frogs on the pond go ribbit ribbit
    ribbit,
Ribbit ribbit ribbit, ribbit ribbit ribbit.
The frogs on the pond go ribbit ribbit
    ribbit,
All through the day.

The boats on the pond go paddle paddle
    paddle,
Paddle paddle paddle, paddle paddle
    paddle.
The boats on the pond go paddle paddle
    paddle,
All through the day.

"In a Boat"

When you get into a boat
You must sit down to keep it afloat.
If you stand up in a flash
The boat will tip you with a SPLASH!

PROPS

*Flannelboard Rhyme

"Lilypad Match"

PIECES NEEDED: *5 large lilypads in different colors; frog shapes in the same 5 colors, enough for each child to hold one*

Here is a green lilypad
Sitting on the pond.
If you have a green frog
Make him hop on!

Repeat with other colors.

*Flannelboard Rhyme

"Five Big Boats"

PIECES NEEDED: *5 boats*

5 big boats sailing from the shore.
1 stopped to catch some fish, and then there
   were 4.
4 big boats sailing out to sea.
1 stopped to look around, and then there
   were 3.
3 big boats with so much to do.
1 stopped at an island, and then there were 2.
2 big boats sailing under the sun.
1 stopped in a port, and then there was 1.
1 big boat, sailing all alone.
That one turned around, and sailed for home.

*Prop Story: "Teddy's Trip"

PIECES NEEDED: *teddy bear; small plastic laundry basket for boat; dowel rod with white paper attached to represent sail; small souvenir items from various countries, such as foreign coins, knick-knacks, etc. If you wish, you may pass out the souvenirs to the children before the story and have the bear sail around the room to pick them up.*

My teddy bear decided to sail around the world! He made himself a little boat with a sail, and here it is. He said he would get me a present in each place that he visited. The day that he left, I was so sad. I gave him a big hug and a kiss and said, "Bon voyage! Be careful! Come home soon!" And Teddy set sail. Some days it was easy sailing, and the waters were smooth. And some days it rained and rained and the waves tossed the little boat. *(Shake laundry basket.)* But Teddy kept going. He visited China and got me a pretty kimono to wear. Next he visited India and got me a little carving of an elephant.

Repeat until all items have been collected.

Then he decided it was time to sail toward home. When he got home, I gave him a big hug and a kiss and said, "Welcome back! I missed you so much!" and he showed me all the things he had gotten for me in his travels. I said, "Teddy, thank you for these wonderful presents. But the best present of all is that you are back home safe with me!"

*Flannelboard Story   *Moonbear's Canoe* by Frank Asch. New York: Simon and Schuster, 1993.

PIECES NEEDED: *bear, canoe, paddle, bird, turtle, pig, lion, moose, water*

*Flannelboard Story   *Mr. Gumpy's Outing* by John Burningham. New York: Henry Holt, 1970.

PIECES NEEDED: *man, boat, children, rabbit, cat, dog, pig, sheep, chickens, calf, goat. Use a spray bottle to spray the children when the boat overturns with a splash.*

CRAFTS

Simple Sailboat Craft

From Enchanted Learning at http://www.enchantedlearning.com/crafts/boats/lid/index.shtml.

Lilypad Frogs

MATERIALS: 1 lilypad shape cut from construction paper for each child, 1 frog die-cut or picture for each child, googly eyes, crayons, glue, decorating materials

DIRECTIONS:
1. Glue the frog onto the lilypad.
2. Glue the googly eyes onto the frog and decorate as desired.

Puddlejumpers

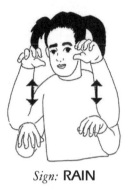

Sign: **RAIN**

BOOKS

Bringing the Rain to Kapiti Plain by Verna Aardema. New York: Dial, 1981.

*Rain Dance by Kathi Appelt. New York: HarperFestival, 2001.

*Rabbits and Raindrops by Jim Arnosky. New York: G. P. Putnam's Sons, 1997.

*Cat and Mouse in the Rain by Tomek Bogacki. New York: Farrar, Straus and Giroux, 1997.

I Love the Rain by Margaret Park Bridges. San Francisco: Chronicle, 2005.

And Then It Rained . . . by Crescent Dragonwagon. New York: Atheneum, 2003.

Rain Song by Lezlie Evans. New York: Houghton Mifflin, 1995.

One Rainy Day by Valeri Gorbachev. New York: Philomel, 2002.

*What Can You Do in the Rain? by Anna Grossnickle Hines. New York: Greenwillow, 1999.

*Kipper's Rainy Day by Mick Inkpen. San Diego: Harcourt, 1991.

The Rainy Day by Felicia Law. Minneapolis: Picture Window Books, 2004.

*Raindrop, Plop! by Wendy Cheyette Lewison. New York: Viking, 2004.

Puddles by Jonathan London. New York: Viking, 1997.

*Here Comes the Rain by Mary Murphy. New York: DK, 2000.

Red Rubber Boot Day by Mary Lyn Ray. San Diego: Harcourt, 2000.

Soggy Saturday by Phyllis Root. Cambridge, MA: Candlewick, 2001.

Rain by Manya Stojic. New York: Crown, 2000.

Sonny's Beloved Boots by Lisa Stubbs. Hauppauge, NY: Barron's, 1997.

*Ducks Like to Swim by Agnes Verboven. New York: Orchard Books, 1996.

RECORDED MUSIC

"Leaky Umbrella" from *Jim Gill Sings The Sneezing Song and Other Contagious Tunes* by Jim Gill. Jim Gill Music, 1993.

*"Rock and Roll Freeze Dance" from *"So Big": Activity Songs for Little Ones* by Hap Palmer. Hap-Pal Music, 1994. *(Make this a "rain dance" by spraying the kids with a water bottle each time they freeze.)*

*"The Eensy Weensy Spider" from *Mainly Mother Goose* by Sharon, Lois, and Bram. Elephant Records, 1984.

FINGERPLAYS/SONGS

"Thunderstorm"

The rain falls from the sky:
Splash splash splash!
The thunder rushes by:
Crash crash crash!
Now lightning, my oh my!
Flash flash flash!

"If It's Raining . . ."
(to the tune of "If You're Happy and You Know It")

If it's raining and you know it, hold up your umbrella.
If it's raining and you know it, hold up your umbrella.
If it's raining and you know it, then your umbrella will show it.
If it's raining and you know it, hold up your umbrella.
. . . put on your raincoat
. . . put on your boots
. . . splash in the puddles

"Puddle Song"
(to the tune of "Row, Row, Row Your Boat")

Splash, splash, splash in puddles,
Splashing all day long.
Splashing's what we do when we
Sing this splashing song.
Jump . . .
Spin . . .
Hop . . .
Clap . . .
Stomp . . .

"You Are My Sunshine"
(traditional)

You are my sunshine, my only sunshine.
You make me happy when skies are gray.
You'll never know, dear, how much I love you.
Please don't take my sunshine away.

"The Wheels on the Bus (on a Rainy Day)"
(adapted traditional)

The wheels on the bus go splash splash splash,
Splash splash splash, splash splash splash.
The wheels on the bus go splash splash splash,
On a rainy day.
The wipers on the bus go swish swish swish . . .
The lights on the bus go on and off . . .
The people on the bus go grumble grumble grumble . . .
The wheels on the bus go splash splash splash . . .

"Rain Is Falling"
(to the tune of "Frère Jacques")

Rain is falling, rain is falling,
On the ground, on the ground,
Watering the flowers, watering the flowers,
All around, all around.

PROPS

*Flannelboard Rhyme

"Counting Raindrops"

PIECES NEEDED: *sun, cloud, 10 raindrops*

A great big cloud was in the sky.
He covered the sun, and by and by,
He sent the raindrops down below.
Raindrops falling to and fro.
How many raindrops can we count?
1, 2, 3, 4, 5, 6, 7, 8, 9, 10!

*Flannelboard Activity

"Colors in the Rain"

PIECES NEEDED: *orange, blue, green, yellow, and red umbrellas*

I took a walk out in the rain
And saw umbrella colors.
What colors do you see?
Orange, blue, green, yellow, and red!
Can you count them? 1, 2, 3, 4, 5!

*Prop Story   *Rainy Day* by Janet Morgan Stoeke. New York: Dutton, 1999.

PIECES NEEDED: *chicken, sheep, spray bottle of water*

CRAFTS

Puddlejumper Picture

MATERIALS: 1 piece of construction paper for each child, 1 circle cut from aluminum foil for each child, cupcake liners precut into halves, chenille stems, die-cuts of children, glue, crayons, glitter

DIRECTIONS:
1. Glue the aluminum foil circle onto the paper to represent a puddle.
2. Glue the die-cut of the child onto the paper.
3. Make an umbrella from half of a cupcake liner and use a curved length of chenille stem for the handle. Glue onto the picture.
4. Use glitter to represent rain.
5. Decorate with crayons as desired.

Rainstick

MATERIALS: 1 paper towel tube for each child, aluminum foil, beans or beads, scissors, stickers

DIRECTIONS:
1. Cut a length of aluminum foil about 8 inches by 22 inches. Fold it in half lengthwise. Continue to fold it until it is about 1–2 inches wide.
2. Using a large piece of aluminum foil, cover the paper towel roll leaving one end uncovered.
3. Accordion-fold the long piece of aluminum foil, then slide it into the tube.
4. Pour beans or beads into the tube, just enough to create some noise.
5. Cover the open end of the tube with aluminum foil. Use tape or glue to secure the foil over the ends.
6. Decorate the tube with stickers.
7. Turn the tube over to create a rain noise.

Puppy Tales

Sign: **DOG**

BOOKS

The Day the Dog Dressed Like Dad by Tom Amico and James Proimos. New York: Bloomsbury, 2004.

Stanley's Party by Linda Bailey. Toronto, ON: Kids Can Press, 2003.

Dear Zoo by Rod Campbell. New York: Four Winds Press, 1982.

Woof! Woof! by David A. Carter. New York: Little Simon, 2006.

Slippers at Home by Andrew Clements. New York: Dutton, 2004.

Wiggle by Doreen Cronin. New York: Atheneum, 2005.

Grumpy Gloria by Anna Dewdney. New York: Viking, 2006.

Bark George by Jules Feiffer. New York: HarperCollins, 1999.

Buster by Denise Fleming. New York: Henry Holt, 2003.

Please, Puppy, Please by Spike Lee and Tonya Lewis Lee. New York: Simon and Schuster, 2005.

Show Dog by Meghan McCarthy. New York: Viking, 2004.

Puppies! Puppies! Puppies! by Susan Meyers. New York: Abrams, 2005.

Dogs, Dogs, Dogs! by Leslea Newman. New York: Simon and Schuster, 2002.

I Love Dogs by Barney Saltzberg. Cambridge, MA: Candlewick, 2005.

The Stray Dog by Marc Simont. New York: HarperCollins, 2001.

Madlenka's Dog by Peter Sís. New York: Farrar, Straus and Giroux, 2002.

Cool Cat, Hot Dog by Sandy Turner. New York: Atheneum, 2005.

Unlovable by Dan Yaccarino. New York: Henry Holt, 2001.

RECORDED MUSIC

"Do Your Ears Hang Low?" from *Stay Tuned* by Sharon, Lois, and Bram. Elephant Records, 1987.

"My Dog Rags" from *Sing Along with Bob #1* by Bob McGrath. Bob's Kids Music, 2000.

FINGERPLAYS/SONGS

"Little Poodle"

I had a little poodle,
His coat was silver gray.
One day I thought I'd bathe him,
To wash the dirt away.
I washed my little poodle,
Then dried him with a towel.
My poodle seemed to like his bath,
He didn't even growl.

"Call the Puppy"
(traditional)

Call the puppy and give him some milk,
Brush his coat till it shines like silk,
Call the puppy and give him a bone,
Take him for a walk and then bring him
    home.

"My Puppy"
(traditional)

I like to pat my puppy,
He has such nice soft fur,
And if I don't pull his tail,
He won't say grrrrrrrr!

"Digging in the Dirt"
(traditional)

Ten little doggies went out one day
    (hold 10 fingers up)
To dig in the dirt and play, play, play.
    *(pretend to dig like a dog with
    both hands)*
Five were spotted, and five were not,
    (hold up one hand at a time)
And at dinner time they ate a lot!
    (pretend to eat)

"If You're a Puppy and You Know It"
(to the tune of "If You're Happy and You Know It")

If you're a puppy and you know it, clap
    your paws.
If you're a puppy and you know it, clap
    your paws.
If you're a puppy and you know it, then
    you really ought to show it.
If you're a puppy and you know it, clap
    your paws.
. . . wag your tail.
. . . pant with your tongue.
. . . chase your tail.

PROPS

*Flannelboard Rhyme

"Old Mother Hubbard"

Patterns can be found in The Flannelboard Storytelling Book *by Judy Sierra (New York: H. W. Wilson, 1997).*

Old Mother Hubbard went to the
    cupboard,
To fetch her poor dog a bone.
But when she got there, the cupboard
    was bare,
And so the poor dog had none.

*Flannelboard Song

"BINGO"

PIECES NEEDED: *large felt shapes for the letters of Bingo's name. Remove each letter as the song progresses.*

There was a farmer, had a dog
And Bingo was his name, oh.
B-I-N-G-O, B-I-N-G-O, B-I-N-G-O,
And Bingo was his name, oh.

Repeat, gradually replacing each letter with a clap.

*Flannelboard Song

"Five Little Dogs"

PIECES NEEDED: *5 dogs*

1 little dog went out to play,
Outside in the grass one day.
He had such enormous fun,
He called for another dog to come.
2 little dogs . . .
3 little dogs . . .
4 little dogs . . .
5 little dogs went out to play,
Outside in the grass one day.
They had such enormous fun,
And they ran home when the day was done.

*Flannelboard Story   *Dog's Colorful Day* by Emma Dodd. New York: Dutton, 2000.

PIECES NEEDED: *white dog with black spot on left ear; 9 dots in red, blue, green, brown, yellow, pink, gray, orange, and purple; bathtub*

CRAFTS

Puppy Ears

MATERIALS: 1 long strip of construction paper to form a headband for each child, 2 dog-ear shapes for each child, crayons, glue, stapler

DIRECTIONS:
1. Staple the ends of the construction paper strip together to form a headband.
2. Color the ears as desired.
3. Glue or staple the ears to the sides of the headband so they point downward.
4. Wear your puppy ears.

Dog Spoon Puppets

MATERIALS: 1 white plastic spoon for each child, glue, 1 small black pom-pom for each child, googly eyes, 2 ears cut from construction paper for each child, 1 small red sticker for mouth

DIRECTIONS:
1. Turn the spoon upside down. The back of the bowl of the spoon will form the dog's face.
2. Glue the black pom-pom on for a nose, then glue on googly eyes and ears. Place the red sticker for a mouth.

Rhyme Time

Sign: **RHYTHM**

BOOKS

Hickory Dickory Dock by Keith Baker. San Diego: Harcourt, 2007.

My Granny Went to Market: A Round-the-World Counting Rhyme by Stella Blackstone. Cambridge, MA: Barefoot Books, 2005.

Rhyming Words by Karen Bryant-Mole. Strongsville, OH: Gareth Stevens, 2000.

*Hello, Sun! by Dayle Ann Dodds. New York: Dial, 2005.

Is Your Mama a Llama? by Deborah Guarino. New York: Scholastic, 1989.

*Bears on the Stairs: A Beginner's Book of Rhymes by Muriel and Lionel Kalish. New York: Scholastic, 1993.

*New Friends, True Friends, Stuck-Like-Glue Friends by Virginia Kroll. Grand Rapids, MI: Eerdmans, 1994.

There's a Cow in the Road! by Reeve Lindbergh. New York: Dial, 1993.

*Time to Say Goodnight by Sally Lloyd-Jones. New York: HarperCollins, 2006.

Chicka Chicka Boom Boom by Bill Martin Jr. and John Archambault. New York: Simon and Schuster, 1989.

A Huge Hog Is a Big Pig: A Rhyming Word Game by Francis McCall. New York: Greenwillow, 2002.

*Play Day: A Book of Terse Verse by Bruce McMillan. New York: Holiday House, 1991.

*What Does Bunny See? by Linda Sue Park. New York: Clarion, 2005.

Sam's Sandwich by David Pelham. New York: Dutton, 1991.

Piggy in the Puddle by Charlotte Pomerantz. New York: Macmillan, 1974.

Dunk Skunk by Michael Rex. New York: G. P. Putnam's Sons, 2005.

One Fish, Two Fish, Red Fish, Blue Fish by Dr. Seuss. New York: Random House, 1960.

*Dinosaur Roar! by Paul and Henrietta Stickland. New York: Puffin, 1994.

*Tanka Tanka Skunk! by Steve Webb. New York: Orchard, 2003.

*Overboard! by Sarah Weeks. San Diego: Harcourt, 2006.

RECORDED MUSIC

"Yes, No, Maybe" from *Jim Gill Sings Do Re Mi on His Toe Leg Knee* by Jim Gill. Jim Gill Music, Inc., 1999.

"The Rhyme Family" from *Leaping Literacy* by Dr. Pam Schiller. Kimbo Educational, 2005. *(use with rhythm sticks)*

*"Five Little Monkeys" from *"So Big": Activity Songs for Little Ones* by Hap Palmer. Hap-Pal Music, 1994.

*"One, Two, Buckle My Shoe" from *Tony Chestnut and Fun Time Action Songs* by The Learning Station. Kaladon Publishing, 1997.

FINGERPLAYS/SONGS

"Silly Style Nursery Rhymes"

Present the silly rhymes below as if you think they are the real versions, and let the children correct you after each line.

Little Miss Muffet sat on . . . an easy chair,
Eating her . . . pepperoni pizza.
Along came a . . . monkey,
And sat down beside her . . . and asked
    her out to dinner!

Old Mother Hubbard went to the . . .
    refrigerator
To get her poor dog a . . . soda.
But when she got there, the cupboard
    was . . . full of elephants
And so her poor dog had . . . ice cream.

*"Teddy Bear, Teddy Bear"
(traditional)

Teddy Bear, Teddy Bear, turn around.
Teddy Bear, Teddy Bear, touch the
    ground.
Teddy Bear, Teddy Bear, show your shoe.
Teddy Bear, Teddy Bear, that will do.
Teddy Bear, Teddy Bear, go upstairs.
Teddy Bear, Teddy Bear, say your prayers.
Teddy Bear, Teddy Bear, turn out the light.
Teddy Bear, Teddy Bear, say good night.

"1, 2 Buckle My Shoe"
(traditional)

1, 2 buckle my shoe.
3, 4 shut the door.
5, 6 pick up sticks.
7, 8 lay them straight.
9, 10 a big fat hen!

"Rhymin' Simon"

Use your ears, use your ears and listen
    carefully.
Figure out the rhyming words and play
    along with me!
Can you touch something that rhymes
    with egg?
You were right if you touched your leg!
Can you touch something that rhymes
    with sky?
You were right if you touched your eye!
. . . linger . . . finger
. . . swarm . . . arm
. . . yummy . . . tummy
. . . sea . . . knee
. . . tear . . . ear
. . . care . . . hair

"I Went to the Pet Store"

Pause before the last word of each verse to let the children guess the rhyme.

I went to the pet store
And made a special wish.
The pet that I wanted
Was a very special . . . fish!

I went to the pet store.
I went there at a jog,
To get a pet with a wagging tail.
It was a little . . . dog!

I went to the pet store.
I went there just like that,
Because I heard a little purr.
It was a little . . . cat!

I went to the pet store.
It had become a habit.
The pet I wanted now
Was a soft, white, fluffy . . . rabbit!

I went to the pet store.
I'm sure this sounds absurd.
But the pet I wanted was
A colorful flying . . . bird!

I went to the pet store.
It was no mistake.
What I really wanted now
Was a hissing green . . . snake!

PROPS

*Prop Rhyme

"Jack Be Nimble"

PIECES NEEDED: *real candlestick, or fake candlestick made from a paper-covered toilet paper roll with a paper flame taped to the top*

Jack be nimble, Jack be quick.
Jack jump over the candlestick.
_____ be nimble, _____ be quick.
_____ jump over the candlestick.

Give each child a turn to jump over the candlestick as everyone repeats the rhyme with his or her name in it.

*Stick Puppet Rhyme

"Two Little Blackbirds"

PIECES NEEDED: *2 blackbirds*

2 little blackbirds sitting on a hill,
One named Jack and one named Jill.
Fly away, Jack! Fly away, Jill!
Come back, Jack! Come back, Jill!

*Flannelboard Rhyme

"The Old Woman Who Lived in a Shoe"
(adapted traditional)

PIECES NEEDED: *shoe; old woman; child shapes in various colors, enough for each child to hold one*

There was an old woman who lived in a
    shoe.
She had so many children, but she knew
    just what to do.
She read them sweet stories, and gave
    them some bread
And gathered up her red children, and
    put them to bed.

Repeat with additional colors, inviting children to place their pieces on the flannelboard as you call their colors.

Flannelboard Story: "Sally O'Malley"

Pieces needed: *girl, mother, father, plate of spaghetti, red hat, blue hat, hamburger, teacher*

Once upon a time there was a girl named Sally O'Malley. Sally loved to rhyme more than anything in the world. If someone asked her a question, she would only answer with a rhyme. If her mother said, "Dinnertime, are you ready?" Sally would say, "I would like some spaghetti." If her father said, "Which hat do you want for your head?" Sally would say, "I would like the one that's red."

And every day her parents would ask her the same questions, and every day Sally would answer with a rhyme. And Sally was so tired of eating spaghetti . . . but she couldn't think of another food that rhymed with "ready" when her mother said "Are you ready?" And she really wanted to wear her blue hat sometimes, but "blue" didn't rhyme with "head."

Then one day in school her teacher read her a poem. The poem went like this:

"The wind is in the trees.
The trees blow all around.
The leaves fall everywhere."

"What kind of a poem is that?" said Sally. "It doesn't even rhyme, and that's a fact!"

"Poetry doesn't always have to rhyme," said her teacher. "There are lots of words that sound very pretty, even if they don't rhyme."

Sally thought about that. She loved rhyming, but maybe, just maybe, sometimes it was okay if things didn't rhyme.

When she got home that evening, her mother said, "Dinnertime, are you ready?" And Sally said, "I would like a hamburger, please."

The next morning, her father said, "Which hat do you want for your head?" And Sally said, "I would like the one that's blue." But then she added, "I think blue is pretty too."

Because, you see, some habits are hard to break, and no one's perfect.

Magnetic Letters

Use magnetic letters to demonstrate rhyming words. For example, show the word "cat," then show how you can change the *c* to *b* to make "bat," which rhymes.

*Flannelboard Story   *Brown Bear, Brown Bear, What Do You See?* by Bill Martin Jr. New York: Holt, Rinehart, and Winston, 1983.

Pieces needed: *brown bear, red bird, yellow duck, blue horse, green frog, purple cat, white dog, black sheep, goldfish, teacher*

CRAFTS

Humpty Dumpty

MATERIALS: 1 piece of construction paper for each child, red rectangular book processing stickers, 1 oval cut from white construction paper for each child, paper strips to serve as arms and legs, scissors, 1 paper fastener for each child, crayons, glue

DIRECTIONS:
1. Cut the oval shape into 2 pieces with a zigzag line.
2. Fasten the 2 pieces together at the corner with a paper fastener so that the egg can hinge open and shut.
3. Glue arms and legs onto Humpty Dumpty.
4. Create a brick wall on the paper by using the red rectangular stickers for bricks.
5. Glue Humpty Dumpty onto the page and decorate as desired.

Jack and Jill Pictures

MATERIALS: a simple coloring sheet showing a hill and a well for each child, 2 craft sticks for each child, Jack and Jill shapes for each child (patterns can be found in *The Complete Resource Book for Toddlers and Twos* by Pamela Byrne Schiller, Beltsville, MD: Gryphon House, 2003), glue, crayons or markers

DIRECTIONS:
1. Cut a slit in the coloring sheets leading up the hill.
2. Decorate the Jack and Jill shapes, then glue them to the craft sticks to make stick puppets.
3. Decorate the coloring sheet.
4. Poke the sticks through the slit in the paper to act out the rhyme.

Snowflake Dance

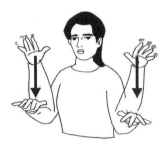

Sign: **SNOW**

BOOKS

Snowmen at Night by Caralyn Buehner. New York: Penguin Putnam, 2002.

There Was a Cold Lady Who Swallowed Some Snow by Lucille Colandro. New York: Scholastic, 2003.

It Feels Like Snow by Nancy Cote. Honesdale, PA: Boyds Mills Press, 2003.

*In the Snow by Sharon Philips Denslow. New York: Greenwillow, 2005.

Snow Dance by Lezlie Evans. New York: Houghton Mifflin, 1997.

The First Day of Winter by Denise Fleming. New York: Henry Holt, 2005.

*Time to Sleep by Denise Fleming. New York: Henry Holt, 1997.

*A Winter Day by Douglas Florian. New York: Greenwillow, 1987.

First Snow by Bernette Ford. New York: Holiday House, 2005.

*Snow by Christine Ford. New York: HarperCollins, 1999.

*Oh! by Kevin Henkes. New York: Greenwillow, 1999.

*What Can You Do in the Snow? by Anna Grossnickle Hines. New York: Greenwillow, 1999.

Stranger in the Woods by Carl R. Sams II and Jean Stoick. Milford, MI: Carl R. Sams Photography, 2000.

Snow by Steve Sanfield. New York: Philomel, 1995.

*Millions of Snowflakes by Mary McKenna Siddals. New York: Clarion, 1998.

Little Fern's First Winter by Jane Simmons. New York: Little, Brown, 2001.

Snow by Manya Stojic. New York: Knopf, 2002.

*Mouse's First Snow by Lauren Thompson. New York: Simon and Schuster, 2005.

Hello, Snow! by Hope Vestergaard. New York: Farrar, Straus and Giroux, 2004.

*Sledding by Elizabeth Winthrop. New York: Harper and Row, 1989.

RECORDED MUSIC

*"Snow Song" from *Hello Everybody! Playsongs and Rhymes from a Toddler's World* by Rachel Buchman. A Gentle Wind, 1986.

*"Snow Fun" from *Preschool Action Time* by Carol Hammett. Kimbo Educational, 1988.

*"Rock and Roll Freeze Dance" from *"So Big": Activity Songs for Little Ones* by Hap Palmer. Hap-Pal Music, 1994.

"Mitten Weather" and "Let's Play in the Snow" from *Sing a Song of Seasons* by Rachel Buchman. Rounder Kids, 1997.

*"I'm a Little Snowflake" from *Whaddaya Think of That?* by Laurie Berkner. Two Tomatoes, 2001.

FINGERPLAYS/SONGS

"Here's a Snowball"

You start out with a bunch of snow,
Then you pick it up just so.
Pat that snow into a ball,
Now throw that little snowball!

"Snow Is Falling"

Snow is falling from the sky.
It's so pretty, me oh my.
Snow is something I would miss
If I didn't get to see it DANCE like this.
. . . TWIST
. . . TURN
. . . FALL

"Ten Little Snowflakes"
(to the tune of "Ten Little Indians")

1 little, 2 little, 3 little snowflakes,
4 little, 5 little, 6 little snowflakes,
7 little, 8 little, 9 little snowflakes,
10 little snowflakes drifting down.

"I'm a Little Snowman"
(to the tune of "I'm a Little Teapot")

I'm a little snowman short and fat.
Here is my scarf and here is my hat.
When the snow is falling come and play.
Sun comes up, I melt away.

"I'm Going to Play in the Snow"
(to the tune of "We're All Together Again")

I'm going to play in the snow, in the snow.
I'm going to play in the snow, in the snow.
What do I need to play in the snow?
First I need my coat.

Repeat with other items of clothing.

"Snow Down My Back"
(to the tune of "Spider on the Floor")

I've got snow down my back, down my back.
I'm gonna have a heart attack.
I've got snow down my back.
I've got snow down my back, down my back.
I've got snow in my shoe, in my shoe / What am I gonna do? . . .
I've got snow in my ear, in my ear / Oh, I really really fear . . .
I've got snow down my leg, down my leg / Oh, help me I beg . . .
I've got snow on my face, on my face / It's quite a hopeless case . . .

PROPS

*Flannelboard or Prop Rhyme

"Five Little Snowmen"

PIECES NEEDED: *5 snowmen with red, blue, green, yellow, and purple scarves or 5 snowman masks and red, blue, green, yellow, and purple scarves for volunteers to wear*

I made 1 little snowman.
I put a hat on his head.
I gave him eyes of coal,
And a scarf of red

I made another snowman,
So now I had 2.
I gave him eyes of coal,
And a scarf of blue.

I made another snowman,
So now how many? 3.
I gave him eyes of coal,
And a scarf of green.

I made another snowman,
He was my 4th fellow.
I gave him eyes of coal,
And a scarf of yellow.

I made one last snowman,
That made 5 snowpeople.
I gave the last one eyes of coal,
And a scarf of purple.

The sun came up, I'm sad to say,
And the snowman with the red
    scarf melted away.
How many are left? 4!

The sun was very bright that day,
And the snowman with the blue
    scarf melted away.
How many are left? 3!

Even though I still wanted to play,
The snowman with the green scarf
    melted away.
How many are left? 2!

I asked the snowmen to please stay,
But the snowman with the yellow
    scarf melted away.
How many are left? 1!

The sun still shone on that day,
And the snowman with the purple
    scarf melted away.
How many are left? None!
Goodbye snowmen!

*Flannelboard Rhyme

"Five Little Snowflakes"

PIECES NEEDED: *5 snowflakes*

The air was cold in the town,
And 1 little snowflake started drifting
    down.
The air grew colder in the town.
Now 2 little snowflakes are drifting down.
The wind started blowing in the town.
Now 3 little snowflakes are drifting down.
The air grew frosty in the town.
Now 4 little snowflakes are drifting down.
It's colder than ever in the town,
And 5 little snowflakes are drifting down.

*Flannelboard Rhyme

"Color Mittens"

PIECES NEEDED: *pairs of mitten shapes in felt, 2 of each color or pattern. Place one of each pair on the flannelboard, and give the others to the children.*

I have two little mittens.
I wear them on my hands.
But I have lost a mitten.
Please help me if you can.
Look at your mitten, what do you see?
If your mitten is _____, please bring it
    to me.

Repeat with other colors, inviting the children to place their mittens on the flannelboard.

Prop Story: "Getting Dressed to Play in the Snow"

PIECES NEEDED: *coat, scarf, sweater, snowpants, socks, boots, hat, mittens. Either select a volunteer to play the main character and put on/take off the clothes throughout the story, or do this yourself as you tell it. Invite the children to mime the actions too.*

One day I wanted to play in the snow. I put on my coat and said, "Mom, I'm ready to go play in the snow." And my mom said, "No, you're not. You've forgotten something."

So I thought about it, and then I said, "Oh, right! My scarf!" So I took off my coat, put on my scarf, put my coat back on, and said, "Mom, I'm ready to go play in the snow." And my mom said, "No, you're not. You've forgotten something."

Repeat the pattern, adding on the sweater, snowpants, socks, boots, hat, and mittens.

"Now are you ready to go play in the snow?" said my mom.
    And I said, "No. Now I'm too tired!"

*Flannelboard Story   *The Mitten* by Jan Brett. New York: Putnam, 1989.

PIECES NEEDED: *boy, grandmother, pair of small white mittens, 3 white mittens in gradually larger sizes, mole, rabbit, hedgehog, owl, badger, fox, bear, mouse*

*Flannelboard Story   *Time to Sleep* by Denise Fleming. New York: Henry Holt, 1997.

PIECES NEEDED: *bear, snail, skunk, turtle, woodchuck, ladybug*

ADDITIONAL SUGGESTIONS

*Parachute Play

PIECES NEEDED: *parachute, rolled-up socks*

Pull out the parachute. Throw rolled-up socks in the center to represent snowballs and let the children bounce them all around.

CRAFTS

Cotton Swab Snowflakes

MATERIALS: 1 piece of blue construction paper for each child, cotton swabs, glue, glitter

DIRECTIONS:
1. Glue the cotton swabs onto the paper to make a snowflake design.
2. Decorate with glitter.

Cupcake Liner Snowmen

MATERIALS: 1 piece of construction paper for each child, 3 cupcake liners for each child, glue, crayons

DIRECTIONS:
1. Glue the 3 cupcake liners onto the paper to form a snowman.
2. Decorate with crayons as desired.

Spring Cleaning

Sign: **CLEAN**

BOOKS

Let's Clean Up! by Peggy Perry Anderson. New York: Houghton Mifflin, 2002.

Gray Rabbit's Odd One Out by Alan Baker. Boston: Kingfisher, 1999.

Mr. Tuggle's Troubles by LeeAnn Blankenship. Honesdale, PA: Boyds Mills Press, 2005.

Five Little Monkeys with Nothing to Do by Eileen Christelow. New York: Clarion, 1996.

Maisy Cleans Up by Lucy Cousins. Cambridge, MA: Candlewick, 2002.

Clean Your Room, Harvey Moon! by Pat Cummings. New York: Bradbury Press, 1991.

This Is the Van That Dad Cleaned by Lisa Campbell Ernst. New York: Simon and Schuster, 2005.

Tidy Titch by Pat Hutchins. New York: Greenwillow, 1991.

I Stink! by Kate and Jim McMullen. New York: HarperCollins, 2002.

Smash! Mash! Crash! There Goes the Trash! by Barbara Odanaka. New York: Simon and Schuster, 2006.

Tom and Pippo Make a Mess by Helen Oxenbury. New York: Macmillan, 1988.

The Car Washing Street by Denise Lewis Patrick. New York: William Morrow, 1993.

When the Fly Flew In . . . by Lisa Westberg Peters. New York: Dial, 1994.

Tracy's Mess by Elise Petersen. Boston: Whispering Coyote Press, 1996.

Nice and Clean by Anne and Harlow Rockwell. New York: Macmillan, 1984.

Mrs. Potter's Pig by Phyllis Root. Cambridge, MA: Candlewick, 1996.

This Is the House That Was Tidy and Neat by Teri Sloat. New York: Henry Holt, 2005.

Car Wash by Sandra Steen and Susan Steen. New York: G. P. Putnam's Sons, 2001.

Fritz and the Mess Fairy by Rosemary Wells. New York: Dial, 1991.

Max Cleans Up by Rosemary Wells. New York: Viking, 2000.

RECORDED MUSIC

*"Clean Up" from *Barney's Favorites.* Barney Music, 1993.

"Clean It Up" from *Buzz Buzz* by Laurie Berkner. Two Tomatoes, 2001.

"I Took a Bath in a Washing Machine" from *Jim Gill Sings The Sneezing Song and Other Contagious Tunes* by Jim Gill. Jim Gill Music, 1993.

"Clean-Up Time" from *Preschool Action Time* by Carol Hammett. Kimbo Educational, 1988.

"Stuff It in the Closet" from *Rhythms on Parade (Revised Expanded Version)* by Hap Palmer. Hap-Pal Music, 1995.

*"Clean-Up Freeze" from *Rock the Day Away* by Stephen Fite. Melody House, 2003.

"Shiny Clean Dance" from *Tony Chestnut and Fun Time Action Songs* by The Learning Station. Kaladon Publishing, 1997.

FINGERPLAYS/SONGS

"Recycling Cheer"

If you've got an old box, don't throw it away.
It can be used in another way.
Recycle it! Recycle it! Hooray!
If you've got a soda can . . .
If you've got an old tire . . .
If you've got an old computer . . .

"Clean Up Everywhere"

It's cleaning time! It's cleaning time!
Let's clean up everywhere!
Let's clean down low, let's clean in the middle.
Let's clean high in the air.
Let's make sure we clean the floors,
The walls and ceiling too.
And when we are done with cleaning,
They will sparkle just like new!

"Clean It Up"
(to the tune of "The Addams Family Theme")

It's dirty and it's dusty.
Your room is looking musty.
It really is quite yucky
With all the mess in here.
Clean it up (clap clap).
Clean it up (clap clap).
Clean it up, clean it up, clean it up
    (clap clap).

"This Is the Way"
(to the tune of "Here We Go 'Round the Mulberry Bush")

This is the way we pick up our toys,
Pick up our toys, pick up our toys.
This is the way we pick up our toys,
When we're cleaning up.
. . . sweep the floor
. . . wipe the table
. . . run the vacuum
. . . dust the shelves
. . . take a rest

"Are You Sweeping?"
(to the tune of "Frère Jacques")

Are you sweeping? Are you sweeping?
Brother John? Brother John?
With a broom and dustpan,
With a broom and dustpan,
Clean, clean, clean.
Clean, clean, clean.

"C-L-E-A-N"
(to the tune of "BINGO")

There was a man who had a house
And he wanted to clean it.
C-L-E-A-N, C-L-E-A-N, C-L-E-A-N
And he wanted to clean it.
Repeat, gradually replacing each letter with claps.

PROPS

*Flannelboard Rhyme

"Bugs under My Rug"

PIECES NEEDED: *5 bugs, rug*

There are 5 bugs hiding under my rug.
Little bugs run away! Today is cleaning day!
Shoo, little bug! 1 ran away from the rug.
There are 4 bugs . . .
There are 3 bugs . . .
There are 2 bugs . . .
There is 1 bug . . .
There are no more bugs hiding under my rug.
Hooray, hooray for cleaning day!

*Prop Story: "Hanging Up My Laundry"

PIECES NEEDED: *laundry basket, clothesline, clothespins, shirt, socks, scarf, squirrel puppet, bird puppet, rabbit puppet. Tie the clothesline between 2 chairs and hang the clothes on it with clothespins as you begin the story.*

One day I took my laundry outside to hang it up on the line. I hung up my pretty scarf, my shirt, and my favorite socks, and left them there to dry.

Along came a squirrel. He looked at my shirt and said, "That would make a perfect rug for my home in the hollow tree." And he took my shirt down and took it home.

A bird flew by next. She saw my pretty scarf and thought it would be perfect to weave into her nest. So she pulled it free and flew away.

Along came a bunny rabbit. He said to himself, "I could use those nice ear-warmers." And took my socks right off the line and put them over his ears. He hopped away, his ears toasty warm.

Later, I came outside to get my laundry off the line. Hey! Who took my clothes? Do you know?

*Prop Game: Pick It Up

PIECES NEEDED: *laminated paper shapes in various colors, each with a magnet attached; dowel rods with circular magnets glued to the ends, enough for each child to hold one*

Scatter the shapes on the floor and invite the children to pick up the pieces you ask for with their magnetic poles. Depending on your audience, you can focus on shapes or colors.

What a mess! What a mess! (Colors/Shapes) are everywhere!
Can you find the (specific color or shape) pieces, and bring them
right up here?

Spring Cleaning   157

CRAFTS

Feather Duster Magnet

MATERIALS: small feathers, a 2-inch length of drinking straw for each child, glue, adhesive magnet strips, googly eyes

DIRECTIONS:
1. Glue feathers to the end of the length of drinking straw.
2. Glue googly eyes onto the feather duster.
3. Attach a length of magnetic strip to the back.

Recycled Trash Collages

MATERIALS: 1 piece of construction paper for each child; glue; pieces of trash materials such as old magazines, grocery bags, tin-can labels, junk mail, aluminum foil, old buttons, etc.

DIRECTIONS: Glue pieces of recycled materials onto the paper to make a design.

Spring Fling

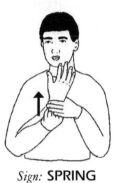

Sign: **SPRING**

 **BOOKS**

In the Spring by Craig Brown. New York: Greenwillow, 1994.

Fran's Flower by Lisa Bruce. New York: HarperCollins, 1999.

The Crunching Munching Caterpillar by Sheridan Cain. Wilton, CT: Tiger Tales, 2000.

The Very Hungry Caterpillar by Eric Carle. New York: Philomel, 1969.

Splish, Splash, Spring by Jan Carr. New York: Holiday House, 2001.

Wake Up, It's Spring! by Lisa Campbell Ernst. New York: HarperCollins, 2004.

Sunflower by Miela Ford. New York: Greenwillow, 1995.

It's Spring! by Linda Glaser. Brookfield, CT: Millbrook Press, 2002.

The Surprise Garden by Zoe Hall. New York: Scholastic, 1998.

Hurray for Spring! by Patricia Hubbell. Minnetonka, MN: NorthWord, 2005.

It's Spring! by Else Holmelund Minarik. New York: Greenwillow, 1989.

Caterpillar's Wish by Mary Murphy. New York: DK, 1999.

Spring Things by Bob Raczka. Morton Grove, IL: Albert Whitman, 2007.

Mud by Mary Lynn Ray. San Diego: Harcourt Brace, 1996.

My Spring Robin by Anne Rockwell. New York: Macmillan, 1989.

Spring Song by Barbara Seuling. San Diego: Harcourt, 2001.

Mouse's First Spring by Lauren Thompson. New York: Simon and Schuster, 2005.

When Will It Be Spring? by Catherine Walters. New York: Dutton, 1997.

Bear Wants More by Karma Wilson. New York: Simon and Schuster, 2003.

Do Zebras Bloom in the Spring? by Viki Woodworth. New York: The Child's World, 1998.

RECORDED MUSIC

"Caterpillar—Cocoon—Butterfly" from *Animal Walks* by Georgiana Stewart. Kimbo Educational, 1987.

"The Bunny Hop" from *Disney's Dance Along, Volume 1.* Walt Disney Records, 1997.

*"Let's Go Fly a Kite" from *Musical Scarves and Activities* by Georgiana Stewart. Kimbo Educational, 2002. *(use kite streamers)*

"Five Little Butterflies" from *Run, Jump, Skip, and Sing* by Barney. Koch Records, 2003.

*"When the Pod Went Pop!" from *Sing a Song of Seasons* by Rachel Buchman. Rounder Kids, 1997.

*"Hop Like a Bunny" from *Toddlers on Parade* by Carol Hammett and Elaine Bueffel. Kimbo Educational, 1999.

*"I Fly My Kite" from *We've Got Harmony!* Kimbo Educational, 2006. *(use kite streamers)*

"Mr. Rabbit" from *Wiggles, Jiggles, and Giggles* by Stephen Fite. Melody House, 2000.

FINGERPLAYS/SONGS

"Caterpillar, Caterpillar"

Caterpillar, caterpillar, turn around.
Caterpillar, caterpillar, on the ground.
Caterpillar, caterpillar, climb up high.
Soon you'll be a butterfly!

"If I Were a Butterfly"

If I were a butterfly,
I would flutter way up high.
I'd flutter left and flutter right,
Flutter flutter through the night.
I'd swoop up high,
Then swoop down low,
Then swoop down to the floor just so.

"This Is the Way . . ."
(to the tune of "Here We Go 'Round the Mulberry Bush")

This is the way the sun does shine,
Sun does shine, sun does shine.
This is the way the sun does shine,
In the spring time.
. . . rain does fall
. . . flowers grow
. . . bunnies hop
. . . birdies fly
. . . caterpillars crawl

"Baby Bumblebee"
(adapted traditional)

I'm bringing home a baby bumblebee.
Won't my mommy be so proud of me?
I'm bringing home a baby bumblebee.
Ouch! It stung me.

I'm letting go my baby bumblebee.
Won't my mommy be so proud of me?
I'm letting go my baby bumblebee.
And I'm never bringing one home again!

"In the Spring"

In the spring the sun does shine,
The birds fly to and fro.
The frogs say "Ribbit" in the pond,
And the flowers grow!

"I'm a Little Seed"
(to the tune of "I'm a Little Teapot")

I'm a little seed, growing in the ground.
I huddle up and I don't make a sound.
If the rain falls and the sun shines just so,
I push my leaves up to say hello!

"The Wind"
(to the tune of "Spider on the Floor")

The wind is blowing my head, blowing my head.
The wind is blowing my head, blowing my head.
Oh, I really dread the wind blowing my head.
The wind is blowing my head, blowing my head.
The wind is blowing my hands . . . help me if you can . . .
The wind is blowing my knees . . . it's quite a strong breeze . . .
The wind is blowing my feet . . . Isn't it neat . . .
The wind is blowing my bottom . . . don't think that I forgot 'em . . .
The wind is blowing all of me . . . I'm sure that you can see . . .

PROPS

*Flannelboard Rhyme

"Five Little Flowers"

PIECES NEEDED: *5 flowers*

5 little flowers grew by my door.
I picked one for my mother, and then there were 4.
4 little flowers pretty as can be.
I picked one for my father, and then there were 3.
3 little flowers, what could I do?
I picked one for my sister, and then there were 2.
2 little flowers out in the sun.
I picked one for my brother, and then there was 1.
1 little flower, isn't this fun?
I picked one for you, and then there were none.

*Prop Story: "Rabbit's Flowers"

PIECES NEEDED: *2 rabbit puppets, bee puppet, mouse puppet, cat puppet, dog puppet, bear puppet, 5 artificial flowers in yellow and 4 other colors*

One day Rabbit picked 5 flowers for his mother: *(name colors)*. He hopped home to give them to his mother, but on the way he met Bee. "Bzzzz," said Bee, "what a pretty yellow flower. It's the same color as pollen, and that's my favorite thing in the world. Could I have it, please?" "Well, OK," said Rabbit. So he gave the flower to Bee. "Thank you!" said Bee.

"At least I still have 4 flowers to give to my mother," Rabbit thought, and he hopped toward home.

Continue pattern, with rabbit giving flowers away to the following:

Mouse: "That flower is my favorite color."
Cat: "Today is my birthday."
Dog: "We're best friends."
Bear: "I just woke up from my long winter's nap—is that a present for me?"

When Rabbit arrived home, he had no flowers for his mother. He was very sad. He decided to draw a picture of a flower for her instead. And do you know what? She loved it, and she hung it right up on the refrigerator!

*Kite Streamers

Use with kite songs listed above. Cut small rectangles from construction paper and tape them to a length of curling ribbon for a handle. Tape a shorter length of ribbon to one side to flutter out like a tail. Make enough for each child to have one.

*Flannelboard Story   *The Most Wonderful Egg in the World* by Helme Heine. New York: Aladdin, 1987.

Flannelboard patterns can be found in Books in Bloom: Creative Patterns and Props That Bring Stories to Life *by Kimberly K. Faurot (Chicago: American Library Association, 2003).*

*Flannelboard Story   *The Very Hungry Caterpillar* by Eric Carle. New York: Philomel, 1969.

Flannelboard patterns can be found in 2's Experience Felt Board Fun *by Liz and Dick Wilmes (Elgin, IL: Building Blocks, 1994).*

CRAFTS

Lunch Bag Kites

MATERIALS: 1 lunch bag for each child, strips of crepe streamers, yarn, stickers, crayons, gluesticks, hole punch, reinforcement circles

DIRECTIONS:
1. Punch a hole on each side of the bag, about half an inch from the edge.
2. Place a reinforcement circle on each of the holes.
3. Tie a piece of yarn to each of the holes, then tie the ends of the strings together to form the kite handle.
4. Decorate the bag with stickers and crayons.
5. Attach lengths of crepe streamers to the ends of the bag.
6. To fly the kite, open the bag completely, hold the kite handle, and run. The wind will catch the bag and make it fly up.

Sandwich-Bag Butterflies

MATERIALS: 1 plastic sandwich bag for each child, small squares of tissue paper in various colors, 1 pipe cleaner for each child

DIRECTIONS:
1. Fill the sandwich bag with pieces of tissue paper.
2. Close the bag and pinch the middle of it. Twist the pipe cleaner around the middle of the bag and twist the ends up to look like antennae.

Sticky Stories

Sign: **STICKY**

BOOKS

At Grandpa's Sugar Bush by Margaret Carney. Toronto, ON: Kids Can Press, 1997.

*Where There's a Bear, There's Trouble! by Michael Catchpool. Wilton, CT: Tiger Tales, 2002.

*Jamberry by Bruce Degen. New York: HarperCollins, 1983.

Mr. Wolf's Pancakes by Jan Fearnley. Wilton, CT: Little Tiger Press, 1999.

Bread and Jam for Frances by Russell Hoban. New York: HarperCollins, 1964.

*Sticky People by Tony Johnston. New York: HarperCollins, 2006.

The Beeman by Laurie Krebs. Washington, DC: National Geographic, 2002.

The Bear Who Didn't Like Honey by Barbara Maitland. New York: Orchard Books, 1996.

*If You Give a Pig a Pancake by Laura Numeroff. New York: HarperCollins, 1998.

*Curious George Makes Pancakes by H. A. Rey. New York: Houghton Mifflin, 1998.

*One Duck Stuck by Phyllis Root. Cambridge, MA: Candlewick, 1998.

The Bubble Gum Kid by Stu Smith. Philadelphia: Running Press Kids, 2006.

*Yum, Yum, Yummy by Martin Waddell. Cambridge, MA: Candlewick, 1998.

*Hey, Pancakes! by Tamson Weston. San Diego: Harcourt, 2003.

Bubble Gum, Bubble Gum by Lisa Wheeler. New York: Little, Brown, 2004.

Perfect Pancakes, If You Please by William Wise. New York: Dial, 1997.

RECORDED MUSIC

*"Peanut Butter and Jelly" from *Fun and Games* by Greg and Steve. Greg and Steve Productions, 2002.

*"Stick to the Glue" from *Jim Gill Makes It Noisy in Boise, Idaho* by Jim Gill. Jim Gill Music, 1995.

"My Lollipop" from *Fabulous Food*. Schiller Educational Resources, 2005.

FINGERPLAYS/SONGS

"Bubblegum, Bubblegum"

Bubblegum, Bubblegum, stretch up high.
Bubblegum, Bubblegum, touch the sky.
Bubblegum, Bubblegum, stretch
    down low.
Bubblegum, Bubblegum, bubbles blow . . .
POP!

"Melting Ice Cream"
(to the tune of "Frère Jacques")

Licking my ice cream, licking my ice
    cream.
It can't wait. It can't wait.
I don't want it to melt. I don't want it to
    melt.
Oops! Too late. Oops! Too late.

"Sticky, Sticky Bubblegum"
(traditional)

Sticky sticky sticky bubblegum,
Bubblegum, bubblegum.
Sticky sticky sticky bubblegum,
Sticking my hand to my knee.
Pull it off!

Repeat, sticking other body parts together.

"Lollipop"

My lollipop is delicious, it's true.
It is turning my tongue bright blue.
I lick and I lick till my lolly's all gone.
Now my hands are all sticky. MOM!

"Making Pancakes Call and Response Chant"

Inspired by "The Muffin Game" from If You Give a Moose a Muffin/
Doin' the Moose/The Muffin Game *by Laura Numeroff (audiobook;
New York: HarperCollins, 1997).*

If you want to make pancakes in a special way
Just do what I do and say what I say.
Shoop, shoop, in goes the flour. (Shoop, shoop, in goes the flour.)
Crack, crack, in go the eggs. (Crack, crack, in go the eggs.)
Pour, pour, pour in the milk. (Pour, pour, pour in the milk.)
Drip, drop in goes the butter. (Drip, drop in goes the butter.)
Sprinkle, sprinkle the salt. (Sprinkle, sprinkle the salt.)
Pour, pour baking powder. (Pour, pour baking powder.)
Now stir it up, stir it up, stir it up. (Now stir it up, stir it up, stir
    it up.)
Sizzle, sizzle, the pan is hot. (Sizzle, sizzle, the pan is hot.)
Pour, pour, pour in the batter. (Pour, pour, pour in the batter.)
Now wait . . . and wait . . . (Now wait . . . and wait . . .)
Flip, flip, flipping the pancakes. (Flip, flip, flipping the pancakes.)
And wait . . . and wait . . . (And wait . . . and wait . . .)
Pancakes are ready! (Pancakes are ready!)
Flip, slip onto a plate. (Flip, slip onto a plate.)
Sticky, sticky, pour on the syrup. (Sticky, sticky, pour on the syrup.)
Now eat 'em up, eat 'em up, eat 'em up! (Now eat 'em up, eat
    'em up, eat 'em up!)
Mmmmm, PANCAKES!

"The Gluey Jump Dance Wiggle"
(to the tune of "The Hokey Pokey")

You put your right hand in, you put your right hand out.
You put your right hand in, then you stick it to your head.
You jump, dance, wiggle, and you turn yourself around.
That's what it's all about.

Keep right hand on head as you continue the song. Each time another 2 body parts get stuck together, they remain that way for the rest of the song.

Left hand . . . stick it to your tummy
Knees . . . stick together
Elbow . . . stick it to your neighbor
Backside . . . stick it to the floor

PROPS

*Prop Song

"There's a Sticker on My Knee"
(to the tune of "Spider on the Floor")

PIECES NEEDED: *stickers*

There's a sticker on my knee, on my knee, on my knee.
There's a sticker on my knee, on my knee, on my knee.
Oh, won't you please help me? There's a sticker on my knee.
There's a sticker on my knee, on my knee, on my knee.
. . . on my nose . . . everybody knows . . .
. . . on my elbow . . . won't you help me, fellow? . . .
. . . on my chin . . . it makes me grin . . .

*Flannelboard Story: "Pancake Man"

PIECES NEEDED: *pancake man, woman, man, little girl, little boy, dog, cat, fox, river*

One day a lady was making pancakes. Her little girl asked her to make a special pancake shaped like a little man, so she did. But as soon as she flipped it over in the pan, that pancake jumped right up out of the pan and started dancing around the kitchen. The Pancake Man said, "Run, run, as fast as you can! You can't catch me, I'm the Pancake Man!" The Pancake Man ran out of the house. The lady chased the Pancake Man out the door. She ran into her husband, and said "Help!" So the man chased the lady, and the lady chased the Pancake Man, and the Pancake Man said, "Run, run, as fast as you can! You can't catch me, I'm the Pancake Man!"

Continue pattern, adding all characters except the fox and the river.

Then the Pancake Man came to a wide river. There was a fox there, and as the Pancake Man stood by the water trying to figure out how to cross the river, the fox said, "Hop on my back! I will carry you across!" So the Pancake Man jumped onto the fox's back, and the fox started swimming across the river. But soon the Pancake Man said, "I'm getting wet!" So the fox said, "Climb up onto my head." So the Pancake Man climbed up onto the fox's head. Soon the Pancake Man said again, "I'm getting wet!" So the fox said, "Poor Pancake Man, climb up onto my snout, and you will stay dry." And just as the Pancake Man climbed up to the fox's snout, the fox opened up his mouth and SNAP, ate the Pancake Man in one big bite.

*Flannelboard Story   *Dog's Colorful Day* by Emma Dodd. New York: Dutton, 2000.

PIECES NEEDED: *white dog with black spot on left ear; 9 dots in red, blue, green, brown, yellow, pink, gray, orange, and purple; bathtub; small scrubber for each child made from netting material tied together in a bunch. At the end of the story, invite the children to scrub the air with their scrubbers as you remove the dots from the dog.*

ADDITIONAL SUGGESTIONS

Poetry

"Bubble Gum, Bubble Gum" from *Schoolyard Rhymes* by Judy Sierra. New York: Knopf, 2005.

CRAFTS

Bumblebee Hive

MATERIALS: 1 coloring sheet with a picture of a hive on it (an excellent one can be found at http://www.coloring.ws/animals/hive.gif), rectangular yellow library processing stickers, rectangular black library processing stickers cut into strips, crayons

DIRECTIONS:
1. Place the yellow stickers on the page, then add black stripes to make bees.
2. Color as desired.

Stickers

MATERIALS: 2 circles of contact paper (about 5 inches in diameter) for each child, 1 circle of construction paper (about 4 inches in diameter) for each child, tape, scissors, crayons or markers

DIRECTIONS:
1. Decorate the construction paper as desired.
2. Place a loop of tape on top of one of the contact paper circles.
3. Press the construction paper to the tape, design side up.
4. Remove the backing from the second circle of contact paper.
5. Place the contact paper over the construction paper. If the edges don't line up, trim them with scissors once the top sheet of contact paper is in place. Press your fingers down all over the image to stick the contact paper on well.
6. To stick the sticker somewhere, remove the backing on the bottom sheet of contact paper.

Stories of Denise Fleming

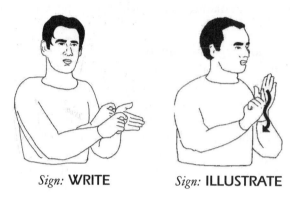

Sign: **WRITE**   *Sign:* **ILLUSTRATE**

 **BOOKS**

Alphabet Under Construction by Denise Fleming. New York: Henry Holt, 2002.

*Barnyard Banter by Denise Fleming. New York: Henry Holt, 1994.

Beetle Bop by Denise Fleming. New York: Henry Holt, 2007.

Buster by Denise Fleming. New York: Henry Holt, 2003.

Count by Denise Fleming. New York: Henry Holt, 1997.

The Cow Who Clucked by Denise Fleming. New York: Henry Holt, 2006.

The Everything Book by Denise Fleming. New York: Henry Holt, 2000.

The First Day of Winter by Denise Fleming. New York: Henry Holt, 2005.

*In the Small, Small Pond by Denise Fleming. New York: Henry Holt, 1993.

*In the Tall, Tall Grass by Denise Fleming. New York: Henry Holt, 1991.

*Lunch by Denise Fleming. New York: Henry Holt, 1998.

*Mama Cat Has Three Kittens by Denise Fleming. New York: Henry Holt, 1998.

*Pumpkin Eye by Denise Fleming. New York: Henry Holt, 2001.

*Time to Sleep by Denise Fleming. New York: Henry Holt, 1997.

Where Once There Was a Wood by Denise Fleming. New York: Henry Holt, 1996.

RECORDED MUSIC

*"Old MacDonald" from *More Playgroup Favorites* by Mommy & Me. Concord, 2004.

*"Jumping and Counting" from *Jim Gill's Irrational Anthem and More Salutes to Nonsense* by Jim Gill. Jim Gill Music, 2001.

"Three Little Kittens" from *Three Little Kittens.* Kimbo Educational, 2002.

*"I Love My Rooster" from *Whaddaya Think of That?* by Laurie Berkner. Two Tomatoes, 2001.

FINGERPLAYS/SONGS

"In a Cabin, In a Wood"
(traditional)

In a cabin, in a wood, *(form a roof with your hands)*
Little man by the window stood. *(hold pretend binoculars up to your eyes)*
Saw a rabbit hopping by, *(use 2 fingers in a V and hop them along)*
Knocking at the door. *(pretend to knock)*
"Help me! Help me! Help!" it said,
"Before the hunter shoots me dead." *(throw your hands up in the air and look scared)*
"Come little rabbit, come inside, safely you'll abide." *(motion for the rabbit to come inside and pretend to gently rock it)*

"Lunchtime"

Lunchtime is my favorite time
Because I like to eat!
I eat some apples and some crackers
And drink some juice so sweet.

"Here Is a Nest for Robin"
(traditional)

Here's a nest for robin, *(cup hands)*
Here's a hive for bee, *(place fingers together)*
Here's a hole for rabbit, *(fingers together to form hole)*
And here's a house for me. *(interlock fingers to make house)*

"In the Forest"

In the forest, day after day,
See the little animals play.
Birds fly, bunnies hop,
Squirrels climb without a stop.
Beaver slaps water with his tail,
Deer run in the dale.
Nighttime comes and owls say "Whooo."
Good night forest, good night to you.

PROPS

*Flannelboard Song

"Rooster Feathers"
(to the tune of "Do You Know the Muffin Man?")

PIECES NEEDED: *rooster body, enough feathers in various colors for each child to hold one*

Oh, do you have a red feather, red feather, red feather?
Oh, if you have a red feather, bring that feather up here.

Repeat with other colors, inviting the children to place their feathers on the rooster when you call their colors.

*Puppet Song

"When Ducks Get Up in the Morning"
(traditional)

PIECES NEEDED: *ducks, pigs, cows, other animals*

When ducks get up in the morning, they always say good day.
When ducks get up in the morning, they always say good day.
"Quack, quack, quack, quack." That is what they say, they say.
"Quack, quack, quack, quack." That is what they say.

Repeat with other animals.

*Flannelboard Song

"Three Little Kittens"

PIECES NEEDED: *3 kittens, mama cat, 3 sets of mittens, pie*

3 little kittens, they lost their mittens,
And they began to cry.
"Oh, mother dear, we sadly fear
Our mittens we have lost."
"What? Lost your mittens, you naughty
kittens!
Then you shall have no pie!"
Meow, meow, meow, meow.

3 little kittens, they found their mittens,
And they began to cry.
"Oh, mother dear, see here, see here,
Our mittens we have found."
"What? Found your mittens, you lovely
kittens!
Then you shall have some pie!"
Meow, meow, meow, meow.

*Flannelboard Song

"Alphabet Sounds"

(to the tune of "As I Was Walking to Town One Day" from *The Baby Record* by Bob McGrath and Katharine Smithram, Bob's Kids Music, 2000)

PIECES NEEDED: *letters of the alphabet. If desired, pass out the letters to the children before singing the song. Invite the children to identify the correct letters during the song and place them on the flannelboard.*

While I was walking to school one day, I
met a "D" along the way.
And what do you think that "D" did say?
"Da, da da."

*Flannelboard or Stick Puppet Story   *In the Small, Small Pond* by Denise Fleming. New York: Henry Holt, 1993.

> **PIECES NEEDED:** *tadpoles, frog, geese, dragonfly, turtle, heron, minnows, waterbugs, swallows, crawfish, ducks, raccoon, muskrats*

*Flannelboard Story   *Time to Sleep* by Denise Fleming. New York: Henry Holt, 1997.

> **PIECES NEEDED:** *bear, snail, skunk, turtle, woodchuck, ladybug*

ADDITIONAL SUGGESTIONS

Denise Fleming's Illustrations

Use information from the author's website (www.denisefleming.com) to share information about Fleming's unique pulp painting method.

CRAFTS

Denise Fleming's Website: www.denisefleming.com

Check out this site for lots of wonderful craft suggestions relating to Denise Fleming's books. The selection includes printable coloring sheets, activity sheets, and full instructions and templates for all the crafts.

Storytime Classics

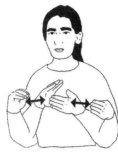

Sign: **STORY**

BOOKS

Madeline by Ludwig Bemelmens. New York: Viking, 1939.

*Goodnight Moon by Margaret Wise Brown. New York: Harper and Row, 1947.

Mike Mulligan and His Steam Shovel by Virginia Lee Burton. New York: Houghton Mifflin, 1967.

*The Very Hungry Caterpillar by Eric Carle. New York: Philomel, 1969.

Strega Nona by Tomie dePaola. New York: Simon and Schuster, 1975.

*Corduroy by Don Freeman. New York: Viking, 1968.

Millions of Cats by Wanda Gág. New York: Coward-McCann, 1928.

Harold and the Purple Crayon by Crockett Johnson. New York: HarperCollins, 1955.

*The Snowy Day by Ezra Jack Keats. New York: Viking, 1968.

The Story of Ferdinand by Munro Leaf. New York: Viking, 1936.

Make Way for Ducklings by Robert McCloskey. New York: Viking, 1941.

The Day Jimmy's Boa Ate the Wash by Trinka Hakes Noble. New York: Dial, 1980.

*If You Give a Mouse a Cookie by Laura Numeroff. New York: HarperCollins, 1985.

*The Little Engine That Could by Watty Piper. New York: Platt and Munk, 1930.

Curious George by H. A. Rey. New York: Houghton Mifflin, 1973.

Where the Wild Things Are by Maurice Sendak. New York: HarperCollins, 1963.

Caps for Sale by Esphyr Slobodkina. New York: Harper and Row, 1968.

Dr. DeSoto by William Steig. New York: Farrar, Straus and Giroux, 1982.

*The Itsy Bitsy Spider by Iza Trapani. Watertown, MA: Charlesbridge, 1993.

A Chair for My Mother by Vera B. Williams. New York: Greenwillow, 1982.

*The Little Mouse, the Red Ripe Strawberry, and the Big Hungry Bear by Don and Audrey Wood. New York: Scholastic, 1984.

RECORDED MUSIC

*"I'm a Little Teapot" from *Early Childhood Classics: Old Favorites with a New Twist* by Hap Palmer. Hap-Pal Music, Inc., 2000.

*"Nursery Rhyme Tap" from *Leaping Literacy* by Dr. Pam Schiller. Kimbo Educational, 2005. *(use with rhythm sticks)*

*"The Eensy Weensy Spider" from *Mainly Mother Goose* by Sharon, Lois, and Bram. Elephant Records, 1984.

"She'll Be Comin' 'Round the Mountain" from *One Elephant Went Out to Play* by Sharon, Lois, and Bram. A&M, 1978.

*"Where Is Thumbkin?" from *Preschool Action Time* by Carol Hammett. Kimbo Educational, 1988.

"Skip to My Lou" from *We All Live Together, Volume 1* by Greg and Steve. Youngheart Music Education, 1975.

FINGERPLAYS/SONGS

*"Teddy Bear, Teddy Bear"
(traditional)

Teddy Bear, Teddy Bear, turn around.
Teddy Bear, Teddy Bear, touch the
    ground.
Teddy Bear, Teddy Bear, show your shoe.
Teddy Bear, Teddy Bear, that will do.
Teddy Bear, Teddy Bear, go upstairs.
Teddy Bear, Teddy Bear, say your prayers.
Teddy Bear, Teddy Bear, turn out
    the light.
Teddy Bear, Teddy Bear, say good night.

*"I Have Ten Little Fingers"
(traditional)

I have 10 little fingers.
They all belong to me.
I can make them do things.
Would you like to see?
I can close them up tight.
I can open them wide.
I can hold them up high.
I can put them by my side.
I can wave them to and fro.
I can lay them in my lap just so.

*"Open, Shut Them"
(traditional)

Open, shut them,
Open, shut them,
Give a little clap, clap, clap.
Open, shut them,
Open, shut them,
Lay them in your lap, lap, lap.
Creep them, creep them,
Creep them, creep them,
Right up to your chin.
Open wide your little mouth,
But do not let them in!

*"The More We Get Together"
(traditional)

The more we get together, together,
    together,
The more we get together, the happier
    we'll be.
'Cause your friends are my friends
And my friends are your friends.
The more we get together, the happier
    we'll be.
The more we play together . . .
The more we read together . . .
The more we sing together . . .

*"Charlie over the Water"
(traditional)

Charlie over the water,
Charlie over the sea,
Charlie catch a blackbird,
But you can't catch me!

Repeat with children's names.

*"Hands on Shoulders"
(traditional)

Hands on shoulders, hands on knees,
Hands behind you, if you please.
Touch your shoulders, touch your nose,
Touch your head and touch your toes.
Put your hands up in the air,
Now at your sides, now touch your hair.
Hands up high just like before,
Now clap those hands: 1, 2, 3, 4!

*"Head, Shoulders, Knees and Toes"
(adapted traditional)

Head, shoulders, knees and toes, knees
   and toes.
Head, shoulders, knees and toes, knees
   and toes.
Eyes and ears and mouth and nose.
Head, shoulders, knees and toes, knees
   and toes.
Shake your head, shoulders, knees and
   toes, knees and toes . . .
Tickle your head, shoulders, knees and
   toes, knees and toes . . .

PROPS

*Flannelboard Song

"BINGO"

PIECES NEEDED: *large felt shapes for the letters
of Bingo's name. Remove each letter as the song
progresses.*

There was a farmer, had a dog,
And Bingo was his name, oh.
B-I-N-G-O, B-I-N-G-O, B-I-N-G-O,
And Bingo was his name, oh.

*Repeat, gradually replacing each letter with
a clap.*

*Flannelboard Rhyme

"Baa Baa [Color] Sheep"

PIECES NEEDED: *sheep shapes in a variety of
colors, enough for each child to hold one*

Baa Baa Black Sheep, have you any wool?
Yes sir, yes sir, three bags full.
One for my master, one for the dame,
One for the little boy who lives down
   the lane.

*Repeat with various colors and invite the
children to place their sheep on the flannelboard
as you call their color.*

*Flannelboard Story   *The Napping House* by Audrey Wood. New York: Harcourt Brace,
1984.

PIECES NEEDED: *bed, house, granny, child, dog, cat, mouse, flea*

*Flannelboard Story   *The Very Hungry Caterpillar* by Eric Carle. New York: Philomel,
1969.

*Flannelboard patterns can be found in 2's Experience Felt Board Fun by Liz and Dick
Wilmes (Elgin, IL: Building Blocks, 1994).*

*Flannelboard Story   *Caps for Sale* by Esphyr Slobodkina. New York: Harper and Row, 1968.

Pieces needed: *peddler; monkeys; large tree; 1 checkered cap for peddler; caps in blue, red, gray, and brown*

*Flannelboard Story   *Brown Bear, Brown Bear, What Do You See?* by Bill Martin Jr. New York: Holt, Rinehart, and Winston, 1983.

Pieces needed: *brown bear, red bird, yellow duck, blue horse, green frog, purple cat, white dog, black sheep, goldfish, teacher*

Crafts

Bookmarks

Materials: 1 precut strip of cardstock (6 by 2 inches) for each child, hole punch, 1 8-inch strip of ribbon for each child, crayons or markers, stickers

Directions:
1. Decorate your bookmark with stickers, crayons, etc.
2. Punch a hole on the top, about ½ inch from the edge.
3. Fold the ribbon in half, and push the folded end through the hole. Push the loose ends through the loop formed by the folded end, and pull them tight.

Sheep Shapes

Materials: sheep shapes cut from posterboard, cotton balls, glue, crayons

Directions:
1. Glue the cotton balls onto the sheep to form the wool.
2. Decorate as desired.

Summer Fun

Sign: **SUMMER**

BOOKS

Watermelon Day by Kathi Appelt. New York: Henry Holt, 1996.

Sand Cake by Frank Asch. Strongsville, OH: Gareth Stevens, 1978.

Grandma's Beach by Rosalind Beardshaw. New York: Bloomsbury, 2001.

Maisy Makes Lemonade by Lucy Cousins. Cambridge, MA: Candlewick, 2002.

Maisy's Pool by Lucy Cousins. Cambridge, MA: Candlewick, 1999.

One Hot Summer Day by Nina Crews. New York: Greenwillow, 1995.

A Summer Day by Douglas Florian. New York: Greenwillow, 1988.

Summer Beat by Betsy Franco. New York: Simon and Schuster, 2007.

Sea, Sand, Me! by Patricia Hubbell. New York: HarperCollins, 2001.

Kipper's Sunny Day by Mick Inkpen. San Diego: Harcourt, 1991.

At the Beach by Huy Voun Lee. New York: Henry Holt, 1994.

When the Fireflies Come by Jonathan London. New York: Dutton, 2003.

How Will We Get to the Beach? by Brigitte Luciani. New York: North-South, 2000.

Splash! by Flora McDonnell. Cambridge, MA: Candlewick, 1999.

Watermelon Wishes by Lisa Moser. New York: Clarion, 2006.

Senses at the Seashore by Shelley Rotner. Brookfield, CT: Millbrook Press, 2006.

Minerva Louise at the Fair by Janet Morgan Stoeke. New York: Dutton, 2000.

Ten Flashing Fireflies by Philemon Sturges. New York: North-South, 1995.

Mouse's First Summer by Lauren Thompson. New York: Simon and Schuster, 2004.

RECORDED MUSIC

"Going on a Picnic" from *The Corner Grocery Store* by Raffi. Rounder/UMGD, 1979.

"Firefly" from *Makin' Music: Come Outside to Play.* Makin' Music Rockin' Rhythms, 2002.

*"Swimmy Swim" from *Sing a Song of Seasons* by Rachel Buchman. Rounder Kids, 1997.

*"Having Fun at the Beach" from *Splish Splash Big Red Boat* by The Wiggles. HIT Entertainment, 2006.

"Let's Go Swimming" from *Top of the Tots* by The Wiggles. HIT Entertainment, 2004.

*"A Walking We Will Go" from *We All Live Together, Volume 5* by Greg and Steve. Youngheart, 1994.

FINGERPLAYS/SONGS

"Watermelon, Watermelon"

Watermelon, watermelon, big and round.
Watermelon, watermelon, touch the
    ground.
Watermelon, watermelon, pink and
    yummy.
Watermelon, watermelon in my tummy.

"I'm a Little Firefly"
(to the tune of "I'm a Little Teapot")

I'm a little firefly,
On a summer night.
I light up my tail and I flash so bright.
When it's dark I stay and play.
Sun comes up, I fly away.

"I Took a Walk on the Beach"
(to the tune of "I Took a Walk
to Town One Day")

I took a walk on the beach one day
And met a crab along the way.
And what do you think that crab did say?
    SNIP SNIP.
. . . fish . . . GLUG GLUG
. . . seagull . . . AWK AWK

"This Is the Way"
(to the tune of "Here We Go 'Round the
Mulberry Bush")

This is the way we dig in the sand, dig in
    the sand, dig in the sand.
This is the way we dig in the sand when
    we're at the beach.
This is the way we splash in the ocean . . .
This is the way we put on our
    sunscreen . . .
This is the way we brush off the sand . . .

"Vacation Rhyme"

I am going on vacation.
It's so much fun to do.
I'm going with my family.
And you can come too.
First we pack our suitcase.
Then we get in the car.
We always say, "Are we there yet?"
Because it seems so far.
But finally we do arrive.
We get out of the car.
We hug our friends and family.
Oh! How happy we are!

"Chocolate Ice Cream Cone"
(to the tune of "Baby Bumblebee")

I'm bringing home a chocolate ice cream cone.
I'm so glad I've got my very own.
I'm bringing home a chocolate ice cream cone.
MMMM! Yummy!

I'm licking up my chocolate ice cream cone.
I'm so glad I've got my very own.
I'm licking up my chocolate ice cream cone.
Brain freeze! OW!

I'm crunching up my chocolate ice cream cone.
I'm so glad I've got my very own.
I'm crunching up my chocolate ice cream cone.
Now it's all over my hands!

I'm cleaning up my chocolate ice cream cone.
I'm so glad I had my very own.
I'm cleaning up my chocolate ice cream cone.
All gone!

PROPS

*Flannelboard Rhyme

"Five Beach Umbrellas"

PIECES NEEDED: *5 beach umbrellas in blue, red, yellow, green, and purple*

I went to the beach and sat under the sun.
I put up my blue umbrella, and that was number 1.
My sister came along, she brought an umbrella too.
She set up her red umbrella, and that was number 2.
My brother came next, he called and waved to me.
And he set up a yellow umbrella, and that was number 3.
My mother finally got there, now we only need one more.
She set up a green umbrella, and that was number 4.
At last my father came, the last one to arrive.
He set up a purple umbrella, and that was number 5.

*Prop Story: "Going on a Picnic"

PIECES NEEDED: *picnic basket, teddy bear, picnic blanket, plastic plates and utensils, fake food, ant puppet*

I am going on a picnic with my bear. Would you like to come? I have everything we need right here in my basket. First we'll put down our blanket.

Take out items one by one and discuss the purpose of each. Invite the children to tell you their favorite picnic foods. Pull out the ant last.

Hey, who invited him?

*Stick Puppet Story   *The Twelve Days of Summer* by Elizabeth Lee O'Donnell. New York: Morrow, 1991.

PIECES NEEDED: *1 purple sea anemone, 2 pelicans, 3 jellyfish, 4 sandpipers, 5 flying fish, 6 squid, 7 starfish, 8 crabs, 9 seals, 10 dolphins, 11 waves, 12 gulls*

CRAFTS

Sand Art

MATERIALS: coloring sheets depicting summer scenes, school glue, paintbrushes, sand in various colors, empty bowls. (To decrease mess, place the sand in condiment bottles.)

DIRECTIONS:
1. Paint each area of the picture with a thick layer of glue.
2. Spread the desired color of sand over the area.
3. Slide the excess sand into an empty bowl.

Rising Sun Pop-Up Cup

MATERIALS: 1 Styrofoam or paper cup with a hole poked in the bottom for each child, 1 craft stick for each child, glue, 1 precut sun shape for each child, crayons or markers

DIRECTIONS:
1. Decorate the sun as desired.
2. Glue the sun to the craft stick.
3. Place the sun in the cup so that the stick goes through the hole in the bottom. Move the stick to make the sun rise.

Super Sign Language

Sign: **I LOVE YOU**

BOOKS

Handtalk Zoo by George Ancona and Mary Beth Miller. New York: Four Winds Press, 1989.

*Signs for Me: Basic Sign Vocabulary for Children, Parents, and Teachers by Ben Bahan and Joe Dannis. San Diego: DawnSign Press, 1990. *(use this book to learn the signs listed in the songs and fingerplays below)*

I Can Sign My ABCs by Susan Gibbons Chaplin. Washington, DC: Gallaudet University Press, 1986.

Handtalk Birthday: A Number and Story Book in Sign Language by Remy Charlip, Mary Beth, and George Ancona. New York: Four Winds Press, 1987.

Handsigns: A Sign Language Alphabet by Kathleen Fain. New York: Chronicle, 1993.

Victory Week by Walter P. Kelley. Rochester, NY: Deaf Life Press, 1998.

Dad and Me in the Morning by Patricia Lakin. New York: Whitman, 1994.

*Beyond Words: Great Stories for Hands and Voice by Valerie Marsh and Patrick K. Luzadder. Fort Atkinson, WI: Alleyside Press, 1995.

Handtalk School by Mary Beth Miller and George Ancona. New York: Four Winds Press, 1991.

Moses Goes to a Concert by Isaac Millman. New York: Farrar, Straus and Giroux, 1998.

Moses Goes to School by Isaac Millman. New York: Farrar, Straus and Giroux, 2000.

*Moses Goes to the Circus by Isaac Millman. New York: Farrar, Straus and Giroux, 2003.

Moses Sees a Play by Isaac Millman. New York: Farrar, Straus and Giroux, 2004.

The Handmade Alphabet by Laura Rankin. New York: Dial, 1991.

Secret Signs: Along the Underground Railroad by Anita Riggio. Honesdale, PA: Boyds Mills Press, 1997.

The Best Worst Brother by Stephanie Stuve-Bodeen. Bethesda, MD: Woodbine House, 2005.

The Printer by Myron Uhlberg. Atlanta, GA: Peachtree, 2003.

*More Simple Signs by Cindy Wheeler. New York: Viking, 1998.

*Simple Signs by Cindy Wheeler. New York: Puffin, 1995.

RECORDED MUSIC

"Magic Words," "Look at My Hands," and "Silly Pizza Song" from *Signing Time Songs, Volumes 1–3* by Rachel de Azevedo Coleman. Two Little Hands Productions, 2002.

CD-ROM

American Sign Language Clip and Create 4. Institute for Disabilities Research and Training (www.idrt.com), 2003. *(This program contains a vast dictionary of ASL sign clip art, as well as templates for games and activities to use with the signs.)*

FINGERPLAYS/SONGS

Sign the words in capital letters.

"Sign to Me"

You sign to me,
and I'll sign to you.
When we talk to each other,
there's so much we can do.
We can say HELLO!
We can say I LOVE YOU!
We can say to each other
You're my FRIEND too!

"Let's All Do Sign Language"
(to the tune of "Mary Had a Little Lamb")

Let's all do some sign language,
Sign language, sign language.
Let's all do some sign language.
We'll use our hands to talk.

"Friends"
(to the tune of "Row, Row, Row Your Boat")

Here's the sign for "YOU,"
Here's the sign for "ME."
I hook my fingers together like this,
'Cause "FRIENDS" we'll always be!

"If You're Happy and You Know It"
(adapted traditional)

In American Sign Language, what we do with our faces is just as important as what we do with our hands.

If you're happy and you know it, make a
    happy face.
If you're happy and you know it, make a
    happy face.
If you're happy and you know it, then
    your face will surely show it.
If you're happy and you know it, make a
    happy face.
If you're sad . . .
If you're scared . . .
If you're angry . . .
If you're excited . . .

"The More We SIGN Together"

The more we get TOGETHER, TOGETHER, TOGETHER,
The more we get TOGETHER, the HAPPIER we'll be.
'Cause your FRIENDS are my FRIENDS
And my FRIENDS are your FRIENDS.
The more we get TOGETHER, the HAPPIER we'll be.

The more we SIGN TOGETHER, TOGETHER, TOGETHER,
The more we SIGN TOGETHER, the HAPPIER we'll be.
'Cause your FRIENDS are my FRIENDS
And my FRIENDS are your FRIENDS.
The more we SIGN TOGETHER, the HAPPIER we'll be.

PROPS

*Stick Puppet Rhyme

"Hands Can"

PIECES NEEDED: *4 large hands cut out of posterboard. Attach each hand to a paint stirrer. Leave hands #1 and #2 as they are. On hand #3, glue down the thumb, middle, ring, and pinky fingers. On hand #4, glue down the middle and ring fingers.*

Hands can say STOP. *(hold up hand #1)*
Hands can say GO. *(wave #1 toward you)*
Hands can say SHHH. *(hold #3 to your lips)*
Hands can wave to and fro. *(wave #1 and #2 above your head)*
But of all the things that hands can do,
The best is when they say I LOVE YOU. *(hold up #4)*

*Prop Story: "Katie's Toys"

PIECES NEEDED: *large bag containing a doll, a toy car, a ball, a teddy bear, a train, a drum, a duck, and a book. Show signs for the toys as you pull them from the bag.*

Katie has a bag with all of her favorite toys in it. Katie likes her DOLL best of all . . . except for her CAR. Then when she sees her BALL, she thinks that might be her favorite. Yes, she likes her BALL better than anything . . . except her BEAR. But maybe the TRAIN is really her favorite. Oh, look, it's Katie's DRUM! She likes that the best. Except for her DUCK. Yes, the DUCK is her favorite, except for her BOOK. Katie likes her BOOK better than anything in the whole world, except for her MOMMY and DADDY!

Flannelboard Song   "Silly Pizza Song" from *Signing Time Songs, Volumes 1–3* by Rachel de Azevedo Coleman. Two Little Hands Productions, 2002.

PIECES NEEDED: *pizza crust, apple, cracker, ice cream, cereal, bread, cookies, banana, candy*

ADDITIONAL SUGGESTIONS

Website

For a 3-D way to learn the signs needed above, check out the ASL video dictionary at www.aslpro.com.

Dramatic Play

After reading *Moses Sees a Play* by Isaac Millman (New York: Farrar, Straus and Giroux, 2004), act out a favorite fairy tale such as "Little Red Riding Hood." Have the children act out Red Riding Hood packing her basket and walking through the woods, the wolf talking to her and putting on grandmother's clothes, and so on.

CRAFTS

I LOVE YOU Sign Language Stick Puppets

MATERIALS: 1 piece of construction paper for each child, scissors, craft sticks, glue, decorating materials

DIRECTIONS:
1. Have each child trace his or her hand onto construction paper and cut out the shape. (You may wish to provide precut handshapes instead.)
2. Have the children fold down and glue the middle and ring fingers to make the ILY sign.
3. Attach a craft stick and decorate.

Handmade Letters

MATERIALS: large printouts of letters from the American Sign Language manual alphabet (search the Internet for "Gallaudet font," a free download, to easily print out large handshapes for each letter from your word processing program), crayons

DIRECTIONS: Give each child a sheet with the handshape for the first letter of his or her name on it. Invite the children to draw other items on the page that start with that letter. If desired, you can point out the pictures in *The Handmade Alphabet* by Laura Rankin (New York: Dial, 1991) for inspiration.

Surprise!

Sign: **SURPRISE**

BOOKS

Duckie's Rainbow by Frances Barry. Cambridge, MA: Candlewick, 2004.

Hedgie's Surprise by Jan Brett. New York: G. P. Putnam's Sons, 2000.

Hoppity Skip Little Chick by Jo Brown. Wilton, CT: Tiger Tales, 2004.

A Dark Dark Tale by Ruth Brown. New York: Puffin, 1981.

The Secret Birthday Message by Eric Carle. New York: HarperCollins, 1972.

Peek-a-Moo! By Marie Torres Cimarusti. New York: Dutton, 1998.

Mrs. Hen's Big Surprise by Christel Desmoinaux. New York: Simon and Schuster, 2000.

Watch Out! by Jan Fearnley. Cambridge, MA: Candlewick, 2004.

Flora's Surprise! by Debi Gliori. New York: Orchard, 2002.

Animal Surprise! by Christopher Gunson. New York: Transworld, 2002.

The Surprise Garden by Zoe Hall. New York: Scholastic, 1998.

The Surprise Party by Pat Hutchins. New York: Aladdin, 1969.

Boomer's Big Surprise by Constance W. McGeorge. San Francisco: Chronicle, 1999.

Let's Do That Again! by Hiawyn Oram. New York: Dutton, 2001.

A Surprise for Rosie by Julia Rawlinson. Wilton, CT: Tiger Tales, 2005.

Three Kind Mice by Vivian Sathre. San Diego: Harcourt Brace, 1997.

The Surprise by George Shannon. New York: Greenwillow, 1983.

Grandma Rabbitty's Visit by Barry Smith. New York: DK, 1999.

Happy Birthday, Dotty! by Tim Warnes. Wilton, CT: Tiger Tales, 2003.

Claude's Big Surprise by David Wojtowycz. New York: Dutton, 2001.

RECORDED MUSIC

*"If You're Surprised and You Know It" from *Start Smart Songs for 1's, 2's, and 3's* by Dr. Pam Schiller. Kimbo Educational, 2006.

FINGERPLAYS/SONGS

"Jack-in-the-Box"

Pop up! Big surprise!
Jack appears before my eyes.
Hunch down, back inside.
Now it's time for Jack to hide.

"Egg Surprise"

I am a little egg.
I have a secret I hide.
I have a big surprise
Right inside.
When the time is right
You'll hear a tap tap tap
And a baby chick will pop out
Just like that!

"Everyone Forgot"

It's my birthday today
But I am pretending it's not,
Because it's my birthday today
And everyone forgot.
No one said, "Happy Birthday!"
When I woke up today.
They just said "Good Morning"
And went on their way.
Wait—what's this I see before my eyes?
Cake, balloons, and streamers? A party!
    SURPRISE!

*"Caterpillar, Caterpillar"

Caterpillar, caterpillar, turn around.
Caterpillar, caterpillar, on the ground.
Caterpillar, caterpillar, climb up high.
Soon you'll be a butterfly!
Surprise!

*"Peek-a-boo Game"

1, 2, 3,
You can't see me!
4, 5, 6,
I'm playing tricks.
7, 8, 9,
This game is fine!
Peek-a-boo!

"Yes, I Will"
(traditional)

Jack-in-the box sits so still. (*hunch down*)
Won't you come out?
Yes, I will. (*jump up*)

"Wrap the Presents"
(to the tune of "Row, Row, Row Your Boat")

Wrap, wrap, wrap the presents,
Wrapping all day long.
We are wrapping birthday presents
To surprise our mom.

Props

*Flannelboard Song

"Counting Candles"
(to the tune of "Happy Birthday")

PIECES NEEDED: *cake with 5 candles, separate flame piece for each candle*

How many candles on the cake?
How many candles on the cake?
I wish you could tell me
How many candles on the cake?
1 candle on the cake . . .

Repeat with higher numbers.

Now let's make a wish.
Now let's make a wish.
We'll blow out the candlestick
And then make a wish.
Blow out 1 candle, *(remove flames as the candles go out)*
Blow out 2 candles,
Blow out 3 and 4 candles,
And now number 5. *(leave 5th flame in place)*
Oh no! It won't go out. We have to blow harder! Good job!

*Prop Story: "The Present"

PIECES NEEDED: *small note that says "I love you!"; 6–7 boxes of progressively larger sizes, sized so that each box can fit into the next largest. As you tell the story, open each box in turn.*

My mom gave me this present. She says it's got the best thing in the world in it. I wonder what it will be. Maybe a train set! Or a new doll. What do you think it is?

Invite children to speculate, then open first box.

It's another box inside! It looks too small to be a train set. What could be in this box?

Continue pattern, opening the boxes as they get smaller and smaller.

Well, this box is so small, I wonder what could be inside? My mom said it's the best thing in the world.

Open box.

It's a note that says "I love you!" Mom was right! Love *is* the best thing in the world, better than any present!

*Magnetboard Story: "What Present Is This?"

PIECES NEEDED: *ball, bear, car, frog wearing a hat. Laminate a piece of wrapping paper in the exact shape and size of each piece and place magnets on the back so that the wrapping paper can be put over the shapes on the magnetboard.*

I am opening my birthday presents. Would you like to help? What do you think this shape is? Let's see . . . it's a bear! Wow!

Repeat with other shapes, saving the frog for last.

*Prop Story   *Wrapping Paper Romp* by Patricia Hubbell. New York: HarperFestival, 1998.

PIECES NEEDED: *wrapped box containing tissue paper and 3 teddy bears, piece of wrapping paper and tissue paper for each child*

*Prop Story   *Old Bear's Surprise Painting* by Jane Hissey. New York: Philomel, 2001.

PIECES NEEDED: *overhead projector, transparencies, transparency film markers. Draw the various patterns in the book, each on its own transparency, then put the films together at the end to show the completed design.*

 # CRAFTS

Clown Pop-Up Cup

MATERIALS: 1 Styrofoam or paper cup with a hole poked in the bottom for each child, 1 craft stick for each child, glue, 1 precut picture of a clown for each child, crayons or markers

DIRECTIONS:
1. Color the clown.
2. Glue the clown to the craft stick.
3. Place the clown in the cup so that the stick goes through the hole in the bottom. Move the stick to make the clown pop up for a surprise.

Birthday Candles Picture

MATERIALS: 1 coloring sheet of a cake for each child, candles cut from various colors of construction paper, glue, crayons, decorating materials

DIRECTIONS:
1. Glue the candles onto the cake.
2. Draw in flames and decorate as desired.

Sweet Tooth

Sign: **SWEET**

BOOKS

Cocoa Ice by Diana Appelbaum. New York: Orchard, 1997.

*The Chocolate-Covered-Cookie Tantrum by Deborah Blumenthal. New York: Clarion, 1996.

*Maisy Makes Gingerbread by Lucy Cousins. Cambridge, MA: Candlewick, 1999.

*The Doorbell Rang by Pat Hutchins. New York: Greenwillow, 1986.

Chocolatina by Erik Kraft. Cambridge, MA: BridgeWater Books, 1998.

The Candystore Man by Jonathan London. New York: Lothrop, Lee, and Shepard, 1999.

Chocolate: A Sweet History by Sandra Markle. New York: Grosset and Dunlap, 2005.

Princess Chamomile Gets Her Way by Hiawyn Oram. New York: Dutton, 1999.

The Sweet Tooth by Margie Palatini. New York: Simon and Schuster, 2004.

*Curious George Goes to a Chocolate Factory by Margret and H. A. Rey. New York: Houghton Mifflin, 1998.

The Last Chocolate Cookie by Jamie Rix. Cambridge, MA: Candlewick, 1997.

Lucky Pennies and Hot Chocolate by Carol Diggory Shields. New York: Dutton, 2000.

*Chocolate Chip Cookies by Karen Wagner. New York: Henry Holt, 1990.

*Mr. Cookie Baker by Monica Wellington. New York: Dutton, 2006.

*Max's Chocolate Chicken by Rosemary Wells. New York: Puffin, 1989.

RECORDED MUSIC

**"Ice Cream Cone" and "Rum Sum Sum" from *Buzz Buzz* by Laurie Berkner. Two Tomatoes, 2001.

"Hot Chocolate" from *Wintersongs* by John McCutcheon. Rounder, 1995. *(use with scarves)*

**"Brush Your Teeth" from *Singable Songs for the Very Young* by Raffi. Rounder/UMGD, 1976.

FINGERPLAYS/SONGS

"Lollipop"

My lollipop is delicious, it's true.
It is turning my tongue bright blue.
I lick and I lick till my lolly's all gone.
Now my hands are all sticky. MOM!

"Who Stole the Cookies from the Cookie Jar?"
(traditional)

Who stole the cookies from the cookie
    jar?
Who, me? Yes, you!
Can't be! Then who?
_____ stole the cookies from the
    cookie jar!
Who, me? Yes, you!
Can't be! Then who?

Repeat until all children's names have been used. For a funny ending, use your name last, and when you say "Can't be!" pull real or fake cookies out of your pockets.

"Sticky, Sticky Bubblegum"
(traditional)

Sticky sticky sticky bubblegum,
Bubblegum, bubblegum.
Sticky sticky sticky bubblegum,
Sticking my hand to my knee.
Pull it off!

Repeat, sticking other body parts together.

"Melting Ice Cream"
(to the tune of "Frère Jacques")

Licking my ice cream, licking my ice
    cream.
It can't wait. It can't wait.
I don't want it to melt. I don't want it
    to melt.
Oops! Too late. Oops! Too late.

"Ate a Cookie"
(to the tune of "Ate a Peanut")

Ate a cookie, ate a cookie,
Ate a cookie just now.
Just now I ate a cookie, ate a cookie
    just now.

I ate another one, ate another one,
Ate another one just now.
Just now I ate another one, ate another
    one just now.

Got a tummyache, got a tummyache,
Got a tummyache just now.
Just now I got a tummyache, got a
    tummyache just now.

"Sweet Treat"

My brother loves to eat candy
But I don't give a hoot
Because my favorite treat to eat
Is sweet and yummy fruit!

PROPS

*Flannelboard Rhyme

"Five Pieces of Candy"

PIECES NEEDED: *5 pieces of candy*

5 pieces of candy at the store.
I bought one for my mother, and then there were 4.
4 pieces of candy, yummy as can be.
I bought one for my father, and then there were 3.
3 pieces of candy and I knew what to do.
I bought one for my sister, and then there were 2.
2 pieces of candy are so much fun.
I bought one for my brother, and then there was 1.
1 piece of candy sitting all alone.
I bought that one for me, and I took the candy home.

*Prop Story   *Lilly's Chocolate Heart* by Kevin Henkes. New York: Greenwillow, 2004.
PIECE NEEDED: *chocolate heart*

*Prop Story   *The Doorbell Rang* by Pat Hutchins. New York: Greenwillow, 1986.
PIECES NEEDED: *12 cookies*

CRAFTS

Lollipop Circles

MATERIALS: 1 large circle (about 6 inches in diameter) cut from white posterboard for each child, crayons, glue, craft sticks

DIRECTIONS:
1. Color the entire circle using various light colors such as yellow, orange, and pink.
2. Cover the entire colored surface of the posterboard with dark red crayon.
3. Using a craft stick, etch away the red crayon in designs to show the lighter colors underneath.
4. Glue the circle to a craft stick to make it a "lollipop."

Tootsie Roll Sculptures

MATERIALS: Tootsie Rolls, sprinkles or other cake decorating materials, frosting

DIRECTIONS:
1. Rub the candy between your palms to make it warm and pliant, then mold it into whatever shape you like.
2. Use a dab of frosting to stick on sprinkles or other decorating materials for eyes, nose, and so on.

Trick or Treat

Sign: **HALLOWEEN**

📖 **BOOKS**

Clifford's First Halloween by Norman Bridwell. New York: Scholastic, 1995.

Happy Halloween, Biscuit! by Alyssa Satin Capucilli. New York: HarperCollins, 1999.

Here They Come! by David Costello. New York: Farrar, Straus and Giroux, 2004.

Trick-or-Treat, Smell My Feet! by Lisa Desimini. New York: Scholastic, 2005.

A Trick or a Treat? A Not-Too-Scary Window Surprise Book by Keith Faulkner. New York: Dutton, 2001.

Pumpkin Eye by Denise Fleming. New York: Henry Holt, 2001.

Halloween by Gail Gibbons. New York: Holiday House, 1984.

T. Rex Trick-or-Treats by Lois G. Grambling. New York: HarperCollins, 2005.

When the Goblins Came Knocking by Anna Grossnickle Hines. New York: Greenwillow, 1995.

The Halloween Queen by Joan Holub. Morton Grove, IL: Albert Whitman, 2004.

Trick or Treat Countdown by Patricia Hubbard. New York: Holiday House, 1999.

Froggy's Halloween by Jonathan London. New York: Viking, 1999.

Trick or Treat, It's Halloween! by Linda Lowery and Richard Keep. New York: Random House, 2000.

Who Will I Be? A Halloween Rebus Story by Shirley Neitzel. New York: Greenwillow, 2005.

Sweets and Treats by Toni Trent Parker. New York: Scholastic, 2002.

Halloween Mice! by Bethany Roberts. New York: Clarion, 1995.

Five Little Pumpkins by Iris Van Rynbach. Honesdale, PA: Boyds Mills Press, 1995.

Sheep Trick or Treat by Nancy Shaw. New York: Houghton Mifflin, 1997.

Pumpkin Day by Nancy Elizabeth Wallace. New York: Marshall Cavendish, 2002.

Monster, Monster by Melanie Walsh. Cambridge, MA: Candlewick, 2002.

What Is Halloween? by Harriet Ziefert. New York: HarperCollins, 1992.

RECORDED MUSIC

*"Ten Little Pumpkins" from *Preschool Action Time* by Carol Hammett. Kimbo Educational, 1988.

*"Five Little Pumpkins" from *Singable Songs for the Very Young* by Raffi. Rounder/UMGD, 1976.

"Ten Little Goblins" from *Toddlers on Parade* by Carol Hammett and Elaine Bueffel. Kimbo Educational, 1999.

*"Spooky Loo," "I'm a Pumpkin," and "Fly Little Bats" from *Wee Sing for Halloween* by Pamela Conn Beall and Susan Hagen Nipp. Price Stern Sloan, 2002.

FINGERPLAYS/SONGS

"Costume Guessing Game"

What will I be on Halloween night?
Listen to the clues and try to guess right.
I'll wear a red nose and jump up and
　　down.
In long shoes and a wig, I'll be a . . .
　　clown!

What will I be on Halloween night?
Listen to the clues and try to guess right.
I'll wear an eye patch and on my shoulder
　　a parrot.
With my peg leg, I will be a . . . pirate!

What will I be on Halloween night?
Listen to the clues and try to guess right.
I'll wear whiskers and ears and a tail
　　like that.
I'll say meow, because I'm a . . . cat!

"Pumpkin, Pumpkin"

Pumpkin, pumpkin, turn around.
Pumpkin, pumpkin, touch the ground.
Pumpkin, pumpkin, stomp your feet.
Pumpkin, pumpkin, trick or treat!

"Answering the Door"

Knock knock knock on the door.
Here come the trick-or-treaters, 1, 2, 3, 4.
Someone opens the door, and we say
　　"Trick or Treat!"
Isn't it amazing, all the creatures that
　　you meet?

"Black Cat"

The black cat sat on the fence
And arched her furry back.
She stretched out her claws
And gave a MEOW
And jumped down just like that.

"I Like Candy"

I like candy, yes I do.
I like candy, how about you?
When it goes into my bag, I know what
　　to do.
I give a big smile, and I say, "Thank you!"

PROPS

*Flannelboard Rhyme

"Five Little Pumpkins"
(traditional)

PIECES NEEDED: *5 pumpkins*

5 little pumpkins sitting on a gate.
The first one said, "Oh my, it's getting late."
The second one said, "There are witches in the air."
The third one said, "But we don't care."
The fourth one said, "Let's run and run and run."
The fifth one said, "I'm ready for some fun."
Then whoosh went the wind and out went the lights
And the 5 little pumpkins rolled out of sight!

*Flannelboard Story   *Julius's Candy Corn* by Kevin Henkes. New York: HarperCollins, 2003.

PIECES NEEDED: *Julius, 8 cupcakes, 8 candy corns*

*Flannelboard Story   *10 Trick-or-Treaters: A Halloween Counting Book* by Janet Schulman. New York: Knopf, 2005.

PIECES NEEDED: *10 children in costumes, spider, toad, bat, ghost, skeleton, witch, monster, vampire, mummy, bed*

CRAFTS

Pumpkin Treat Cartons

Instructions can be found on the DLTK Kids website: http://www.dltk-holidays.com/halloween/mpumpkincarton.htm.

Masquerade Masks

MATERIALS: 1 rounded rectangle about 6 inches by 3½ inches cut from black posterboard for each child, tongue depressors, glue, book processing stickers in various shapes, star stickers, various shapes cut from posterboard, masking tape

DIRECTIONS:
1. Precut eyeholes in the rectangle of black posterboard.
2. Decorate the mask using stickers and the various shapes. (Large white stickers, for example, could be white hair for a wizard, while a large triangle could be set atop the wizard's head for a hat and decorated with stars.)
3. Use the masking tape to attach the tongue depressor to one side of the mask for a handle.

Wearin' of the Green

Sign: **GREEN**

BOOKS

Fiona's Luck by Teresa Bateman. Watertown, MA: Charlesbridge, 2007.

Harp o' Gold by Teresa Bateman. New York: Holiday House, 2001.

*The Field of Buttercups by Alice Boden. New York: Henry Z. Walck, 1974.

St. Patrick's Day in the Morning by Eve Bunting. New York: Clarion, 1980.

Fin M'Coul: The Giant of Knockmany Hill by Tomie dePaola. New York: Holiday House, 1981.

Jamie O'Rourke and the Big Potato: An Irish Folktale by Tomie dePaola. New York: G. P. Putnam's Sons, 1992.

Jamie O'Rourke and the Pooka by Tomie dePaola. New York: G. P. Putnam's Sons, 2000.

The Leprechaun's Gold by Pamela Duncan Edwards. New York: HarperCollins, 2004.

King Puck by Michael Garland. New York: HarperCollins, 2007.

*St. Patrick's Day by Gail Gibbons. New York: Holiday House, 1994.

St. Patrick's Day by Brenda Haugen. Minneapolis: Picture Window Books, 2004.

Saint Patrick and the Peddler by Margaret Hodges. New York: Orchard Books, 1993.

The Last Snake in Ireland: A Story about St. Patrick by Sheila MacGill-Callahan. New York: Holiday House, 1999.

Tim O'Toole and the Wee Folk by Gerald McDermott. New York: Viking, 1990.

The St. Patrick's Day Shillelagh by Janet Nolan. Morton Grove, IL: Albert Whitman, 2002.

*Clever Tom and the Leprechaun by Linda Shute. New York: Lothrop, Lee, and Shepard, 1988.

A Fine St. Patrick's Day by Susan Wojciechowski. New York: Random House, 2004.

*St. Patrick's Day Countdown by Salina Yoon. New York: Price Stern Sloan, 2006.

RECORDED MUSIC

"'Tis Irish I Am/Irish Washerwoman" from *Holiday Songs Around the World* by Catherine Slonecki. Educational Activities, Inc., 1994. *(use with shamrock streamers)*

"St. Patrick's Day Is Here" from *Holiday Songs for All Occasions.* Kimbo Educational, 1978.

"Ireland (Piper Piper)" from *Multicultural Rhythm Stick Fun* by Georgiana Stewart. Kimbo Educational, 2006.

"Doing the Reel" (and many others!) from *St. Patrick's Day Songs That Tickle Your Funnybone* by Ruth Roberts and Bill Katz. Michael Brent Publications, 1998.

World of Kids: Ireland. Big Blue Dog Records, 2002. *(use with shamrock streamers)*

"Unicorn: Galloping" from *A World of Parachute Play* by Georgiana Stewart. Kimbo Educational, 1997.

FINGERPLAYS/SONGS

"Leprechaun, Leprechaun"

Leprechaun, Leprechaun, turn around.
Leprechaun, Leprechaun, touch the ground.
Leprechaun, Leprechaun, show your shoe.
Leprechaun, Leprechaun, that will do.
Leprechaun, Leprechaun, reach up high.
Leprechaun, Leprechaun, touch the sky.
Leprechaun, Leprechaun, jump this way.
Soon it will be St. Patrick's Day!

"On St. Patrick's Day"
(to the tune of "Here We Go 'Round the Mulberry Bush")

This is the way we dance a jig, dance a jig, dance a jig.
This is the way we dance a jig on St. Patrick's Day.
This is the way we wish you luck . . .

"Are You Wearing Green Today?"
(to the tune of "Mary Had a Little Lamb")

Are you wearing green today, green today, green today?
Are you wearing green today? It is St. Patrick's Day.
_____ has a green shirt on, green shirt on, green shirt on.
_____ has a green shirt on, it is St. Patrick's Day.

Repeat with additional names and items of clothing.

"Have You Seen a Leprechaun?"
(to the tune of "Do You Know the Muffin Man?")

Have you seen a leprechaun, a leprechaun, a leprechaun,
Oh, have you seen a leprechaun on St. Patrick's Day?

PROPS

*Flannelboard Rhyme

"Five Little Shamrocks"

PIECES NEEDED: *5 shamrocks*

5 little shamrocks grew by my door.
I picked one for my mother, and then there were 4.
4 little shamrocks pretty and green.
I picked one for my father, and then there were 3.
3 little shamrocks, what could I do?
I picked one for my sister, and then there were 2.
2 little shamrocks out in the sun.
I picked one for my brother, and then there was 1.
1 little shamrock, isn't this fun?
I picked one for you, and then there were none.

*Shamrock Streamers

Cut out shamrock shapes from green construction paper. Attach a length of curling ribbon to each shape. To make your streamers more durable, laminate the shapes before attaching the ribbon. Pass out one shamrock streamer to each child and use with the music listed above.

Paper-Cutting Story   "Barney's Mission" from *Is Your Storytale Dragging?* by Jean Stangle. Belmont, CA: Fearon Teacher Aids, 1989.

*Flannelboard Story   *Lucky Leprechaun* by Dawn Bentley. New York: Price Stern Sloan, 2003.

PIECES NEEDED: *leprechaun, coins, snow-covered mountains, boat, trees, fairy, four-leaf clovers, rainbow, pot of gold*

CRAFTS

Harp Craft

MATERIALS: 1 harp shape cut from posterboard for each child, precut lengths of green yarn for strings, glue, crayons, decorating materials

DIRECTIONS:
1. Glue the green yarn across the harp to make the strings.
2. Decorate as desired.

Shamrock Puzzle

Materials: 1 shamrock precut from green cardstock for each child (with pre-drawn lines for cutting into puzzle pieces—these can be copied onto the cardstock using a photocopier), decorating materials, scissors

Directions:
1. Decorate shamrocks as desired.
2. Cut along the lines to create puzzle pieces.

Welcome to My Web

Sign: **SPIDER**

BOOKS

Are You a Spider? by Judy Allen. Boston: Kingfisher, 2000.

*The Very Busy Spider by Eric Carle. New York: Philomel, 1984.

*Itsy Bitsy Spider by Keith Chapman. Wilton, CT: Tiger Tales, 2006.

Diary of a Spider by Doreen Cronin. New York: HarperCollins, 2005.

Spiders by Gail Gibbons. New York: Holiday House, 1993.

Be Nice to Spiders by Margaret Bloy Graham. New York: HarperCollins, 1967.

*Itsy Bitsy the Smart Spider by Charise Mericle Harper. New York: Dial, 2004.

*The Eensy-weensy Spider by Mary Ann Hoberman. New York: Little, Brown, 2000.

The Spider and the Fly by Mary Botham Howitt. New York: Simon and Schuster, 2002.

Anansi and the Moss-Covered Rock by Eric Kimmel. New York: Holiday House, 1988.

Miss Spider's Tea Party by David Kirk. New York: Scholastic, 1994.

*Itsy Bitsy Spider by Annie Kubler. Auburn, ME: Child's Play, 2004.

The Spider Who Created the World by Amy MacDonald. New York: Orchard Books, 1996.

Aaaarrgghh! Spider! by Lydia Monks. New York: Houghton Mifflin, 2004.

*Spider on the Floor by Bill Russell. New York: Crown, 1993.

*The Itsy Bitsy Spider by Iza Trapani. Strongsville, OH: Gareth Stevens, 1996.

RECORDED MUSIC

**"The Itsy-Bitsy Spider" from *Early Childhood Classics: Old Favorites with a New Twist* by Hap Palmer. Hap-Pal Music, Inc., 2000.

**"The Eensy Weensy Spider" from *Mainly Mother Goose* by Sharon, Lois, and Bram. Elephant Records, 1984.

**"Do the Daddy Long Legs" from *Racing to the Rainbow* by The Wiggles. Koch Records, 2007.

**"Spider on the Floor" from *Singable Songs for the Very Young* by Raffi. Rounder/UMGD, 1976.

FINGERPLAYS/SONGS

"Miss Muffett, Silly Style"

Present the silly rhyme below as if you think it is the real version, and let the children correct you after each line.

Little Miss Muffet sat on . . . an easy
    chair,
Eating her . . . pepperoni pizza.
Along came a . . . monkey
And sat down beside her . . . and asked
    her out to dinner!

"Willaby Wallaby Woo"
(traditional)

Willaby wallaby woo,
A spider sat on you.
Willaby wallaby wee,
A spider sat on me.
Willaby wallaby wara,
A spider sat on Sarah . . . *(continue with
    other children's names)*

"Little Spider"
(traditional)

See the little spider climb up the wall.
    (move fingers up arm)
See the little spider tumble and fall.
    (make fingers fall)
See the little spider tumble down the
    street. *(move fingers down leg)*
See the little spider stop at my feet.
    (place fingers on shoe)

"1, 2, 3, There's a Spider on Me"

1, 2, 3, there's a spider on me.
He's crawling up my side.
I wish that I could hide.
He's crawling up my fingers.
I wish he wouldn't linger.
He's crawling up my arm,
But he does me no harm.
He's crawling on my shoulder,
He grows ever bolder.
He's crawling on my face.
Oh what a disgrace!
Now he's on my hair
But I really don't care.
Until he starts to spin a web.
Enough, spider! Go away!

"If You're a Spider"
(to the tune of "If You're Happy
and You Know It")

If you're a spider and you know it, wave
    your legs.
If you're a spider and you know it, wave
    your legs.
If you're a spider and you know it, then
    you really ought to show it.
If you're a spider and you know it, wave
    your legs.
. . . spin a web.

PROPS

*Rhythm Stick Song

"The Spider Went over the Mountain"

PIECES NEEDED: *rhythm sticks, enough for each child to hold 2. Have the children hold the sticks vertically, as if they were long spider legs, and make the spiders "walk" while you sing the song.*

The spider went over the mountain,
The spider went over the mountain,
The spider went over the mountain,
To see what he could see.

He saw another mountain,
He saw another mountain,
He saw another mountain,
And that's what he could see.

*Black Pom-Poms

Have enough for each child to hold one. Use these as "spiders" when you sing "Spider on the Floor" or do the rhyme "1, 2, 3, There's a Spider on Me."

Prop Activity: Webspinning

PIECES NEEDED: *a ball of white yarn*

Have everyone sit in a big circle on the floor. Hold one end of the yarn and announce a fact or something you like about spiders. Throw the ball of yarn to someone else across the circle. That person should tell a fact or something she likes about spiders, and then throw the ball of yarn to someone else, making sure to hold on to her part of the yarn. Eventually this will form a cool web pattern on the floor. Leave the web on the floor and have everyone stand up and do your favorite freeze dance as spiders in their web.

*Flannelboard Story   *The Very Busy Spider* by Eric Carle. New York: Philomel, 1984.

PIECES NEEDED: *fencepost, spider, horse, cow, sheep, goat, pig, dog, cat, duck, rooster, owl, web, fly*

ADDITIONAL SUGGESTIONS

*Sign Language

Using the illustrations in *Itsy Bitsy Spider* by Annie Kubler (Auburn, ME: Child's Play, 2004), teach the signs for the song.

CRAFTS

Itsy Bitsy Spider Rainspout

MATERIALS: 1 toilet paper roll for each child, hole punch, black yarn, black pom-poms, googly eyes, yarn, crayons, decorating materials

DIRECTIONS:
1. Punch a hole in one end of the toilet paper roll, about half an inch from the edge.
2. Tie an 8-inch length of black yarn to the toilet paper roll through the hole.
3. Tie the other end of the yarn around the black pom-pom.
4. Glue the googly eyes on the pom-pom.
5. Decorate the "rainspout" as desired.
6. Use the spider and rainspout to act out "The Itsy Bitsy Spider."

Paper Plate Spider

MATERIALS: 1 small paper plate for each child, 8 strips (1 by 4 inches) of black construction paper for each child, black yarn, pencil, crayons, glue, googly eyes

DIRECTIONS:
1. Using the pencil, punch 2 small holes side by side in the center of the paper plate.
2. Turn the plate upside down, and thread a length of black yarn through one hole and back up through the other. Tie the ends of the yarn together. This should allow the plate to hang horizontally when you lift the string.
3. Accordion-fold the strips of black construction paper and glue them to the sides of the paper plate for legs. The legs should hang down when you lift the string to raise the spider up.
4. Glue googly eyes to the front of the plate and decorate as desired.

Zoo Escape!

Sign: **ANIMAL**

BOOKS

Monkey Do! by Allan Ahlberg. Cambridge, MA: Candlewick, 1998.

Gladys Goes Out to Lunch by Derek Anderson. New York: Simon and Schuster, 2005.

The Escape of Marvin the Ape by Caralyn and Mark Buehner. New York: Dial, 1992.

Dear Zoo by Rod Campbell. New York: Four Winds Press, 1982.

Peek-a-Zoo! by Marie Torres Cimarusti. New York: Dutton, 2003.

The Dumb Bunnies Go to the Zoo by Sue Denim. New York: Scholastic, 1997.

Last Night at the Zoo by Michael Garland. Honesdale, PA: Boyds Mills Press, 2001.

I Went to the Zoo by Rita Golden Gelman. New York: Scholastic, 1993.

If Anything Ever Goes Wrong at the Zoo by Mary Jean Hendrick. San Diego: Harcourt Brace, 1993.

The Seals on the Bus by Lenny Hort. New York: Henry Holt, 2000.

Bouncing Time by Patricia Hubbell. New York: HarperCollins, 2000.

Smile If You're Human by Neal Layton. New York: Dial, 1999.

Polar Bear, Polar Bear, What Do You Hear? by Bill Martin Jr. New York: Henry Holt, 1991.

My Camera at the Zoo by Janet Perry Mitchell. New York: Little, Brown, 1989.

Our Class Took a Trip to the Zoo by Shirley Neitzel. New York: Greenwillow, 2002.

Bad Bears Go Visiting by Daniel Pinkwater. New York: Houghton Mifflin, 2007.

Good Night Gorilla by Peggy Rathmann. New York: G. P. Putnam's Sons, 1994.

Curious George Visits the Zoo by H. A. Rey. New York: Houghton Mifflin, 1985.

Sam Who Never Forgets by Eve Rice. New York: Greenwillow, 1977.

Wild about Books by Judy Sierra. New York: Knopf, 2004.

RECORDED MUSIC

"New Zoo Review" from *Big Fun* by Greg and Steve. Youngheart, 2000.

*"Dancing Animals" from *Choo Choo to the Zoo: Creative Movement and Play* by Georgiana Stewart. Kimbo Educational, 2006.

FINGERPLAYS/SONGS

"Five Little Monkeys Jumping on the Bed"
(traditional)

5 little monkeys jumping on the bed.
1 fell off and bumped his head.
Mama called the doctor and the doctor said,
"No more monkeys jumping on the bed!"
4 little monkeys . . .
3 little monkeys . . .
2 little monkeys . . .
1 little monkey . . .
No little monkeys . . .

"Elephant, Elephant"

Elephant, Elephant, stomp stomp stomp.
Elephant, Elephant, chomp chomp chomp. *(mime bringing food to mouth with trunk)*
Elephant, Elephant, turn around.
Elephant, Elephant, make a sound!
(trumpet like an elephant)

"If I Were an Animal in the Zoo"

If I were an animal in the zoo
I would always know just what to do.
If I were an elephant, I would wave my trunk.
If I were a kangaroo, I'd jump jump jump.
If I were an ostrich, I would run and run and run.
If I were a lizard, I would sit in the sun.
If I were a bird, I would spread my wings and soar.
And if I were a lion, I would give a loud ROAR!

"If You're a . . ."
(to the tune of "If You're Happy and You Know It")

If you're a monkey and you know it, say "eee eee."
If you're a monkey and you know it, say "eee eee."
If you're a monkey and you know it, then you really ought to show it.
If you're a monkey and you know it, say "eee eee."
If you're an elephant and you know it, swing your trunk . . .
If you're a giraffe and you know it, stretch your neck . . .
If you're a flamingo and you know it, stand on one leg . . .
If you're a lion and you know it, give a roar . . .
If you're a penguin and you know it, waddle around . . .

"Old MacDonald's Zoo"
(to the tune of "Old MacDonald")

Old MacDonald had a zoo, EIEIO.
And in this zoo he had a lion, EIEIO.
With a roar here and a roar there,
Here a roar, there a roar, everywhere a roar.
Old MacDonald had a zoo, EIEIO.

Repeat with elephant, snake, monkey, etc.

PROPS

*Flannelboard Song

"One Elephant Went Out to Play"
(adapted traditional)

PIECES NEEDED: *5 animals*

1 elephant went out to play outside of the
    zoo one day.
He had such enormous fun, he called for
    another elephant to come.
2 elephants . . .
3 elephants . . .
4 elephants . . .
5 elephants went out to play outside of
    the zoo one day.
They had such enormous fun, and went
    home to the zoo when the day was
    done.

Prop Song

"P-A-N-D-A"
(to the tune of "BINGO")

PIECES NEEDED: *panda puppet*

There is an animal that's black and white
And panda is its name, oh.
P-A-N-D-A, P-A-N-D-A, P-A-N-D-A,
And panda is its name, oh.

Repeat, gradually replacing letters with claps.

*Mask Story: "The Great Zoo Escape"

MASKS NEEDED: *elephant, zebra, lion, tiger, bear, penguin, giraffe,
monkey, hippopotamus, macaw, snake, zookeeper*

The animals at the zoo were tired of being cooped up all the time.
They wanted to go on a trip! The elephant said to the zookeeper,
"Please, zookeeper, please can we go on a trip?" But the zookeeper
said, "NO!"

*Repeat the pattern with the other animals. Invite audience members to
play the parts of the animals.*

But now the zookeeper was starting to feel sorry for the animals.
So he called the bus company and set up a trip. And do you know
where the animals went on their field trip? They went to visit a
school!

Flannelboard Game: Habitat Match

PIECES NEEDED: *iceberg, penguin, tree, monkey, desert scene, snake, cave,
bear, watering hole, hippopotamus*

Oh no! The animals have escaped! Can you help me put them back
in the right homes? Does a monkey live on an iceberg? No! Where
does a monkey live? In a tree!

Continue until all animals have been matched to the correct habitats.

Flannelboard Story   *Polar Bear, Polar Bear, What Do You Hear?* by Bill Martin Jr. New York: Henry Holt, 1991.

PIECES NEEDED: *polar bear, lion, hippopotamus, flamingo, zebra, boa constrictor, elephant, leopard, peacock, walrus, zookeeper*

Prop Story   *Our Class Took a Trip to the Zoo* by Shirley Neitzel. New York: Greenwillow, 2002.

PIECES NEEDED: *coat, lunchbox, button, jeans, hat, shirt, shoes, dime*

CRAFTS

Paper Plate Lions

MATERIALS: paper plates; 4-inch-long strips of yellow and orange crepe streamers; glue; pre-cut pieces for nose, eyes, and mouth; strips of black construction paper for whiskers

DIRECTIONS:
1. Glue crepe streamers around the edge of the plate for the lion's mane.
2. Glue on eyes, nose, mouth, and whiskers and decorate as desired.

Slithering Snakes

MATERIALS: paper plates, crayons or markers, googly eyes, glue, scissors, red curling ribbon

DIRECTIONS:
1. Cut paper plate into a spiral, stopping about 4 inches from the center. The center piece will be the snake's head.
2. Color as desired.
3. Glue on googly eyes.
4. Glue on a small piece of red ribbon for the tongue.

Appendix

Recommended Resources
for Story Box Preparation

Resource Books

Baltuck, Naomi. *Crazy Gibberish and Other Story Hour Stretches.* Hamden, CT: Linnet Books, 1993.

Benton, Gail, and Tricia Waichulaitis. *Ready-to-Go Storytimes: Fingerplays, Scripts, Patterns, Music, and More.* New York: Neal-Schuman, 2003.

Briggs, Diane. *52 Programs for Preschoolers: The Librarian's Year-Round Planner.* Chicago: American Library Association, 1997.

Briggs, Diane. *101 Fingerplays, Stories, and Songs to Use with Finger Puppets.* Chicago: American Library Association, 1999.

Castellano, Marie. *Simply Super Storytimes: Programming Ideas for Ages 3–6.* Fort Atkinson, WI: Upstart Books, 2003.

Chupela, Dolores C. *Once Upon a Childhood: Fingerplays, Action Rhymes, and Fun Times for the Very Young.* Lanham, MD: Scarecrow Press, 1998.

Cobb, Jane. *I'm a Little Teapot! Presenting Preschool Storytime.* Vancouver, BC: Black Sheep Press, 1996.

Cooper, Cathie Hilterbran. *The Storyteller's Cornucopia.* Fort Atkinson, WI: Alleyside Press, 1998.

Cullum, Carolyn N. *The Storytime Sourcebook: A Compendium of Ideas and Resources for Storytellers.* New York: Neal-Schuman, 1999.

Davis, Robin Works. *Toddle On Over: Developing Infant and Toddler Literature Programs.* Fort Atkinson, WI: Alleyside Press, 1998.

Dowell, Ruth E. *Move Over, Mother Goose! Finger Plays, Action Verses, and Funny Rhymes.* Mt. Rainier, MD: Gryphon House, 1987.

Esche, Maria Bonfanti, and Clare Bonfanti Braham. *Kids Celebrate! Activities for Special Days throughout the Year.* Chicago: Chicago Review Press, 1998.

Faurot, Kimberly K. *Books in Bloom: Creative Patterns and Props That Bring Stories to Life.* Chicago: American Library Association, 2003.

Frey, Yvonne Amar. *One-Person Puppetry Streamlined and Simplified.* Chicago: American Library Association, 2005.

Fujita, Hiroko. *Stories to Play With: Kids' Tales Told with Puppets, Paper, Toys, and Imagination.* Little Rock, AR: August House, 1999.

Ghoting, Saroj Nadkarni, and Pamela Martin-Diaz. *Early Literacy Storytimes @ your library: Partnering with Caregivers for Success.* Chicago: American Library Association, 2006.

Hamilton, Leslie. *Child's Play: 200 Instant Crafts and Activities for Preschoolers.* New York: Crown, 1989.

Hamilton, Leslie. *Child's Play Around the World: 170 Crafts, Games, and Projects for Two-to-Six-Year-Olds.* New York: Perigee, 1996.

Lima, Carolyn and John. *A to Zoo: Subject Access to Children's Picture Books.* Westport, CT: Libraries Unlimited, 2001.

MacDonald, Margaret Read. *Bookplay: 101 Creative Themes to Share with Young Children.* North Haven, CT: Library Professional Publications, 1995.

MacDonald, Margaret Read. *Twenty Tellable Tales.* Chicago: American Library Association, 2005.

MacMillan, Kathy. *Try Your Hand at This: Easy Ways to Incorporate Sign Language Into Your Programs.* Lanham, MD: Scarecrow Press, 2006.

Nichols, Judy. *Storytimes for Two-Year-Olds,* 3rd ed. Chicago: American Library Association, 2007.

Reid, Rob. *Children's Jukebox, Second Edition: The Select Subject Guide to Children's Musical Recording.* Chicago: American Library Association, 2007.

Reid, Rob. *Family Storytime: Twenty-four Creative Programs for All Ages.* Chicago: American Library Association, 1999.

Ring A Ring O'Roses. Flint (MI) Public Library, 2000. (810) 232-7111.

Roberts, Lynda. *Mitt Magic.* Beltsville, MD: Gryphon House, 1985.

Schiller, Pam, and Jackie Silberg. *The Complete Book of Activities, Games, Stories, Props, Recipes, and Dances for Young Children.* Beltsville, MD: Gryphon House, 2003.

Schiller, Pamela Byrne. *The Complete Resource Book for Toddlers and Twos.* Beltsville, MD: Gryphon House, 2003.

Sierra, Judy. *The Flannelboard Storytelling Book.* New York: H. W. Wilson, 1997.

Silberg, Jackie, and Pam Schiller. *The Complete Book of Rhymes, Songs, Poems, Fingerplays, and Chants.* Beltsville, MD: Gryphon House, 2002.

Stangle, Jean. *Is Your Storytale Dragging?* Belmont, CA: Fearon Teacher Aids, 1989.

Story-Hoffman, Ru. *Nursery Rhyme Time.* Fort Atkinson, WI: Alleyside Press, 1996.

Warren, Jean, ed. *Storytime Theme-a-Saurus.* Everett, WA: Warren Publishing House, 1993.

Warren, Jean, ed. *Nursery Rhyme Theme-a-Saurus.* Torrance, CA: Totline Publications, 1993.

Wilmes, Liz and Dick. *Felt Board Fingerplays with Patterns and Activities.* Elgin, IL: Building Blocks, 1997.

Wilmes, Liz and Dick. *2's Experience Felt Board Fun.* Elgin, IL: Building Blocks, 1994.

Wilmes, Liz and Dick. *2's Experience Fingerplays.* Elgin, IL: Building Blocks, 1994.

Software

American Sign Language Clip and Create 4. Institute for Disabilities Research and Training (www.idrt.com), 2003.

Websites

Story Box Planning

ASL Pro (American Sign Language Video Dictionary): www.aslpro.com

The Best Kids Book Site (thematic book recommendations, crafts, fingerplays): http://www.thebestkidsbooksite.com/storytimes.htm

Child Care Lounge (fingerplays): http://www.childcarelounge.com/Caregivers/main.htm

ChildFun (fingerplays, crafts, and activities): www.childfun.com

DLTK Kids (crafts and fingerplays): www.dltk-kids.com

Enchanted Learning (crafts and fingerplays): www.enchantedlearning.com (subscription of $20 per year is required to print craft templates and coloring pages)

First-School (crafts and fingerplays): www.first-school.ws

Gayle's Preschool Rainbow (crafts and fingerplays): www.preschoolrainbow.org

The Idea Box (activities and crafts): www.theideabox.com

Kids' Chalkboard (crafts and fingerplays): www.kidschalkboard.com

Let's Create a Flannelboard!: http://members.aol.com/Ivinsart/handbook.html

Miss Lisa's Theme Sharing (crafts and fingerplays): http://www.geocities.com/Heartland/Acres/7875/themes.html

Nuttin' But Kids (crafts and fingerplays): www.nuttinbutkids.com

Songs for Teaching (fingerplays and songs): www.songsforteaching.com

Vendors of Prepackaged Flannelboards, Big Books, and Other Props

Book Props, LLC: www.bookprops.com

Brodart: www.shopbrodart.com

Demco: www.demco.com

The Felt Source: www.thefeltsource.com

Folkmanis Puppets: www.folkmanis.com

Highsmith: www.highsmith.com

Holcomb's Education Resource: www.holcombscatalog.com

Lakeshore Learning: www.lakeshorelearning.com

The Library Store: www.thelibrarystore.com

MerryMakers, Inc: www.merrymakersinc.com

School Specialty: www.schoolspecialtyonline.net

Teacher's Paradise: www.teachersparadise.com

Index

Note: Titles in italics indicate books or music albums. Authors/performers are displayed within parentheses.

KATHY MACMILLAN wears many hats: librarian, American Sign Language (ASL) interpreter and instructor, author, and signing storyteller. She started her library career at Howard County (MD) Library, followed by Carroll County (MD) Public Library, where she managed the children's department at the Eldersburg branch in between presenting storytimes and coaching CCPL's Bookcart Precision Drill Team. In 2001, Kathy became the library/media specialist at the Maryland School for the Deaf in Columbia, MD, where she honed her visual, hands-on storytelling style through work with deaf children with multiple disabilities. In 2004, Kathy founded Stories By Hand (www.storiesbyhand.com), which brings the magic of ASL to hearing audiences through participation stories and music. Kathy has been a reviewer for *School Library Journal* since 1999 and is the author of *Try Your Hand at This! Easy Ways to Incorporate Sign Language into Your Programs* (Scarecrow Press, 2005), as well as many articles on programming and ASL collection development. A passionate believer in the idea that being a librarian is something you *are,* not just something you do, she continues to work as a substitute at Carroll County Public Library and as a consultant for public and school libraries. Kathy earned her master's degree in library science at the University of Maryland, College Park.